Teacher's Guide

Revised Framework Edition

HATHERSHAW TECHNOLOGY COLLEGE
BELLFIELD AVENUE
OLDHAM
OL8 3EP

Jeannie McNeill • Steve Williams

www.pearsonschools.co.uk

✓ Free online support
✓ Useful weblinks
✓ 24 hour online ordering

0845 630 33 33

Heinemann

Part of Pearson

Heinemann is an imprint of Pearson Education Limited, a company incorporated in England and Wales, having its registered office at Edinburgh Gate, Harlow, Essex, CM20 2JE. Registered company number: 872828

www.pearsonschoolsandfecolleges.co.uk

Heinemann is a registered trademark of Pearson Education Limited.

© Pearson Education Limited 2010

First published 2010

14 13 12 11 10
10 9 8 7 6 5 4 3 2 1

British Library Cataloguing in Publication Data is available from the British Library on request.

ISBN 978 0 435088 46 0

Edited by Melanie Birdsall
Designed by Artistix
Typeset by Saxon Graphics Ltd, Artistix and TechType
Cover design by Wooden Ark Studio
Cover photo © Imagestate
Printed in the UK by Ashford Colour Press Ltd

We would like to thank Julie Green and Jenny Gwynne for their contributions to this new edition.

Acknowledgements
Every effort has been made to contact copyright holders of material reproduced in this book. Any omissions will be rectified in subsequent printings if notice is given to the publishers.

CD-ROM
Important notice
This software is suitable for use on PCs only. It will not run on a Mac.

If the CD is loaded into a CD drive on a PC it should autorun automatically. If it does not, please click on RB32.exe (D:EchoEx1TGRFSoW.exe).

Active content
Your browser security may initially try to block elements of this product. If this problem occurs, please refer to the Troubleshooting document which can be found in the root of this CD (D:EchoEx1TGRFSoW/Troubleshooting.doc).

Installation instructions
This product may be installed to your local hard drive or to the network. Further instructions on how to do this are available from the main menu.

VLE Pack
The root of this CD contains the content from this product as a zipped SCORM 1.2 Content Pack to allow for convenient uploading to your VLE.

Please follow the usual instructions specific to your VLE system to upload this content pack.

Contents

Introduction

Echo Express is the tried, tested and successful Key Stage 3 course for pupils starting German in Year 8. This New Edition has been updated in line with the Key Stage 3 Programme of Study for Modern Foreign Languages (2007) and the MFL Framework (2009). References to the Key Stage 3 Framework are also provided throughout. *Echo Express* is designed for middle- to higher-ability pupils, providing differentiated activities throughout the course. *Echo Express 1* is for Year 8 and *Echo Express 2* is for Year 9.

Teaching Foundation Subjects MFL and the MFL Framework (2009) using *Echo Express*

Framework objectives

Echo Express 1 and *2* cover all of the framework objectives for Years 7, 8 and 9. All Year 7 objectives are covered at least twice and Year 8 objectives at least once in Book 1. Year 8 objectives are all met again in Book 2 and Year 9 objectives are covered at least twice in Book 2.

Details of where the objectives are covered are given:

a   in the Framework Overview grids on pages 5 and 6 of this Teacher's Guide to help you with your **long-term planning**;

b   in the Teacher's Guide in the overview grids at the beginning of each chapter (e.g. page 17) to help you with your **medium-term planning**:

c   in the Teacher's Guide in the overview boxes at the start of each teaching unit to help with your **short-term i.e. lesson planning**.

In addition, all activities in the Pupil's Book are cross-referenced to the MFL Framework, to allow you to cover the teaching objectives at different points in the course if you wish. The references are given in the Teacher's Guide at the start of each activity.

The CD-ROM which accompanies this Teacher's Guide provides a customisable scheme of work that includes coverage of the 2009 Framework.

Lesson starters

Two starters are provided for each unit of the Pupil's Book in the Teacher's Guide, the first at the beginning of every unit, the second approximately half-way through the unit at the point when a second lesson is likely to begin. Most of them are simple ideas designed to focus pupils' attention and to promote engagement and challenge. They allow you to recap on previous knowledge or prepare the pupils for new language to be learnt in the unit. Some of the activities have an accompanying worksheet in the Resource & Assessment File.

Plenaries

Every unit in the Pupil's Book ends with a plenary session. Again, these are simple ideas described in the Teacher's Guide. They aim to draw out the key learning points. Pupils are actively involved and are expected to demonstrate and explain what they have learnt in the unit. They identify links with what the pupils have learnt so far and what they will learn later in the course.

Skills development

Throughout the Pupil's Book, Resource & Assessment File, and Workbooks, there are **learning skills** tip boxes as well as activities and worksheets specifically designed to challenge the pupils to think about the language they are learning, the skills required to learn and how to improve those skills.

Thinking skills

In addition, the Pupil's Book, Teacher's Guide, Workbooks and Resource & Assessment File contain specific activities and ideas to develop **thinking skills**, encouraging pupils to engage with language and use their brains in ways that are not traditionally associated with language learning, for example through categorising, lateral thinking and deduction.

Assessment for Learning

Pupils can be assessed formally at the end of every chapter using the *Kontrollen* in the Resource & Assessment File. There is also an end-of-year *Kontrolle 7*. All the tests are matched to the National Curriculum Attainment Target levels. Pupils have the opportunity to reach National Curriculum Level 5 by the end of *Echo Express 1*. Lower-ability pupils who do not progress beyond Levels 1 and 2 can still be formally assessed throughout the whole year. The pattern of assessment is as follows:

Kapitel 1	Levels 1 – 3
Kapitel 2	Levels 1 – 3
Kapitel 3	Levels 1 – 4
Kapitel 4	Levels 1 – 4
Kapitel 5	Levels 1 – 5
Kapitel 6	Levels 1 – 5
End-of-year	Levels 1 – 5

Opportunities for Assessment for Learning:

- At the end of every third unit in each chapter there is a *Mini-Test*, a checklist of what the pupils have learnt so far in the chapter.
- The *Lernzieltest* at the end of each chapter provides the longer checklist of "I can do" statements. These appear in the Resource & Assessment File so that pupils can keep a handy record of their progress.
- *Mein Fortschritt* pages in the Workbooks and the Resource & Assessment File allow pupils to record their National Curriculum level in each Attainment Target and set themselves improvement targets for the next chapter.
- The Workbooks and the Resource & Assessment File both contain the National Curriculum level descriptors in pupil-friendly language to help pupils with their target-setting.
- The plenary sessions focus on what the pupils have learnt in the units and invite pupils to identify key learning points and links with previous learning.

Echo Express 1 Framework Objectives (Year 7) long-term plan

Framework objective		
1.1/Y7 Listening – gist and detail	Chapter 2, Unit 2	Chapter 5, Unit 1
1.2/Y7 Listening – unfamiliar language	Chapter 3, Unit 3	Chapter 3 *Mehr*
1.3/Y7 Listening – (a) interpreting intonation and tone	Chapter 2, Unit 1	Chapter 3, Unit 3
1.3/Y7 Speaking – (b) using intonation and tone	Chapter 2, Unit 1	Chapter 3, Unit 3
1.4/Y7 Speaking – (a) social and classroom language	Chapter 1, Unit 4	Chapter 2, Unit 2
1.4/Y7 Speaking – (b) using prompts	Chapter 2, Unit 4	Chapter 3, Unit 1
1.5/Y7 Speaking – (a) presenting	Chapter 3, Unit 5	Chapter 3 *Mehr*
1.5/Y7 Speaking – (b) expression/non-verbal techniques	Chapter 3, Unit 5	Chapter 3 *Mehr*
2.1/Y7 Reading – main points and detail	Chapter 1, Unit 4	Chapter 5, Unit 4
2.2/Y7 Reading – (a) unfamiliar language	Chapter 1 *Mehr*	Chapter 2 *Mehr*
2.2/Y7 Reading – (b) text selection	Chapter 1 *Mehr* or teachers can provide alternative texts	Chapter 2 *Mehr*
2.3/Y7 Reading – text features	Chapter 2 *Mehr*	Chapter 3, Unit 3
2.4/Y7 Writing – (a) sentences and texts as models	Chapter 2, Unit 4	Chapter 3, Unit 2
2.4/Y7 Writing – (b) building text	Chapter 3, Unit 1	Chapter 3, Unit 4
2.5/Y7 Writing – different text types	Chapter 2, Unit 5	Chapter 4, Unit 3
3.1/Y7 Culture – aspects of everyday life	Chapter 1 *Mehr*	Chapter 2, Unit 3
3.2/Y7 Culture – (a) young people: interests/opinions	Chapter 2, Unit 5	Chapter 3, Unit 5
3.2/Y7 Culture – (b) challenging stereotypes	Chapter 2, Unit 5	Chapter 3, Unit 5
4.1/Y7 Language – letters and sounds	Chapter 1, Unit 1	Chapter 1, Unit 3
4.2/Y7 Language – high frequency words	Chapter 1, Unit 1	Chapter 1, Unit 5
4.3/Y7 Language – gender and plurals	Chapter 1, Unit 3 Chapter 2, Unit 4	Chapter 1, Unit 4 Chapter 3, Unit 4
4.4/Y7 Language – sentence formation	Chapter 3, Unit 2	Chapter 5, Unit 3
4.5/Y7 Language – (a) present tense verbs	Chapter 1, Unit 2	Chapter 2, Unit 3
4.5/Y7 Language – (b) modal verbs	Chapter 4, Unit 5	Chapter 6, Unit 2
4.6/Y7 Language – (a) questions	Chapter 1, Unit 5	Chapter 3, Unit 1
4.6/Y7 Language – (b) negatives	Chapter 2, Unit 5	Chapter 3, Unit 3
5.1 Strategies – patterns	Chapter 2, Unit 4	Chapter 3, Unit 4
5.2 Strategies – memorising	Chapter 1, Unit 2	Chapter 4, Unit 5
5.3 Strategies – English/other languages	Chapter 1, Unit 2	Chapter 4, Unit 1
5.4 Strategies – working out meaning	Chapter 2, Unit 1	Chapter 6, Unit 2
5.5 Strategies – reference materials	Chapter 1 *Mehr*	Chapter 5 *Mehr*
5.6 Strategies – reading aloud	Chapter 2, Unit 5	Chapter 6, Unit 3
5.7 Strategies – planning and preparing	Chapter 2, Unit 5	Chapter 3 *Mehr*
5.8 Strategies – evaluating and improving	Chapter 2, Unit 2	Chapter 4 *Mehr*

Echo Express 1 Framework Objectives (Year 8) long-term plan

Framework objective	
1.1/Y8 Listening – understanding on first hearing	Chapter 6, Unit 1
1.2/Y8 Listening – new contexts	Chapter 6, Unit 5
1.3/Y8 Listening – (a) understanding language for specific functions	Chapter 6, Unit 5
1.3/Y8 Speaking – (b) using language for specific functions	Chapter 5, Unit 1
1.4/Y8 Speaking – (a) classroom exchanges	Chapter 4 *Mehr*
1.4/Y8 Speaking – (b) unscripted conversations	Chapter 4, Unit 1
1.5/Y8 Speaking – (a) unscripted talks	Chapter 5, Unit 2
1.5/Y8 Speaking – (b) using simple idioms	Chapter 5, Unit 2
2.1/Y8 Reading – authentic materials	Chapter 4, Unit 5
2.2/Y8 Reading – (a) longer, more complex texts	Chapter 4 *Mehr*
2.2/Y8 Reading – (b) personal response to text	Chapter 5 *Mehr*
2.3/Y8 Reading – text features: emotive	Chapter 5 unit 5
2.4/Y8 Writing – (a) using text as stimulus	Chapter 6, Unit 4
2.4/Y8 Writing – (b) organising paragraphs	Chapter 6, Unit 1
2.5/Y8 Writing – using researched language	Chapter 5 *Mehr*
3.1/Y8 Culture – changes in everyday life	Chapter 6, Unit 4
3.2/Y8 Culture – (a) young people: aspirations	Chapter 6, Unit 5
3.2/Y8 Culture – (b) customs/traditions	Chapter 4, Unit 5
4.1/Y8 Language – sounds/spelling exceptions	Chapter 4, Unit 2
4.2/Y8 Language – increasing vocabulary	Chapter 5, Unit 3
4.3/Y8 Language – gender	Chapter 5, Unit 4
and plurals	Chapter 6, Unit 2
4.4/Y8 Language – developing sentences	Chapter 4, Unit 4
4.5/Y8 Language – (a) range of verb tenses (past)	Chapter 5, Unit 5
4.5/Y8 Language – (a) range of verb tenses (future)	Chapter 6, Unit 5
4.5/Y8 Language – (b) range of modal verbs	Chapter 4, Unit 4
4.6/Y8 Language – (a) range of questions	Chapter 4, Unit 2
4.6/Y8 Language – (b) range of negatives	Chapter 5, Unit 2
For section 5 objectives see Y7 grid above	

Differentiation

Echo Express 1 and *Echo Express 2* each provide one book for a wide ability range. The range is catered for in the following ways:

- Differentiated activities at a range of AT levels throughout the Pupil's Book.
- Ideas in the Teacher's Guide for simplifying and extending the Pupil's Book activities.
- A *Mehr* unit at the end of every chapter contains longer reading and listening passages to provide opportunities for extension work.
- The *Lesen/Schreiben* section at the back of the book provides extra reading and writing activities at reinforcement and extension levels.

- The Workbooks are differentiated at two levels: reinforcement (*Übungsheft A*) and extension (*Übungsheft B*).

Echo Express 1 takes pupils up to Level 5 of the National Curriculum and *Echo Express 2* takes pupils up to Level 6.

Grammar

Grammar is fully integrated into the teaching sequence in *Echo Express* to ensure that pupils have the opportunity to learn thoroughly the underlying structures of the German language. The key grammar points are presented in the *Echo-Detektiv* boxes in the Pupil's Book, with short explanations. Fuller explanations and practice activities are provided in the *Grammatik* section at the back of the Pupil's Book. In addition, there are worksheets in the Resource & Assessment File which specifically focus on grammar.

Grammar points explained and practised in Echo Express 1:

1 Nouns
Gender
Singular/Plural

2 Articles and cases
The definite article
The indefinite article
The nominative
The accusative
The dative
The negative article (*kein*)
Possessive adjectives

3 Adjectives
Adjectives before and after nouns

4 Pronouns
Nominative pronouns
It
Man
Du and *Sie*

5 Verbs
The infinitive
Regular verbs (present)
Irregular verbs (present)
Sein and *haben* (present)
Present tense for future plans
Talking about the past (*war* and *hatte*)
The imperative
Modal verbs

6 Word order
Normal word order
Verb as second idea

7 Questions
Without question words
With question words

8 *Es gibt*

9 *Gern*

10 Negatives with *nicht*

11 Extras
Numbers
Days
Dates
Times
Adverbs of frequency

List of grammar worksheets (Grammatik) in the Resource & Assessment File

Resource & Assessment File	Grammar	Teacher's Guide
Ch. 1 Arbeitsblatt 1.3	Saying 'the' and 'a'	p.28
Ch. 1 Arbeitsblatt 1.4	*Haben* and *sein*	p.31
Ch. 2 Arbeitsblatt 2.3	Regular verbs	p.56
Ch. 2 Arbeitsblatt 2.4	Accusative: *eine / eine / ein*	p.59
Ch. 3 Arbeitsblatt 3.1	*Haben* and *sein*	p.80
Ch. 3 Arbeitsblatt 3.2	Adjectives	p.83
Ch. 3 Arbeitsblatt 3.4	Plural forms	p.86
Ch. 4 Arbeitsblatt 4.2	Regular and irregular verbs	p.109
Ch. 4 Arbeitsblatt 4.4	Questions	p.109
Ch. 5 Arbeitsblatt 5.3	Word order (verb second)	p.142
Ch. 5 Arbeitsblatt 5.5	*Kein* (accusative)	p.142
Ch. 5 Arbeitsblatt 5.6	Talking about the past	p.148
Ch. 6 Arbeitsblatt 6.6	Talking about the future	p.179

The components
- Pupil's Book
- Audio CDs
- Workbooks
- Resource & Assessment File
- Teacher's Guide
- Flashcards
- Echo Express Elektro 1 Teacher Presentation Package
- Echo Express Elektro 1 Pupil Activity Package

Pupil's Book
The Pupil's Book consists of six chapters, sub-divided as follows:

- Five double-page core units. These units contain the core material in all four skills that must be taught to ensure that all the key language and grammar is covered in Year 8.
- *Lernzieltest* – a checklist of "I can do" statements allowing the pupils to keep a check on their progress as part of assessment for learning (see "Teaching Foundation Subjects MFL" above).
- *Wiederholung* – optional revision activities that can be used preceding the end-of-chapter *Kontrollen* in the Resource & Assessment File.
- One optional two-page extension unit, *Mehr*.
- *Wörter* – two pages of chapter word lists for vocabulary learning and revision plus a *Strategie* tip box to help pupils acquire the skills they need to learn vocabulary more effectively.

At the back of the Pupil's Book there are three further sections:

- *Lesen/Schreiben* – self-access differentiated reading and writing activities. *Lesen/Schreiben A* contains reinforcement activities for lower-ability and *Lesen/Schreiben B* extension activities for higher-ability pupils. These are ideal for use as homework.
- *Grammatik* – the grammar reference and practice section.
- *Wortschatz* – a comprehensive German–English word list, a shorter English–German word list and a list of instructions covered in the Pupil's Book.

Audio CDs

There are three audio CDs for *Echo Express 1*. The material includes dialogues, interviews and songs recorded by native speakers, as well as activities designed for pronunciation practice.

Workbooks (New Edition)

There are two parallel Workbooks to accompany *Echo Express 1*, one for reinforcement (*Übungsheft A*) and one for extension (*Übungsheft B*). The Workbooks fulfil a number of functions:

- They provide enjoyable self-access reading and writing activities to consolidate the language learnt in each unit.
- They give extra practice in grammar and thinking skills with integrated activities throughout the Workbooks.
- Revision pages at the end of each chapter (*Wiederholung*) help pupils revise what they have learnt during the chapter.
- Chapter word lists (*Wörter*) with English translations are invaluable for language-learning homeworks.
- *Mein Fortschritt* pages at the end of each chapter allow pupils to record their National Curriculum level in each Attainment Target and set themselves improvement targets.
- National Curriculum level descriptors in pupil-friendly language allow pupils to see what they must do to progress up through the National Curriculum levels.

Resource & Assessment File

The Resource & Assessment File is organised into chapters for ease of use. It comes with an audio CD and all worksheets on a customisable CD-ROM.

Worksheets (*Arbeitsblätter*) include:

- Lesson Starter sheets to accompany some of the lesson starter suggestions in the Teacher's Notes.
- Learning Skills sheets designed to help pupils become effective and independent language learners.
- Thinking Skills sheets.
- Grammar sheets (*Grammatik*). Page 7 of this Teacher's Guide shows where these sheets fit into the scheme of work.
- Chapter word lists (*Wörter*) in a photocopiable format.

Assessment pages:

- *Lernzieltest*: "I can do" checklist for self-assessment and/or peer-assessment.
- *Kontrollen*: end-of-chapter (and end-of-year) tests for formal assessment.
- *Mein Fortschritt*: target-setting sheets to allow pupils to record their National Curriculum level in each Attainment Target and set themselves improvement targets for the next chapter.
- National Curriculum levels: National Curriculum level descriptors in pupil-friendly language.
- The listening test material is provided on an audio CD with the file.

Teacher's Guide

The Teacher's Guide contains:

- A customisable scheme of work on CD-ROM.
- A long-term plan grid for the teaching objectives of the 2009 MFL Framework.
- Overview grids for each chapter to help with medium-term planning.
- Mapping of activities to the 2007 National Curriculum Programmes of Study.
- Clear teaching notes for short-term planning together with full audio transcript.
- Suggestions for extra activities for reinforcement and extension.
- Indications of how the course offers cross-curricular opportunities (Citizenship, English, ICT, Mathematics).
- Ideas for using the flashcards and other games in the classroom.

Flashcards

There are 96 full-colour single-sided flashcards with the name of the object on the reverse. They can be used for presentation of new language or practice. A full list of the *Echo Express 1* flashcards can be found on page 12. Here are some imaginative methods of using the flashcards to help pupils learn and memorise new vocabulary more effectively.

Method 1

Show one card, say the word or phrase and pupils repeat in fun and varied ways (loud/soft, high/low etc.)

Use four cards. Show one that you've just used and give a choice of two words. Pupils say the correct word. Continue until they know about eight.

Method 2

Once you've been through about 6–9 cards and they've heard the words a few times, stick a selection on the board, numbered. Say one in German; a pupil gives you the number. Then say the number; a pupil gives you the word. This can then be done from pupil to pupil.

You could then read out an easy sum, but use words instead of the numbers (e.g. *ein Hund und eine Katze, macht …?*) The pupils calculate the answers and give a third word, instead of a number.

Method 3

Put nine cards on the board, in rows of three, divide the class into two teams and play noughts and crosses. Pupils choose a card and say the German, the aim being to get three in a row.

Method 4

Stick a series of cards on the board. Two pupils stand by the board. You or another pupil say a word. The two pupils race to be the first to point to the correct card.

Method 5

Guess the card. You conceal a card behind your back (look at it quickly first). The pupils have to guess which one it is by saying the words.

Method 6

After term 1 use the cards to elicit phrases, negatives, opinions. Aim for longer sentences incorporating the word.

Echo Express Elektro 1 Teacher Presentation Package

The Teacher Presentation Package is designed for use with the interactive whiteboard or data-projector. It offers:

- presentations of new language
- grammar sections
- whole-class games
- video activities
- audio activities
- texts ready to read and adapt on screen.

It is divided into ready-made lesson sequences that are aligned with the units in the Pupil's Book, cutting preparation time to a minimum.

Echo Express Elektro 1 Pupil Activity Package

The Pupil Activity Package provides differentiated practice of the language taught, in all four skills. It is ideal for independent use in the computer suite. Scores can be recorded and tracked so that both pupils and teachers have a clear idea of progress being made.

Each sequence consists of the following activity types:

- Listening
- Vocabulary learning
- Word and sentence work, e.g. phonetic practice, sentence building
- Grammar
- Reading and writing.

Integrating ICT

Suggestions for ICT activities have been included in the Teacher's Guide. The following grid shows the location and nature of these activities.

Unit reference	Activity type
Chapter 1, Unit 5	Using a spreadsheet to write up survey results
Chapter 2, Unit 1	Using a spreadsheet to write up survey results
Chapter 2, Unit 5	Planning and writing a mini webpage
Chapter 3, Unit 4	Creating a poster about pets
Chapter 3, Unit 5	Word-processing, writing an email
Chapter 3, *Mehr*	Powerpoint presentation or poster about a celebrity
Chapter 4, Unit 3	Word-processing a letter and importing graphics to illustrate it
Chapter 5, Unit 2	Using a spreadsheet to write up survey results
Chapter 6, Unit 6	Word-processing texts and importing graphics

Games and other teaching suggestions

Reading aloud

1 Set a challenge – 'I bet no-one can read this without making a single mistake' – or ask a volunteer pupil to predict how many mistakes they will make before having a go. See if they can do better than their prediction.

2 Texts could be read round the class with pupils simply reading up to a full-stop and then passing it on to someone else in the room.

3 You can also read texts, pause and the pupils have to say the next word.

Reading follow-up

1 You read aloud and stop for pupils to complete the word or sentence.
2 You read aloud and insert the word 'beep' for pupils to complete.
3 You read aloud and make a mistake (either in pronunciation or saying the wrong word). Pupils put up their hands as soon as they spot a mistake.
4 *Hot potato:* pupils read a bit and pass it on quickly to someone who may not be expecting it.
5 *Marathon:* one pupil reads aloud until he/she makes a mistake. Pupils have to put up their hand as soon as they hear a mistake. The second pupil then takes over, reading *from the beginning* and trying to get further than the previous one.
6 *Random reading:* you read a phrase at random and the pupils have to say the next bit.

Mime activities

Mimes are a motivating way to help pupils to learn words.

1 You say a word and the pupils mime. This could be done as a knockout, starting with six volunteers at the front who mime to the class as you say each word. The ones who do the wrong mime or who are slow to react are knocked out. Impose a two-minute time limit.
2 A pupil says a word or phrase and you mime it – but only if the pupil says it correctly.
3 You mime and pupils say the word or phrase.
4 One person goes out of the room. The rest of the class all mime one characteristic. The volunteer comes back into the room and has to guess the adjective that the class are miming.
5 *Class knock-down:* As above but this time everyone in the class can choose different qualities to mime. The volunteer returns to the room with everyone doing their own mime. The volunteer points to each pupil and says the word or phrase. If correct, the pupil sits down. This works well as a timed or team activity. The aim is to sit your team down as quickly as possible.
6 A version of charades. This is a good activity at the end of the lesson. Organise two teams, A and B. Have words or phrases on separate cards. Put the cards in a pile at the front. A volunteer from Team A comes to the front, picks up the first card and mimes it. Anyone from Team A can put up their hand and say the word. If correct, the volunteer picks up the next card and mimes it. The aim is to get through the whole list as quickly as possible. Note down the time for Team A. Then Team B tries to beat their time.

Exploiting the songs

1 Pupils sing along. You fade out certain parts whilst they continue. When most of them know the song quite well, you can pause the recording whilst they give you the next line from memory. Then try the chorus by heart. Then try a few verses completely from memory.
2 You could try the 'pick up song' game – you fade the song after a few lines, the pupils continue singing and then you fade the song in again towards the end.

Writing follow-up (Text dissection)

1 Display some anagrams of key words from the text and ask pupils to write them correctly. You will need to prepare these in advance and check carefully. Award points for correct answers.
2 Display some jumbled phrases from a text (words in the wrong order), e.g. *ich am spiele Montag Computer am.* Pupils rewrite the phrase correctly in their books or on the board.
3 Display a word or phrase in German. See if pupils can spot a mistake and correct it. This can also be done as 'spot the missing word' or 'spot the word that is in the wrong place'.
4 *Mini dictation.* Read four or five short sentences in German for pupils to write out. Again, this could be a group exercise.
5 If the group is good, give them phrases in English to write down in German.

Vocabulary treasure hunt

1 Find the word for … .
2 Find (3) opinions.

Grammar treasure hunt

1 Find (3) adjectives.
2 Find (2) feminine adjectives.
3 Find a verb in the *wir* form.
4 Find a plural noun.
5 Find a negative.

A variation on pair work

Musical pass the mobile. One pupil operates a CD with music. He/She has to face away from the class. Whilst the music is playing a (toy) mobile phone is passed from pupil to pupil. As soon as the music stops, the CD operator says the first statement of a dialogue. The other pupil who has ended up with the phone replies. They can, if they like, disguise their voices. The CD operator tries to guess who is speaking. The game then continues.

Other games

Wounded soldier

This game can be used to consolidate asking and answering questions on any topic. Draw a soldier on the board and ask pupils to stand in a circle or horseshoe. You ask a question and throw a ball or soft toy to each pupil in turn. He/She must answer as quickly as possible and throw it back to you. (More able pupils could ask the next question themselves, before throwing.) This can be played against the clock. If a pupil does not answer the question correctly, then the soldier loses a leg, an arm or an eye (rub these out on the board) until a correct answer is given.

Wer hat was?

This activity is useful for practising closed questions. Send one pupil out of the room and distribute objects or pictures to some members of the class. The whole class then hide their hands under the desk. The pupil returns and has one minute to find as many objects or pictures as possible by asking a specific question to individual pupils, e.g. *Hast du ein Lineal?* Pupils respond with a full sentence.

Pupils must only hand over the card if the question has been asked accurately and if the answer is yes. The pupil guessing can only continue when his/her question has been answered.

Get your own back

This can be used to practise items of vocabulary or whole phrases. Ask pupils to write or draw (on a piece of paper) a correct sentence using, for example, a particular high-frequency word, such as *mein*. Pupils then pair up with someone else, exchange information and pieces of paper. They then find a new partner and exchange the new information with them. This continues until the pupils get their original papers back.

Sounds hangman

This can be played to practise spelling words with particular sounds in them. Say the word and write up a dash for each letter. Pupils then isolate the sounds in the word and tell you which letters make that sound and where they go (e.g. for *Schwester*: the sound *sch* is spelled s-c-h and that's the first three letters of the word).

Pass the bomb

This can be played to practise items of high-frequency language. Divide the class into two teams. A soft toy or sponge ball is used as the bomb. Write a phrase on the board (e.g. *ich habe*); the pupil holding the toy or ball must make a sentence using that verb. He/She then throws the bomb to someone on the other team, who must make a different sentence using the same phrase. This continues until the bomb goes off. The team holding the bomb when it goes off is given a penalty point. You should allocate a certain amount of time for each verb ranging from 30 to 60 seconds before the bomb goes off. To show when the time has run out, make a noise or set a watch alarm.

Symbols used in the teaching notes

 Extension material/suggestion for extending an activity for the more able.

 Reinforcement material/suggestion for simplifying an activity for the less able.

 Thinking skills activities in the *Übungsheft A/B*, and *Arbeitsblätter* in the Resource & Assessment File, as well as against activities in the teaching notes.

 ICT activity

List of flashcards

1	Deutschland	26	Mathe	51	laut	76	der Dachboden
2	England	27	Naturwissenschaften	52	unpünktlich	77	der Keller
3	Schottland	28	Werken	53	launisch	78	der Balkon
4	Wales	29	Kunst	54	musikalisch	79	der Garten
5	Irland	30	Musik	55	schüchtern	80	die Garage
6	Frankreich	31	Theater	56	lustig	81	mit dem Auto
7	Österreich	32	Erdkunde	57	faul	82	mit dem Zug
8	die Schweiz	33	Geschichte	58	Tennis	83	mit dem Bus
9	der Bleistift	34	Sport	59	Fußball	84	mit dem Taxi
10	das Buch	35	der Orangensaft	60	Basketball	85	mit der U-Bahn
11	die Diskette	36	die Cola	61	Volleyball	86	mit der Straßenbahn
12	das Etui	37	das Wasser	62	Federball	87	mit dem Flugzeug
13	das Heft	38	das Brötchen	63	Tischtennis	88	zu Fuß
14	der Klebstift	39	der Apfel	64	Rugby	89	Hamburger
15	der Kuli	40	die Orange	65	reiten	90	Bratwurst
16	das Lineal	41	die Banane	66	schwimmen	91	Pizza
17	die Schere	42	Chips	67	angeln	92	Schaschlik
18	die Schultasche	43	Kuchen	68	wandern	93	Pommes
19	der Taschenrechner	44	Kekse	69	Snowboard fahren	94	Limonade
20	das Wörterbuch	45	Schokolade	70	das Wohnzimmer	95	Kaffee
21	Deutsch	46	Bonbons	71	das Esszimmer	96	Tee mit Zitrone / mit Milch
22	Englisch	47	freundlich	72	die Küche		
23	Französisch	48	intelligent	73	das Schlafzimmer		
24	Religion	49	sportlich	74	das Badezimmer		
25	Informatik	50	kreativ	75	die Toilette		

Personal Learning and Thinking Skills

The activities and contexts provided throughout the course offer a range of opportunities for students to apply skills from the six groups of the Personal Learning and Thinking Skills framework.

Personal Learning and Thinking Skills	Examples in *Echo 1 Express*
1 Independent enquirers	Pupil's Book activities throughout the course (e.g. Ch2 U5 ex 5 p31, Ch 4 U3 ex 8 p59); ICT-based activities (e.g. ICT suggestions in the TG p9)
2 Creative thinkers	Regular activities developing skills strategies (how to improve listening/reading, etc.) (e.g. Ch3 U5 p47 tip box); starters and plenaries requiring pupils to apply logic and make connections (e.g. Ch3 U4 Starter 1 TG p86)
3 Reflective learners	Ongoing opportunities to assess work and identify areas for improvement (all Mini-tests e.g. p43 PBk), all Plenaries (e.g. Ch6 U3 Plenary TG p173)
4 Team workers	Regular pair work and group work activities (Ch2 U3 ex 3 & 6 pp26-27) including many starters; regular peer assessment, including *Lernzieltest* pages at the end of each chapter (e.g. p16)
5 Self-managers	Ongoing advice on managing learning (e.g. *Strategie* p85 and all other *Strategie* boxes on the *Wörter* pages), including strategies to improve learning (e.g. Ch2 U1 plenary TG p51)
6 Effective participators	Opportunities throughout the course for pupils to contribute (e.g. Ch3 U3 ex. 8 p43), including presentations (e.g. Ch5 U2 ex 4 p73) and all starters and plenaries (e.g. Ch3 U1 starter TG p77 and Ch4 U1 plenary TG p108)

Covering the Programmes of Study

1. Key concepts

There are a number of key concepts outlined in the **QCA Programmes of Study**, which underpin the study of languages. Pupils need to understand these concepts in order to deepen and broaden their knowledge, skills and understanding. These are addressed in all chapters of *Echo Express 1*, so are not included in the tables below, but are listed here for reference.

1.1 Linguistic competence
a developing the skills of listening, speaking, reading and writing in a range of situations and contexts
b applying linguistic knowledge and skills to understand and communicate effectively
1.2 Knowledge about language
a understanding how a language works and how to manipulate it
b recognising that languages differ but may share common grammatical, syntactical or lexical features
1.3 Creativity
a using familiar language for new purposes and in new contexts
b using imagination to express thoughts, ideas, experiences and feelings
1.4 Intercultural understanding
a appreciating the richness and diversity of other cultures
b recognising that there are different ways of seeing the world, and developing an international outlook

The tables below indicate where, in *Echo Express 1*, pupils have the opportunity to progress in the **Key processes**, **Range and content**, and **Curriculum opportunities** prescribed in the QCA Programmes of Study. For each area we have indicated where these appear in the core units of the Pupil's Book. There are further opportunities both in the Pupil's Book and the supplementary components. More detail is provided in the grids at the beginning of each module in this Teacher's Guide.

2. Key processes

These are the essential skills and processes in languages that pupils need to learn to make progress.

2.1 Developing language-learning strategies – pupils should be able to:	
a identify patterns in the target language	Chapter 1 Unit 4, Chapter 1 Unit 5, Chapter 2 Unit 1, Chapter 2 Unit 2, Chapter 4 Unit 4, Chapter 4 Unit 5, Chapter 6 Unit 5
b develop techniques for memorising words, phrases and spellings	Chapter 1 Unit 2, Chapter 2 Unit 1, Chapter 3 Unit 4
c use their knowledge of English or another language when learning the target language	Chapter 2 Unit 1, Chapter 4 Unit 2, Chapter 6 Unit 4
d use previous knowledge, context and other clues to work out the meaning of what they hear or read	Chapter 3 Unit 5, Chapter 4 Unit 2, Chapter 5 Unit 5
e use reference materials such as dictionaries appropriately and effectively	Chapter 3 Unit 5, Chapter 6 Unit 2
2.2 Developing language skills – pupils should be able to:	
a listen for gist or detail	Chapter 2 Unit 4, Chapter 3 Unit 2, Chapter 6 Unit 2
b skim and scan written texts for the main points or details	Chapter 2 Unit 5, Chapter 3 Unit 5, Chapter 5 Unit 2
c respond appropriately to spoken and written language	Chapter 2 Unit 5, Chapter 3 Unit 5, Chapter 4 Unit 5
d use correct pronunciation and intonation	Chapter 1 Unit 2, Chapter 4 Unit 4, Chapter 6 Unit 1
e ask and answer questions	Chapter 1 Unit 5, Chapter 3 Unit 5, Chapter 4 Unit 4
f initiate and sustain conversations	Chapter 1 Unit 5, Chapter 2 Unit 1, Chapter 5 Unit 1
g write clearly and coherently, including an appropriate level of detail	Chapter 2 Unit 5, Chapter 3 Unit 4, Chapter 3 Unit 5, Chapter 5 Unit 3, Chapter 6 Unit 2, Chapter 6 Unit 5
h redraft their writing to improve accuracy and quality	Chapter 3 Unit 5, Chapter 4 Unit 3, Chapter 6 Unit 5

i re-use language that they have heard or read in their own speaking and writing	All chapters
j adapt language they already know in new contexts for different purposes	Chapter 3 Unit 2, Chapter 4 Unit 2, Chapter 6 Unit 5
k deal with unfamiliar language, unexpected responses and unpredictable situations	Chapter 2 Unit 5, Chapter 2 Unit 1, Chapter 5 Unit 1

3. Range and content

This section outlines the breadth of the subject on which teachers should draw when teaching the key concepts and key processes. The study of languages should include:

a the spoken and written form of the target language	All chapters
b the interrelationship between sounds and writing in the target language	Chapter 1 Unit 1, Chapter 3 Unit 1, Chapter 4 Unit 1
c the grammar of the target language and how to apply it	Chapter 1 Unit 3, Chapter 3 Unit 2, Chapter 3 Unit 4, Chapter 5 Unit 2
d a range of vocabulary and structures	Chapter 1 Unit 5, Chapter 3 Unit 5, Chapter 6 Unit 5
e learning about different countries and cultures	Chapter 2 Unit 5, Chapter 6 Unit 1, Chapter 6 Unit 4
f comparing pupils' own experiences and perspectives with those of people in countries and communities where the target language is spoken	Chapter 2 Unit 5, Chapter 6 Unit 1, Chapter 6 Unit 4

4. Curriculum opportunities

During the key stage pupils should be offered the following opportunities that are integral to their learning and enhance their engagement with the concepts, processes and content of the subject. The curriculum should provide opportunities for pupils to:

a hear, speak, read and write in the target language regularly and frequently within the classroom and beyond	All chapters
b communicate in the target language individually, in pairs, in groups and with speakers of the target language, including native speakers, where possible, for a variety of purposes	Chapter 1 Unit 1, Chapter 2 Unit 1, Chapter 3 Unit 5, Chapter 4 Unit 4, Chapter 4 Unit 5
c use an increasing range of more complex language	Chapter 6 Unit 5
d make links with English at word, sentence and text level	Chapter 2 Unit 1, Chapter 4 Unit 2, Chapter 6 Unit 4
e use a range of resources, including ICT, for accessing and communicating information	Chapter 2 Unit 5, Chapter 3 *Mehr*
f listen to, read or view a range of materials, including authentic materials in the target language, both to support learning and for personal interest and enjoyment	Chapter 2 Unit 5, Chapter 4 Unit 5
g use the target language in connection with topics and issues that are engaging and may be related to other areas of the curriculum	Chapter 2 Unit 3, Chapter 3 *Mehr*, Chapter 4 Unit 5, Chapter 5 Unit 5, Chapter 6 Unit 3

Solutions to *Grammatik* exercises (Pupil's Book pp. 112–127)

1

1 Garten – masculine (der), garden   2 Hemd – neuter (das), shirt   3 Hose – feminine plural (die), trousers   4 Kaninchen – neuter (das), rabbit   5 Keks – masculine (der), biscuit   6 Küche – feminine (die), kitchen   7 Lineal – neuter (das), ruler   8 Schere – feminine (die), (pair of) scissors   9 Schlange – feminine (die), snake   10 Wasser – neuter (das), water

2

1 Äpfel   2 Bleistifte   3 Brüder   4 Disketten   5 Katzen   6 Hunde   7 Kaninchen   8 Kekse   9 Autos   10 Stühle

3

1 das Bett   2 das Brötchen   3 der Bruder   4 das Lineal   5 die Orange   6 der Saft

4

1 eine Schlange   2 eine Tante   3 ein Klebstift   4 ein Etui   5 eine Hose   6 ein Goldfisch

5

1 *Ich* finde Mathe langweilig.   2 *Marcus* hat kurze, lockige Haare.   3 *Mein Cousin* spielt Gitarre.   4 *Tanja* isst einen Apfel.   5 Hast *du* einen Bleistift für mich?   6 *Religion* beginnt um elf Uhr.

6
1 *Der* Kuli ist blau.   2 Sind *die* Jeans blau?
3 *Die* Schuhe sind lila.   4 *Das* Pferd ist groß und
braun.   5 *Die* Schuluniform ist schwarz und rot.
6 *Das* Kaninchen ist weiß.

7
1 Sie isst *ein Brötchen*.   2 Ich habe *einen Bleistift*.
3 Hast du *eine Diskette*?   4 Ich trage *eine Jacke*.
5 Susi hat *ein Pferd*.   6 Ich habe *keine Haustiere*.

8
1 Ich habe *einen* Bleistift.   2 Hast du *eine*
Diskette?   3 Ich trage *einen* Rock und *ein* Hemd.
4 Ich esse *ein* Brötchen.   5 Hast du *einen* Kuli für
mich?   6 Ich habe *einen* Wellensittich.

9
1 because of 'auf'   3 because of 'zwischen'
6 because of 'in'

10
1 Die Katze ist hinter *dem* Fernseher.   2 Die
Gitarre ist auf *der* Sofa.   3 Mutti ist in *der* Kuche.
4 Das Esszimmer ist zwischen *der* Kucke and *dem*
Wohnzimmer.   5 Die Stereoanlage ist auf *dem*
Regal.   6 Das Wörterbuch ist neben der
Schultasche.   7 Wo ist der Hund? Unter *dem*
Stuhl.   8 Oma schläft in *dem* Garten.

11
1 Beate hat keinen Computer.   2 Beate hat keine
Gitarre.   3 Beate hat keinen Fernseher.   4 Beate
hat keine Freunde.   5 Beate hat keine Jacke.
6 Beate hat keine Katzen.

12
1 your   2 my   3 his   4 your   5 her   6 my
7 his   8 your

13
1 Mein   2 Ihr   3 deine   4 Meine   5 ihr
6 dein   7 Mein   8 Sein

14
1 braune   2 bunt   3 schicke   4 intelligent
5 blaue   6 graue   7 intelligente   8 kräftig
9 schwierig   10 graue

15
1 Wir   2 Er   3 Sie   4 du   5 Ich   6 Sie
7 Es   8 Sie   9 du   10 Sie

16
1 *Es* ist lecker.   2 *Sie* ist blau und weiß.   3 *Es* ist
sehr langweilig.   4 *Er* ist ziemlich lustig.   5 Wo
ist *er*?   6 Is *es* blau oder lila?   7 *Es* ist super.
8 *Sie* ist sehr intelligent.

17
1 You can cycle.   2 Where can you play football?
3 You can go to the town hall.   4 Can you go to
the cinema?   5 You can go by tram/take the tram.

18
1 du   2 Sie   3 du   4 du   5 Sie   6 Sie

19
essen, hören, gehen, haben, schwimmen, lesen, sein,
trinken, wohnen, heißen

20
1 spiele   2 faulenzt   3 wohnt   4 gehen
5 Wohnen   6 Spielst   7 gehen   8 wohnen
9 hört   10 kochen

21
1 ich nehme   2 du schläfst   3 du siehst   4 er
sieht   5 sie liest   6 du fährst   7 ich esse
8 er isst   9 sie schläft   10 ich schlafe

22
1 Ich *fahre* mit dem Bus.   2 *Liest* du gern Bücher?
3 Du *fährst* mit der U-Bahn.   4 Vati *schläft*
manchmal in Wohnzimmer.   5 Wir *fahren* immer
mit dem Zug.   6 Du *schläfst* im Garten.
7 *Siehst* du gern fern?   8 Max *liest* ein Buch.
9 Was *isst* du gern?   10 Sie *essen* Kuchen und
Schokolade.

23
1 habe   2 Hast   3 Hat   4 haben   5 hast
6 hat   7 haben

24
1 ist   2 bin   3 ist   4 sind   5 bist   6 sind
7 sind

25
1 Ich habe zwei Schwestern.   2 Ich habe keine
Haustiere.   3 Jonas hat eine Gitarre.   4 Wann
hat Julie Geburtstag?   5 Das T-shirt ist grün und
blau.   6 Wir sind sehr intelligent.   7 Sind Sie
Herr Schmidt?   8 Wie alt ist Nina?   9 Hat Andi
Geschwister?   10 Hast du ein Lineal?

26
1 Ich fahre in zwei Wochen nach Irland. – I'm going
  to Ireland in two weeks.
2 Ich spiele am Wochenende Tischtennis. – I'm
  playing table tennis at the weekend.
3 Er geht morgen angeln. – He's going fishing
  tomorrow.
4 Wir kaufen nächste Woche einen Hund. – We're
  buying a dog next week.
5 Er fährt nächstes Jahr nach Amerika. – He's going
  to America next year.
6 Ich bleibe in den Sommerferien zu Hause. – I'm
  staying at home in the summer holidays.

27

1 Ich fahre nächste Woche nach Deutschland.
2 Wir spielen morgen Tennis. 3 Du fährst
nächstes Jahr Ski. 4 Er spielt am Wochenende
Rugby. 5 Sie kauft am Freitag Schuhe. 6 Mein
Bruder spielt nächste Woche Fußball.

28

1 Ich war letztes Jahr zwölf Jahre alt. 2 Sie hatte
letzte Woche Geburtstag. 3 Mein Bruder hatte
letztes Jahr ein Meerschweinchen. 4 Ich war
letzte Woche in Österreich. 5 Meine Schwester
war gestern ziemlich faul. 6 Timo war letzten
Montag in Berlin.

29

1 Nimm die zweite Straße rechts! 2 Nehmen Sie
die erste Straße links! 3 Geh geradeaus!
4 Gehen Sie geradeaus und dann links! 5 Spiel
Fußball! 6 Hör Musik! 7 Sieh nicht fern!
8 Geh ins Kino!

30

1 Man kann ins Kino gehen. 2 Man kann Tennis
spielen. 3 Man kann mit dem Zug fahren.
4 Ich möchte Pommes essen. 5 Man kann Cola
trinken. 6 Man kann in die Disko gehen.
7 Ich mag Mountainbike fahren. 8 Teresa mag
nicht Tischtennis spielen.

31

1 Ich habe zwei Schwestern. 2 Petra ist fünfzehn
Jahre alt. 3 Meine Mutter hat blonde Haare.
4 Wir wohnen in einem Reihenhaus.
5 Geschichte ist mein Lieblingsfach or Mein
Lieblingsfach ist Geschichte. 6 Mein Hund heißt
Wuffi. 7 Ich sehe gern fern. 8 Meine Adresse
ist Ludwigstraße achtzehn.

32

1 In meinem Zimmer habe ich einen Computer.
2 Deutsch ist mein Lieblingsfach. 3 Am Montag
habe ich Geschichte. 4 Mathe finde ich
schwierig. 5 In der Schule trage ich Jeans.
6 In ihrer Schultasche hat sie einen Apfel.

33

1 Mathe finden wir ziemlich langweilig. 2 In der
Pause esse ich Kekse. 3 In deinem Zimmer gibt
es keinen Fernseher. 4 Am Freitag haben wir
Englisch und Religion. 5 In deiner Wohnung gibt
es zwei Badezimmer. 6 Deutsch findet sie sehr
interessant.

34

1 Spielst du gern am Computer? 2 Ist Deutsch
ihr Lieblingsfach? 3 Ist sie dreizehn Jahre alt?
4 Wohnt er in Leipzig? 5 Kann man mit der U-
Bahn fahren? 6 Beginnt Kunst um elf Uhr?
7 Isst du gern Pommes? 8 Ist er groß und kräftig?

35

1 Who are you? *b* 2 Where are you? *e* 3 What
are you like? *d* 4 How old are you? *c* 5 What's
your favourite subject? *g* 6 When's your birthday?
a 7 What's your address? *f* 8 When does break
begin? *h*

36

1 *Wie* heißt deine Schwester? 2 *Wer* isst einen
Apfel? 3 *Wie* alt ist Teresa? 4 *Wo* wohnt Timo?
5 *Was* isst du in der Pause? 6 *Wann* beginnt
Französisch? 7 *Wer* hat Geburtstag? 8 *Was* ist
dein Lieblingsfach?

37

1 Es gibt eine Kuche. 2 Es gibt ein Badezimmer.
3 Es gibt keinen Garten. 4 Es gibt ein Esszimmer.
5 Es gibt eine Garage. 6 Es gibt keinen Keller.

38

1 Ich trinke gern Cola. I like drinking cola. 2 Wir
sehen gern fern. We like watching television.
3 Ingo spielt gern Gitarre. Ingo likes playing the
guitar. 4 Chris fährt gern mit dem Bus. Chris
likes travelling by bus. 5 Anke hört gern Musik.
Anke likes listening to music. 6 Ich spiele nicht
gern Tischtennis. I don't like playing table tennis.
7 Gehst du nicht gern schwimmen? 8 Fährt sie
nicht gern Rad? 9 Gehst du nicht gern in den
Jugendklub 10 Mein Freund Alex trägt nicht
gern Sportschuhe.

39

1 Wir spielen nicht gern Tennis. 2 Man kann
nicht mit dem Bus fahren. 3 Deutsch ist nicht
mein Lieblingsfach. 4 Mein Bruder ist nicht sehr
intelligent. 5 Ich trinke nicht gern Wasser.
6 Sie wohnt nicht in Birmingham. 7 Ich kann
nicht Snowboard fahren. 8 Petra und Susi
faulenzen nicht gern.

40

1 am zehnten September 2 am ersten Dezember
3 am dreiundzwanzigsten April 4 am achten Mai
5 am neunzehnten Februar 6 am dritten
November 7 am fünfzehnten März 8 am
neunundzwanzigsten Oktober 9 am vierten Juni
10 am einundzwanzigsten Juli

41

1 Es ist sieben Uhr zehn. 2 Es ist neun Uhr.
3 Um elf Uhr fünfzig. 4 Um ein Uhr fünfzehn.
5 Es ist zwei Uhr dreiundzwanzig. 6 Um vier Uhr
fünfundfünfzig. 7 Um acht Uhr fünf.
8 Es ist drei Uhr neununddreißig. 9 Um neun
Uhr zwanzig. 10 Es ist zwölf Uhr sechs.

Unit Learning targets	Key framework objectives	NC levels and PoS coverage	Grammar and key language	Skills
1 Wie heißt du? (pp. 6–7) ● Introducing yourself ● Saying how old you are	4.1/Y7 Language – letters and sounds 4.2/Y7 Language – high frequency words	NC levels 1–3 2.1b memorising 2.2a listen for gist 2.2d pronunciation and intonation 2.2e ask and answer questions 3b sounds and writing 3c apply grammar 4b communicate in pairs, etc.	*Wie heißt du?* *Ich heiße … . Und du?* *Hallo!* *Wie geht's?* *Prima, danke.* *Gut, danke.* *Nicht schlecht, danke.* *Nicht so gut.* *Und dir?* Irregular verb *sein: ich bin, du bist* Cardinal numbers 0–19 *Wie alt bist du?* *Ich bin … Jahre alt.*	Pronunciation: *ß* and *w* Social conventions
2 Ich wohne in Deutschland (pp. 8–9) ● Saying where you live ● Using verbs with *ich, du, er* and *sie*	4.5/Y7 Language – (a) present tense verbs 5.2 Strategies – memorising 5.3 Strategies – English/other languages	NC levels 1–3 2.1a identify patterns 2.1b memorising 2.2a listen for gist 2.2b skim and scan 2.2d pronunciation and intonation 2.2e ask and answer questions 3b sounds and writing 3c apply grammar 4b communicate in pairs, etc.	Regular verb *wohnen: ich wohne, du wohnst, er/sie wohnt* Regular verb *heißen: ich heiße, du heißt, er/sie heißt* Irregular verb *sein: ich bin, du bist, er/sie ist* *Wo wohnst du?* *Ich wohne in England, Schottland, Wales, Irland, Deutschland, Österreich, der Schweiz.* *Er/Sie heißt …* *Er/Sie wohnt in …* *Er/Sie ist … Jahre alt*	Pronunciation: *sch/ch*
3 Das Alphabet (pp. 10–11) ● Spelling in German ● Using the definite article (*der, die, das*) to say 'the'	4.1/Y7 Language – letters and sounds 4.3/Y7 Language – gender	NC levels 1–3 2.2d pronunciation and intonation 2.2e ask and answer questions 3b sounds and writing 3c apply grammar 4b communicate in pairs, etc.	Noun gender Definite article in nominative Letters of the alphabet *der Apfel, die Banane, der Computer, der Detektiv, das Eis, der Fußball, die Gitarre, das Haus, die Idee, der Joghurt, die Kamera, die Lampe, die Milch, die Nummer, die Orange, die Party, das Quiz, die Ratte, die Schule, das T-Shirt, die Uniform, der Vater, die Wespe, das Xylophon, die Yacht, der Zoo* *Wie schreibt man … ?* *… schreibt man …* *Der Schal / Die Kappe / Das T-Shirt ist rot, blau, gelb, braun, grün, orange, schwarz, weiß, grau.*	Spelling Asking for help Reviewing progress

Unit Learning targets	Key framework objectives	NC levels and PoS coverage	Grammar and key language	Skills
4 Hast du einen Bleistift? (pp. 12–13) • Describing what you have in your school bag • Using the indefinite article (*ein, eine*) to say – 'a'	**1.4/Y7** Speaking – (a) social and classroom language **2.1/Y7** Reading – main points and detail **4.3/Y7** Language – gender	NC levels 1–3 **2.1a** identify patterns **2.1b** memorising **2.2a** listen for gist **2.2b** skim and scan **2.2e** ask and answer questions **3b** sounds and writing **3c** apply grammar **4b** communicate in pairs, etc.	Irregular verb *haben: ich habe, du hast* Indefinite article in nominative and accusative *der Bleistift, das Buch, die Diskette, das Etui, das Heft, der Klebstift, der Kuli, das Lineal, die Schere, die Schultasche, der Taschenrechner, das Wörterbuch* *Das ist ein/eine/ein …* *Hast du einen/eine/ein … für mich?* *Ja, ich habe einen/eine/ein … .* *Nein.*	
5 Wann hast du Geburtstag? (pp. 14–15) • Learning the numbers from twenty to ninety-nine • Saying when your birthday is	**4.2/Y7** Language – high frequency words **4.6/Y7** Language – (a) questions	NC levels 1–3 **2.1a** identify patterns **2.1b** memorising **2.2a** listen for gist **2.2e** ask and answer questions **2.2f** initiate/sustain conversations **3b** sounds and writing **3c** apply grammar **3d** use a range of vocab/structures **4b** communicate in pairs, etc.	Question words: *wie, wo, wann, was* Irregular verb *haben: ich habe, du hast* Cardinal numbers 20–99 *Wann hast du Geburtstag?* *Ich habe am … … Geburtstag.* *ersten, zweiten, dritten … einunddreißigsten* *Januar, Februar, März, April, Mai, Juni, Juli, August, September, Oktober, November, Dezember*	
Lernzieltest und Wiederholung (pp. 16–17) • Pupils' checklist and practice test		NC levels 2–3 **2.2b** skim and scan **3c** apply grammar **3d** use a range of vocab/structures **4b** communicate in pairs, etc.		
Mehr (pp. 18–19) • Extension material	**2.2/Y7** Reading – (a) unfamiliar language **2.2/Y7** Reading – (b) text selection **3.1/Y7** Culture – aspects of everyday life **5.5** Strategies – reference materials	NC levels 3–4 **2.1d** previous knowledge **2.2a** listen for gist **2.2b** skim and scan **2.2e** ask and answer questions **2.2j** adapt previously-learned language **3c** apply grammar **3d** use a range of vocab/structures	Regular verb *kaufen: ich kaufe, du kaufst* Revision of accusative indefinite article *die Schere, der Klebstift, das Wörterbuch, die CD* *Das macht … Euro.* *Kaufst du einen Bleistift/eine Diskette/ein Wörterbuch?* *Ja. Nein.* *Ich kaufe …* *einen CD-Spieler* *eine Kamera* *ein Handy / Mountainbike / Snowboard / Skateboard* *Inline-Skates*	Reading a longer text for gist
Extra (pp. 100–101) • Self-access reading and writing at two levels		NC levels 1–4 **2.2e** ask and answer questions **3c** apply grammar **3d** use a range of vocab/structures		

Learning targets

- Introducing yourself
- Learning numbers and saying your age

Key framework objectives

4.1/Y7 Language – letters and sounds

4.2/Y7 Language – high frequency words

Grammar

- *sein: ich bin, du bist*

Key language

Wie heißt du?
Ich heiße … . Und du?
Hallo!
Wie geht's?
Prima, danke.
Gut, danke.
Nicht schlecht, danke.
Nicht so gut.
Und dir?
Wie alt bist du?
Ich bin … Jahre alt.
Cardinal numbers 0–19

High-frequency words

wie
ich, du
gut
und
danke
nicht
schlecht
so
bin, bist

Pronunciation

w and *ß*

Mathematics

Cardinal numbers 0–19

Resources

CD 1, tracks 2–7
Workbooks A and B, p.2
Echo Elektro 1 TPP, Express
Mod 1 1.1–1.8

Starter 1   4.2/Y7

Aims

To learn some first expressions in German.
To develop confidence in speaking.
To learn the social conventions of greetings.

Say *Hallo! Ich heiße* …. Write this language on the board and clarify its meaning. Choose a pupil, greet him/her as above and encourage him/her to respond in kind. (You could also shake hands to introduce this typical German custom.) Perform the exchange with a few more pupils. Finally, ask pupils to mingle and perform the exchange amongst themselves.

1 Hör zu. Wer spricht? (1–3) (AT 1/1)

1.1/Y7 4.2/Y7

Listening. Pupils listen to the recording and decide who is speaking in each dialogue. After checking the answers, play the recording again and elicit the meanings of *Ich heiße …*, *Wie heißt du?* and *Und du?*.

1 – *Wie heißt du?*
  – *Ich heiße Niklas. Und du?*
  – *Ich heiße Marie.*
  – *Hallo, Marie!*
  – *Hallo, Niklas!*
2 – *Wie heißt du?*
  – *Ich heiße Alexander. Und du?*
  – *Ich heiße Lea.*
  – *Hallo, Lea!*
  – *Hallo, Alexander!*
3 – *Wie heißt du?*
  – *Ich heiße Valentina. Und du?*
  – *Ich heiße Hamit.*
  – *Hallo, Hamit!*
  – *Hallo, Valentina!*

 2

Answers

1 Marie + Niklas
2 Alexander + Lea
3 Valentina + Hamit

2 Hör zu. Was passt zusammen? (1–3) (AT 1/1)
`4.2/Y7`

Listening. Pupils listen to the recording and match the speech bubbles to the utterances.

Suggestion

After a first playing, establish what the general situation is (asking people how they are) and that *Wie geht's?* means 'How are you?' Ask for ideas about what *Prima, danke, Gut, danke, Nicht schlecht, danke* and *Nicht so gut* might mean, using the pictures in the Pupil's Book to guide the class towards the right answers. Alternatively, present English translations (orally or on the board) and ask the class to match each one to the appropriate German expression.

1 – *Wie geht's?*
– *Nicht schlecht, danke. Und dir?*
– *Gut, danke.*
2 – *Wie geht's?*
– *Nicht so gut. Und dir?*
– *Prima, danke.*
3 – *Wie geht's?*
– *Nicht schlecht, danke. Und dir?*
– *Prima, danke.*

 3

> ### Answers
> **1** a, d   **2** b, c   **3** a, c

Aussprache: w und ß
`4.1/Y7`

Listening. This box explains the pronunciation of *w* and *ß*. Make sure that pupils understand that *ß* is equivalent to *ss* in some words, and do not confuse it with capital B. Pupils listen to the chant and repeat it, to practise the pronunciation of *w* and *ß*. You could get the class to repeat the chant several times in time with the recording, increasing in loudness as you turn down the volume of the recording.

Wie wie wie
Wie heißt du?
Heiße heiße heiße
Ich heiße Sue!

 4

3 Partnerarbeit. (AT 2/3)
`1.4a/Y7  4.1/Y7`

Speaking. Pupils work in pairs to create greeting dialogues based on those in exercises 1 and 2. Encourage pupils to shake hands (as a typical German custom) while introducing themselves. Draw their attention to how the voice rises at the end of *Und du?* and *Und dir?* to signal that they are questions.

4 Schreib einen Dialog. (AT 4/3)
`2.4a/Y7`

Writing. Pupils write their own dialogues, using the language they practised in exercise 3. You could prepare by looking again at exercise 3 with the class and discussing which parts will stay the same and which parts might change.

Starter 2
`1.4a/Y7`

Aims

To revise greetings.
To improve confidence and fluency.

Chorus the dialogue in exercise 3 with the class as a reminder of the structures and sequence to use. Pupils now choose a celebrity name for themselves. They circulate in the class, going through the dialogue with different partners, introducing themselves as the celebrity.

5 Hör zu und wiederhole.
`4.1/Y7  4.2/Y7`

Listening. Pupils listen to the recording and repeat the numbers 0 to 12. After they have listened and repeated a number of times, pause the recording while the class continues chanting. Finally, the class could count down from 12 to 0.

null
eins
zwei
drei
vier
fünf
sechs
sieben
acht
neun
zehn
elf
zwölf

 5

R Prepare some simple sums (all numbers including the answers to be below 13) on an OHT and reveal them one at a time. Elicit the solutions in German from the class.

6 Was passt zusammen? Hör zu und überprüfe es. (AT 3/1 AT 1/1)
`4.2/Y7`

Listening. Pupils match the words to the numbers. This requires them to use their knowledge of the numbers 1–10 to work out the numbers 13–19. (You will probably need to guide a lower-ability class through this exercise step by step, or simply present the numbers on the board or an OHT.) Pupils listen to the recording to check their own answers.

dreizehn
vierzehn
fünfzehn
sechzehn
siebzehn
achtzehn
neunzehn

 6

> **Answers**
> 13 dreizehn; 14 vierzehn; 15 fünfzehn; 16 sechzehn;
> 17 siebzehn; 18 achtzehn; 19 neunzehn

7 Hör zu. Wie alt sind sie? (1–6) (AT 1/2) 1.1/Y7

Listening. Pupils listen to the dialogues and write down the ages of the speakers. After checking answers, play the recording again to focus on the structure of the question and the answer, in preparation for exercise 8.

1 – Wie alt bist du, Ralf?
 – Ich bin dreizehn Jahre alt.
2 – Und du, Emma? Wie alt bist du?
 – Ich bin elf Jahre alt.
3 – Und du, Hasan? Wie alt bist du?
 – Ich bin neunzehn Jahre alt.
4 – Hallo, Hanna! Wie alt bist du?
 – Ich bin zehn Jahre alt.
5 – Hi, Erik! Sag mal, wie alt bist du?
 – Ich bin fünfzehn Jahre alt.
6 – Hallo, Jasmin! Wie alt bist du?
 – Ich bin zwölf Jahre alt.

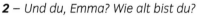 7

> **Answers**
> **1** 13   **2** 11   **3** 19   **4** 10   **5** 15   **6** 12

8 Partnerarbeit (AT 2/2) 1.4a/Y7

Speaking. Pupils work together in pairs to ask each other their ages. In preparation, focus on the formulation of the question and the answer. Drill the question and answer with the whole class.

➕ To achieve more variety in the answers and to practise more numbers, ask pupils to choose an age between 2 and 19. They could circulate in the class asking the question of several classmates. Alternatively, pupils write their chosen age on a piece of paper, then race to find another pupil with the same age. When they find their 'twin', they sit down together.

> **ECHO-Detektiv: sein – *to be*** 4.5a/Y7
> This panel introduces pupils to the conjugation of the verb *sein* in the *ich* and *du* forms. You may wish to take this opportunity to introduce the class to the **Grammatik** section at the back of the Pupil's Book.

9 Schreib über dich. (AT 4/3) 2.4a/Y7

Writing. Pupils write short texts about themselves, using the language they have learned in this unit. You could assist less able pupils by writing the sample answer on the board and eliciting from the class which words could be changed.

Plenary 5.2

Aim
To develop learning strategies.

Pupils work in groups to brainstorm ideas for learning numbers. After a set time limit has expired, ask each group for its best idea. List the ideas on the board or an OHT. Ideas could include:

– Whenever you see a number in the street (e.g. house number, bus number), try to think of the German number.
– Chant the numbers in groups of three.
– Sing the numbers to a well-known tune such as 'Twinkle, twinkle little star'.

Set the class the target of learning the numbers 0 to 19 by the next lesson.

Learning targets
- Saying where you live
- Using verbs with *ich*, *du*, *er* and *sie*

Key framework objectives
4.5/Y7 Language – (a) present tense verbs
5.2 Strategies – memorising
5.3 Strategies – English/ other languages

Grammar
- Present tense of the verbs *wohnen*, *heißen* and *sein* in the *ich*, *du* and *er/sie* forms

Key language
Wo wohnst du?
Ich wohne in …
England
Wales
Schottland
Irland
Frankreich
Deutschland
Österreich
der Schweiz
Er/Sie heißt …
Er/Sie wohnt in …
Er/Sie ist … Jahre alt

High-frequency words
wo?
wie alt?
in
wohne, wohnst, wohnt
heißt
bin
bist
ist
ich
du
er
sie

Pronunciation
sch and *ch*

Citizenship
European countries and the languages spoken by their inhabitants

English
Verb conjugation

Resources
CD 1, tracks 8–11
Workbooks A and B, p. 3
Flashcards 1–8
Echo Elektro 1 TPP, Express Mod 1 2.1–2.6

Starter 1
4.2/Y7

Aim
To revise the numbers 0 to 19.

Bingo: ask pupils to note down any five numbers between 0 and 19 on a mini-whiteboard or a sheet of paper. They must not write the same number twice. Call out numbers at random, repeating each twice. Pupils cross off their numbers when they hear them. The first pupil to cross off all his/her numbers calls out *Lotto!* and holds up his/her board or paper for you to check. The winner could receive a small reward.

Suggestion
To assess the level of geographical knowledge in the class, ask pupils to name European countries in English. Do they know the three countries where German is the main language?

Rate mal: Wie heißt das Land? (AT 3/1) **5.3**

Reading. Pupils study the map and work out which of the German names goes with each country. They complete exercise 2 to check their own answers.

> **Answers**
> **1** Irland
> **2** Wales
> **3** Schottland
> **4** England
> **5** Frankreich
> **6** Deutschland
> **7** Österreich
> **8** die Schweiz

2 Hör zu und überprüfe es. (1–8) (AT 1/1) `1.1/Y7 5.3`

Listening. Pupils listen to the recording to check their answers to exercise 1. To do so, they have to listen for key words (names of countries).

Ask pupils whether they had the right answers before the recording was played. If so, how did they work out the answers? Was it prior knowledge, similarity to English, a process of elimination or a lucky guess? Tell them that all of these things are important in 'decoding' German.

1 *Das ist Irland.*
2 *Das ist Wales.*
3 *Das ist Schottland.*
4 *Das ist England.*
5 *Das ist Frankreich.*
6 *Das ist Deutschland.*
7 *Das ist Österreich.*
8 *Das ist die Schweiz.*

`8`

R List the German names of the countries on the board or an OHT and ask for volunteers to write the English next to each one.

3 Hör zu. Wo wohnen sie? (1–8) (AT 1/2) `1.1/Y7`

Listening. Pupils listen and note which country different people live in. Encourage them to make abbreviated notes while listening and then to convert the notes to full country names afterwards.

1 – *Wo wohnst du, Diarmuid?*
  – *Ich wohne in Irland.*
2 – *Wo wohnst du, Rikki?*
  – *Ich wohne in Deutschland.*
3 – *Wo wohnst du, Elke?*
  – *Ich wohne in Österreich.*
4 – *Anke, hallo! Wo wohnst du?*
  – *Ich wohne in der Schweiz.*
5 – *Wo wohnst du, Rhiannon?*
  – *Ich wohne in Wales.*
6 – *Delphine! Hi! Wo wohnst du?*
  – *Ich wohne in Frankreich.*
7 – *Wo wohnst du, Tom?*
  – *Ich wohne in England.*
8 – *Und du, Harry? Wo wohnst du?*
  – *Ich wohne in Schottland.*

`9`

Answers
1 Irland
2 Deutschland
3 Österreich
4 die Schweiz
5 Wales
6 Frankreich
7 England
8 Schottland

Aussprache: sch/ch `4.1/Y7`

Listening. This panel explains the difference between the pronunciation of *sch* and *ch*. Pupils listen to the recording and distinguish whether the word contains *sch* or *ch*.

1 *Schottland*
2 *Frankreich*
3 *Schule*
4 *acht*
5 *Deutschland*
6 *Schweiz*

`10`

Answers
1 sch 2 ch 3 sch 4 ch 5 sch 6 sch

4 Partnerarbeit: Wer ist das? (AT 2/2) `1.4b/Y7`

Speaking. Pupils create dialogues based on the picture cues. The partner asking the question decides which character is speaking, then the roles are reversed. In preparation, go through the Key Language panel with the class and check that all pupils understand the question and answer. Focus specifically on how they will pronounce words containing any *sch/ch* letter strings.

Suggestion
You could support less able pupils by first eliciting the nationalities symbolised by the flags on the characters' clothes.

Starter 2 `1.4a/Y7`

Aims
To revise giving personal information.
To develop confidence and proficiency in building basic sentences.

On a piece of paper, pupils write a name, a number under 19 and a country in German. They then swap their piece of paper with a partner.

Pupils mingle saying the information on the piece of paper to other pupils using the full sentences in German: *ich heiße …, ich bin … Jahre alt, ich wohne in … .*

Pupils could also ask questions to elicit the information.

When pupils have gained confidence, they could start to swap their pieces of paper each time after exchanging the information, so that they are giving different information each time they talk to somebody new.

5 Hör zu. Wie ist es richtig? (1–3) (AT 1/2) `1.1/Y7`

Listening. Pupils listen to the recording and choose the correct answers for each of the three dialogues. As the sentences are printed in the third person singular, pupils are exposed receptively to these verb forms, but are not yet required to produce them. Before you start listening, go over the sentences and options on the page and see if pupils can deduce the meanings of *er/sie* followed by verbs.

1 – *Wie heißt du?*
  – *Ich heiße Peter.*
  – *Wo wohnst du, Peter?*
  – *Ich wohne in Deutschland.*
  – *Und wie alt bist du?*
  – *Ich bin dreizehn Jahre alt.*
2 – *Wie heißt du?*
  – *Ich heiße Laura.*
  – *Also, Laura, wo wohnst du?*
  – *Ich wohne in der Schweiz.*
  – *In der Schweiz. Und wie alt bist du?*
  – *Ich bin vierzehn Jahre alt.*
3 – *Wie heißt du?*
  – *Ich heiße Alex.*
  – *Und wo wohnst du, Alex?*
  – *Ich wohne in Österreich.*
  – *In Österreich, sehr gut. Und wie alt bist du?*
  – *Ich bin zwölf Jahre alt.*

Answers
1 a, d, h
2 c, f, i
3 b, e, g

6 Lies die Texte und füll die Tabelle aus. (AT 3/3) `2.1/Y7 5.6`

Reading. Pupils read the texts and complete the table with the personal details of the three teenagers.

Answers

Heißt …	… Jahre alt	Wohnt in …
1 Birgit	12	Leipzig, Deutschland
2 Michel	14	Lille, Frankreich
3 Sam	10	Liverpool, England

R Pupils take turns reading the texts out loud to their partners. They could swap roles whenever they reach a punctuation mark. Further ideas to follow up reading exercises can be found in the Introduction on pages 9–10.

+ Pupils write out the contents of the table in full sentences in the third person.

ECHO-Detektiv `4.5a/Y7`

This panel shows *wohnen* and *sein* in the first, second and third person singular. You may wish to check that all pupils can confidently define a verb at this point. This provides a good opportunity to focus on the idea of verbs with regular endings and irregular verbs. Here you could draw on their knowledge from their first foreign language. Pupils could then race to spot and read out sentences containing each of the verb forms from page 9. Refer more able pupils to the **Grammatik** on pages 118 and 120.

7 Schreib Sätze. (AT 4/3) `2.4a/Y7 4.5a/Y7`

Writing. Pupils write short texts in the first person based on the two ID cards.

Answers
1 Ich heiße Jean-Luc Dupont. Ich bin vierzehn Jahre alt. Ich wohne in Frankreich.
2 Ich heiße Lucy McDonald. Ich bin zwölf Jahre alt. Ich wohne in Schottland.

+ As a homework task, more able pupils could write an additional text in the third person about a friend.

Plenary `5.2`

Aim
To develop learning strategies.

Pupils work in pairs to come up with ideas for learning verb forms. Set a time limit of two minutes. After the time limit has expired, ask each pair for its best idea. Ideas could include:

– Write them in a table (as in the Pupil's Book).
– Chant them.
– Write them in a sentence, with words that help to reinforce the patterns, e.g. *Wo wohnst du Stephanie? – Ich wohne in England.*

Learning targets
- Spelling in German
- Using the definite article (*der, die, das*) to say 'the'

Key framework objectives
4.1/Y7 Language – letters and sounds
4.3/Y7 Language – gender

Grammar
- Noun gender
- Definite article: *der, die, das*

Key language
Letters of the alphabet
der Apfel
die Banane
der Computer
der Detektiv
das Eis
der Fußball
die Gitarre
das Haus
die Idee
der Joghurt
die Kamera
die Lampe
die Milch
die Nummer
die Orange
die Party
das Quiz
die Ratte
die Schule
das T-Shirt
die Uniform
der Vater
die Wespe
das Xylophon
die Yacht
der Zoo

Wie schreibt man … ?
Der Schal / Die Kappe / Das T-Shirt ist rot / blau / gelb / braun / grün / orange / schwarz / weiß / grau.

High-frequency words
wie?
der, die, das
man
schreibt
ist

Citizenship
Popular sports in other European countries

English
The alphabet, accurate spelling
Definite and indefinite articles with nouns

Resources
CD 1, tracks 12–14
Workbooks A and B, p. 4
Arbeitsblatt 1.1, p. 4
Echo Elektro 1 TPP, Express Mod 1 3.1–3.8

Starter 1 — 4.2/Y7

Aim
To revise country names in German.
Make an OHT of **Arbeitsblatt 1.1**. (You may also wish to photocopy the worksheet for each pupil to fill in and then stick in their exercise books as a reference.) Pupils work in pairs to write down the country names. With a lower-ability class, you may wish to write the German names in random order on the board for pupils to locate on the map. Set a time limit of about two minutes.

Suggestion
Spell out the name of a pupil in the class, using the German alphabet, writing the letters on the board as you do so. Ask the pupil to put his/her hand up. Spell out further names of class members, without writing them. Pupils put up their hands when they hear their name spelled. Other pupils can prompt them.

Hör zu und lies. — 4.1/Y7
Listening. Pupils listen to the recording and follow the alphabet in their books. Draw their attention to the sounds of E and I, which are easily confused.

As a follow-up activity, pupils work in pairs. Partner A reads out the German pronunciation of each letter (as in the Pupil's Book). Partner B writes the letter in one of two columns: letters that sound similar in German and English, and those that do not (e.g. G, H, J, V, W, Y).

25

R Pupils stand up in pairs. When you call out letters, pairs work together to make the shape of those letters, using just their arms or their whole bodies. Alternatively, pupils 'write' letters on their partner's back with a finger. The partner tries to say the correct letter in German.

> *A, B, C*
> *D, E, F, G*
> *H, I, J*
> *K, L, M*
> *N, O, P, Q*
> *R, S, T, U*
> *V, W, X*
> *Y, Z*

 12

ECHO-Tipp   4.1/Y7

This panel introduces pupils to the Umlaut and reminds them about the letter ß. These pronunciation points are treated in greater detail later in the course. At this point, you could encourage them to look for words where they have already encountered these types of letters.

2 Hör zu und sing den Alphabet-Rap mit.   4.1/Y7

Listening. Pupils listen to the alphabet song and sing along. Further ideas for exploiting songs can be found in the Introduction on page 10. You could divide the class into two groups, singing alternate lines. Draw attention to the fact that all nouns in German start with a capital letter. Elicit from the class that all the words are very close to English. You could also introduce the concept of cognates at this point. What do pupils think the words *der*, *die* and *das* mean? (The definite article is dealt with in detail in the **ECHO-Detektiv** panel.)

Pupils work in pairs to discover ways in which German spelling/pronunciation of cognates differs from English (e.g. -e is not silent, k = c, au = ou, j = y). Collect ideas around the class and discuss.

> *A ist der Apfel.*
> *B ist die Banane.*
> *C ist der Computer.*
> *D ist der Detektiv.*
> *E ist das Eis.*
> *F ist der Fußball.*
> *G ist die Gitarre.*
> *H ist das Haus.*
> *I ist die Idee.*
> *J ist der Joghurt.*
> *K ist die Kamera.*
> *L ist die Lampe.*
> *M ist die Milch.*

13

> *N ist die Nummer.*
> *O ist die Orange.*
> *P ist die Party.*
> *Q ist das Quiz.*
> *R ist die Ratte.*
> *S ist die Schule.*
> *T ist das T-Shirt.*
> *U ist die Uniform.*
> *V ist der Vater.*
> *W ist die Wespe.*
> *X ist das Xylophon.*
> *Y ist die Yacht.*
> *Z ist der Zoo.*

3 Partnerarbeit: Wie schreibt man …? (AT 2/2)   4.1/Y7

Speaking. Pupils work in pairs, asking each other in German how to spell words from exercise 2. Encourage pupils to monitor the accuracy of their partner's pronunciation of the German letters. Higher-ability pupils could attempt to spell the words with their books closed, while their partners monitor their accuracy in the book. The exercise could further be extended to pupils' favourite pop groups or different football teams. Ask pupils when, in real life, they need to spell things to people. See page 10 in the Introduction for a variation on pairwork.

Starter 2   1.1/Y7 4.2/Y7

Aims
To consolidate everyday words.
To practise pronunciation of the alphabet in German.

Play a game of Hangman with the class, using words from exercise 2 on page 10. The class could be divided into two teams, each with a different word. Points could be allocated depending on how quickly the team guesses the word, e.g. 10 points minus the number of wrong letters guessed in order to get the word. Once a letter is guessed wrong, the turn could move to the other team to have a go at their word. If letters are pronounced wrongly, this could equally lead to loss of points. Confirm the word in a whisper before the pupil writes in the spaces on the board.

4 Hör zu. Was passt zusammen? (1–9) (AT 1/1) `4.2/Y7`

Listening. Pupils listen to the recording and match the spoken colours to those in their books. You could use this exercise to focus on the correct pronunciation of *au*.

R To practise the colours, make colour swatches from sheets of coloured paper or card, cut up. Each pupil or pair receives one colour. When pupils hear their colour, they must stand up or hold up their swatch. Pupils holding up the wrong colour are 'out'. Increase the speed of the game until only one pupil or pair remains 'in'.

1 blau
2 grau
3 gelb
4 schwarz
5 grün
6 rot
7 braun
8 orange
9 weiß

14

Answers
1 b   2 i   3 c   4 g   5 e   6 a   7 d   8 f
9 h

ECHO-Detektiv: der, die, das `4.3/Y7`

This panel explains that there are three words for 'the' in German, *der*, *die* and *das*, corresponding to the three noun genders masculine, feminine and neuter. Check comprehension by asking pupils to identify masculine, feminine and neuter nouns in exercise 2 on page 10. After going through the panel with the class, you could refer them to the relevant section of the **Grammatik** at the back of their books (page 113).

5 Lies die Sätze. Welcher Fußball-Fan ist das? (AT 3/2) `4.3/Y7`

Reading. Pupils read the sentences, then decide which football fan is being described. In preparation, establish the meanings of *der Schal* and *die Kappe* and elicit the genders of those two nouns and *das T-Shirt*. Support less able pupils by going through the sample answer.

Answers
1 Frankfurt   2 Bremen   3 Frankfurt
4 Bochum   5 Bremen   6 Bochum

+ Check pupils' cultural knowledge: ask whether they know any other German football teams, or any other sports popular in German-speaking countries (e.g. skiing, motor racing, tennis, handball, hockey and ice hockey; not cricket or rugby).

6 Beschreib den Freiburg-Fan. (AT 4/3) `4.2a/Y7`

Writing. Pupils write sentences to describe the Freiburg fan's clothes. Refer pupils to exercise 5 for model sentences to adapt. Assist less able pupils by providing the start of each sentence.

Suggested answers
Das T-Shirt ist rot. Die Kappe ist rot und weiß. Der Schal ist rot und schwarz.

+ For homework, pupils could draw and label fans of other German or British football teams (e.g. referring to www.bundesliga.de for information).

Plenary `5.8`

Aim
To review language learned to date and identify areas for improvement.

Pupils work in pairs to check the language they have learned so far, using the **Mini-Test** checklist. Ask pupils which points their partners found most difficult. Give them the task of helping their partner to improve those points by next lesson.

Learning targets
- Describing what you have in your school bag
- Using the indefinite article (*ein, eine*) to say 'a'

Key framework objectives
1.4/Y7 Speaking – (a) social and classroom language
2.1/Y7 Reading – main points and detail
4.3/Y7 Language – gender

Grammar
- Using the indefinite article: *ein / eine / ein* and *einen / eine / ein*
- Present tense of the verb *haben* in the *ich* and *du* forms

Key language
der Bleistift
das Buch
die Diskette
das Etui
das Heft
der Klebstift
der Kuli
das Lineal
die Schere
die Schultasche
der Taschenrechner
das Wörterbuch
Das ist ein / eine / ein …
Hast du einen / eine / ein … für mich?
Ja, ich habe einen / eine / ein … .
Nein.

High-frequency words
Was ist das?
das ist ein / eine / ein …
hast du … ?
ich habe einen / eine / ein …
ja, nein
für
mich
danke

Resources
CD 1, tracks 15–16
Workbooks A and B, page 5
Arbeitsblatt 1.2, p. 5
Arbeitsblatt 1.3, p. 6
Arbeitsblatt 1.5, p. 8
Flashcards 9–20
Echo Elektro 1 TPP, Express Mod 1 4.1–4.8

Starter 1
4.2/Y7

Aim
To revise colours.

Brainstorm colours in German to revise those which pupils have met so far (*blau, grau, gelb, schwarz, grün, rot, braun, orange* and *weiß*). Pupils could race to hold up something of the right colour when one is called out. Then call out the following pairs of colours in German. Pupils, working individually or in pairs, write down the colour that is made by mixing the two colours. The first pupil/pair to hold up the correct answer wins a point.

For more practice, simply repeat some of the combinations with the colours reversed.

Blau plus gelb!
Rot plus gelb!
Schwarz plus weiß!
Orange plus schwarz!

Suggestion
Assemble the objects featured in exercise 1. Introduce them one at a time, with the class repeating the name of each object. Then hold up the objects at random (or place them on the OHP, so that their silhouettes can be seen), asking, e.g. *Ist das die Schere?*. Pupils respond with *Ja* or *Nein*. More able groups can add *das ist … .*

Hör zu. Was passt zusammen? (1–12) (AT 1/1)
4.2/Y7

Listening. Pupils listen to the recording and find the corresponding items in their books.

1 das Buch
2 das Heft
3 das Etui
4 das Lineal
5 die Schere
6 die Schultasche
7 die Diskette
8 der Bleistift
9 der Taschenrechner
10 das Wörterbuch
11 der Klebstift
12 der Kuli

 15

Answers

| 1 b | 2 e | 3 d | 4 h | 5 i | 6 j | 7 c | 8 a |
| 9 k | 10 l | 11 f | 12 g | | | | |

R Use the recording to practise pronunciation (listen and repeat).

2 Schreib die Sätze ab und füll die Lücken aus. Welches Bild ist das? (AT 3/2) — 4.3/Y7

Reading. Pupils complete the sentences with *ein* or *eine* and then find the matching pictures. Prepare for this exercise by going through the ECHO-Detektiv panel with the class.

Answers

1. Das ist eine Schere. – b
2. Das ist ein Kuli. – f
3. Das ist ein Lineal. – c
4. Das ist ein Klebstift. – d
5. Das ist ein Wörterbuch. – e
6. Das ist ein Etui. – a

ECHO-Detektiv *the* and *a* — 4.3/Y7

This panel shows the correspondence between noun gender and the form of the indefinite article (nominative). To check pupils' understanding, supply the nouns with the definite articles and elicit the correct indefinite article in each case . Refer pupils to the relevant section of the **Grammatik** at the back of their books (page 113).

3 Partnerarbeit: Was ist das? (AT 2/2) — 4.2/Y7

Speaking. Pupils work together in pairs. They ask each other to identify the pictures from exercise 2, using *Das ist ein/eine … .* Run through the form of the question and the answer with the class first, in preparation.

Starter 2 — 5.1

Aims

To develop thinking skills, e.g. pattern recognition, logic, lateral thinking.
To revise the meaning and gender of everyday words.

Make **Arbeitsblatt 1.2** into an OHT or photocopy it for pupils to use as individual worksheets. Pupils work through the tasks in pairs. If time is short, task C could be set for homework.

4 Hör zu und lies. Was braucht Peter? (AT1/3, AT 3/3) — 1.1/Y7

Listening/Reading. Pupils listen to the recording and follow the dialogue in their books. In order to give the activity more of a listening focus, you could do the listening without the text first to see if pupils can note down the items of stationery mentioned. They then write down in English what Peter needs. Before playing the recording, ask pupils to scan the text and look at the photo. What do they think is going on? Ask for evidence to support their answers. After doing the exercise, ask pupils how this language might be useful for them in the classroom.

– *Julia, hast du einen Bleistift für mich?*
– *Ja, ich habe einen Bleistift.*
– *Danke … Hast du eine Schere für mich?*
– *Ja, ich habe eine Schere.*
– *Danke … Hast du ein Lineal für mich?*
– *Nein!*

16

Answers
Pencil, pair of scissors, ruler

R Pupils practise reading out the dialogue in pairs.

ECHO-Detektiv — 4.5a/Y7

This panel shows the verb *haben* in the *ich* and *du* forms. Ask the class for examples of the two forms in exercise 4. Refer higher-ability pupils to the relevant section in the **Grammatik** at the back of their books, page 120.

ECHO-Detektiv — 4.3/Y7

This panel introduces the indefinite article in the accusative case. Elicit what the difference is from the nominative case, on page 12. Refer higher-ability pupils to the relevant section in the **Grammatik** at the back of their books, page 114.

5 Partnerarbeit. (AT 2/3) `1.4a/Y7`

Speaking. Pupils work in pairs. They ask each other for various items of school equipment, using the Key Language panel. Focus on how to form the question with *haben*. When replying, if practical, they could produce the item itself. Encourage pupils to be accurate in their use of *einen, eine* and *ein* (although less able pupils may not manage this) and on the word order of questions.

+ Pupils can extend the exercise with other nouns they know, e.g. *Hast du einen Apfel für mich?*

6 Lies den Text. Was ist nicht im Bild? (AT 3/3) `2.1/Y7`

Reading. Pupils read the text and compare it with the picture. They identify the items in the text that are not in the picture. Activities to follow up reading with further reading, translation or writing can be found on pages 9–10 of the Introduction.

> **Answers**
> Exercise book (*ein Heft*), pair of scissors (*eine Schere*), football (*einen Fußball*)

7 Was hast du in der Schultasche? (AT 4/3) `2.4a/Y7`

Writing. Pupils write a short text about what they have in their schoolbags. (This does not have to reflect reality exactly!) Remind pupils to think about the gender of each noun and to select *einen, eine* or *ein* as appropriate.

R Support less able pupils by providing them with a simple writing frame. This could be a copy of the text with some words blanked out.

+ Encourage higher-ability pupils to include items from the previous unit and to add extra information, e.g. *Ich habe ein T-Shirt. Das T-Shirt ist rot.*

Plenary `4.2/Y7`

Aims

To consolidate the vocabulary of school objects. To focus on accuracy in written work.

Pupils close their books. Give them two minutes to write down as many German nouns as they can for things in a schoolbag. Encourage pupils to write *der, die* or *das* as appropriate before each noun. Their partners then check their work using the Pupil's Book. They should check for:

1 logic (e.g. *das Haus* is incorrect!)
2 the correct spelling
3 the correct article, if relevant.

If in doubt, they should consult you. Each word scores a maximum of three points; the winner is the pupil with the most points.

Learning targets
- Saying when your birthday is
- Using different question words

Key framework objectives
4.2/Y7 Language – high frequency words
4.6/Y7 Language – (a) questions

Grammar
- Questions with question words
- *haben: ich habe, du hast*

Key language
Cardinal numbers 20–99
Ordinal numbers 1st to 31st
Wann hast du Geburtstag?
Ich habe am … … Geburtstag.
ersten, zweiten, dritten …
einunddreißigsten
Januar
Februar
März
April
Mai
Juni
Juli
August
September
Oktober
November
Dezember

High-frequency words
wie? wo? wann? was?
ich habe, du hast
am

Pronunciation
z

Mathematics
Using cardinal numbers and ordinal numbers (dates)
Gathering and analysing statistics

ICT
Using a spreadsheet application to show survey results

Resources
CD 1, tracks 17–21
Workbooks A and B, p. 6
Arbeitsblatt 1.4, p.7
Echo Elektro 1 TPP, Express Mod 1 5.1–5.10

Starter 1   4.4/Y7

Aims
To practise building sentences.
To launch the concept of high-frequency words.
Write the following words on the board:
habe, bist, wie, in, du, er
Working in pairs, pupils think of a sentence using each word. This could be done as a race. Write the 'winning' sentence on the board and collect a few more suggestions around the class. Explain that the six words are what is called 'high-frequency' words. Can pupils think of why they are called this? Why is it important to make sure they know what they mean?

Suggestion
Write a selection of numbers between 0 and 19 in words on an OHT. Place the OHT back-to-front on the projector, making sure the numbers are covered to start with. Display the numbers one at a time. Pairs of pupils race to decipher the number and write it in figures on a mini-whiteboard or on paper. The first pair to hold up the correct answer wins a point. The pair with most points wins the game.

Hör zu und wiederhole.   4.2/Y7 5.1
Listening. Pupils listen to the recording and repeat the numbers. Elicit from the class what 31 etc. will be, helping pupils as necessary so that they see the pattern, i.e. that Germans write the number as one word, and say 'one-and-twenty' etc. instead of 'twenty-one'.

R Practise numbers up to 99, chorusing or counting round the class.

+ With a higher-ability class, practise counting up or down in twos or threes. As pupils' confidence and fluency increases, move on to further variations, e.g. with a ball or soft toy: the pupil who catches the ball must give the number above or below.

zwanzig, einundzwanzig, zweiundzwanzig, dreiundzwanzig, vierundzwanzig, fünfundzwanzig, sechsundzwanzig, siebenundzwanzig, achtundzwanzig, neunundzwanzig, dreißig, vierzig, fünfzig, sechzig, siebzig, achtzig, neunzig

17

2 Hör zu. Welche Zahl ist das? (AT 1/1)
1.1/Y7

Listening. Pupils listen to the recording and identify which numbers they hear. After checking answers, ask the class which numbers they found most difficult. Discuss what this shows about points of difficulty concerning numbers (e.g. easy to mix up teens and tens – *dreizehn / dreißig*, etc.; easy to confuse tens and units – 34 instead of 43).

a einundzwanzig
b dreiundzwanzig
c vierunddreißig
d siebenundvierzig
e fünfunddreißig
f neunundsechzig
g achtundneunzig
h neunzehn
i fünfzig
j achtzig

18

> **Answers**
> **a** 21   **b** 23   **c** 34   **d** 47   **e** 35   **f** 69   **g** 98   **h** 19
> **i** 50   **j** 80

Aussprache: z
4.1/Y7

Listening. This box explains the pronunciation of *z*. Make sure that pupils understand that *z* is similar in sound to *ts*. Pupils listen to the recording and repeat the phrase to practise the pronunciation of *z*. You could get the class to repeat the phrase several times in time with the recording, increasing in loudness as you turn down the volume of the recording.

Zehn Zebras im Zoo!

19

3 Partnerarbeit: Üb die Zahlen. (AT 2/2)
4.1/Y7 4.2/Y7

Speaking. Pupils work together in pairs. They practise numbers between 20 and 99 using the picture cues in their books. Encourage them to concentrate on the *z* sound as they work.

➕ Higher-ability pupils can write numbers at random for their partners to read out, or write down the number that their partner says.

Alternatively, pupils can write numbers in the air or with a finger on each other's back.

4 Schreib die Monate in der richtigen Reihenfolge auf. Hör zu und überprüfe es. (AT 3/1, AT 1/1)
4.2/Y7 5.3

Writing/Listening. Pupils write the months in the correct order, using their knowledge of cognates to help them. They check their own answers by listening to the recording. Focus their attention on the different pronunciation of the months in German, even when written identically to English. Chorus them with the class.

Januar, Februar, März, April
Mai, Juni, Juli, August
September, Oktober
November, Dezember

20

> **Answers**
> Januar, Februar, März, April, Mai, Juni, Juli, August, September, Oktober, November, Dezember

Starter 2
4.2/Y7

Aim
To consolidate numbers up to 99.

Divide the class into groups of equal size. Each group appoints a secretary, who must sit facing the back of the room. Display six numbers between 13 and 99 as words on the board or an OHT. The numbers should be in jumbled order. The groups dictate the numbers in German, in ascending order, to their secretary, who must write them on a mini-whiteboard or a sheet of paper as figures. As soon as he/she has finished, the secretary comes to the front of the class with the group's answers. The first group with correct answers wins.

5 Hör zu. Wann haben sie Geburtstag? (1–8) (AT 1/2)
1.1/Y7 5.1

Listening. Pupils listen to the recording and identify when the speakers' birthdays are. Before starting, introduce the context by asking pupils what they think this activity will be about – which should be evident from the visuals in their books. By identifying the months, pupils should be able to complete this exercise before the ordinal numbers have been systematically introduced.

After checking the answers, ask the class what they noticed about how to say dates in German. Replaying the recording as necessary, guide the class towards recognising that the rule is *am …ten* for numbers below 20, and *am …sten* for numbers 20 and above, but that there are a few irregular ones (*am ersten, dritten, siebten*). Refer pupils to the Key Language panel.

With a higher-ability class, you may wish to draw attention to the convention for writing dates in German, i.e. with a full stop after the number.

1 – Ingo, wann hast du Geburtstag?
– Ich habe am dritten Dezember Geburtstag.

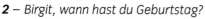 21

2 – Birgit, wann hast du Geburtstag?
– Ich habe am dreizehnten April Geburtstag.

3 – Jonas, wann hast du Geburtstag?
– Ich habe am siebten Mai Geburtstag.

4 – Svenja, wann hast du Geburtstag?
– Ich habe am einundzwanzigsten Juni Geburtstag.

5 – Max, wann hast du Geburtstag?
– Ich habe am vierundzwanzigsten August Geburtstag.

6 – Heike, wann hast du Geburtstag?
– Ich habe am neunundzwanzigsten März Geburtstag.

7 – Kemal, wann hast du Geburtstag?
– Ich habe am dritten Februar Geburtstag.

8 – Ingrid, wann hast du Geburtstag?
– Ich habe am ersten Juli Geburtstag.

Answers
1 am 3. Dezember
2 am 13. April
3 am 7. Mai
4 am 21. Juni
5 am 24. August
6 am 29. März
7 am 3. Februar
8 am 1. Juli

ECHO-Detektiv: Question words

4.6a/Y7

This panel reviews the question words which pupils have met so far in this chapter. Ask for volunteers to give an example of a question with each question word. Refer pupils to the relevant section of the **Grammatik** at the back of their books (page 124).

Suggestion
You could use exercises 6 and 7 as an opportunity to analyse the formation of questions with question words, with reference to the **ECHO-Detektiv** panel.

6 Umfrage. (AT 2/3) 1.4a/Y7 4.6a/Y7

Speaking. Pupils circulate around the class, interviewing each other about their birthdays and ages. If results are to be recorded, pupils should start by writing a list of the months (or abbreviations) in their exercise books to note names, dates and ages next to. You could set pupils the task of finding at least one birthday for each month – is there a month with no class birthdays?

ICT Survey results could be recorded as described above and then represented in a spreadsheet application as a pie chart or bar chart.

Note: You may wish to confer first with the Maths department about the types of charts/graphs which pupils have encountered so far.

7 Beantworte die Fragen (a) für Maren und (b) für David. (AT 3/3) 2.1/Y7 4.6a/Y7

Reading. Pupils answer the questions (a) for Maren and (b) for David, in the first person. This requires them to locate the information in the texts and transform it from the third to the first person. In preparation, support less able pupils by going over the meaning of verbs with *er/sie* in the texts, then working through one or two of the answers as a whole-class activity.

Follow-up reading, translation and writing activities can be found in the Introduction on pages 9–10.

Answers
1a Ich heiße Maren Schmidt.
1b Ich heiße David Krombacher.
2a Ich wohne in Frankfurt, in Deutschland.
2b Ich wohne in Salzburg, in Österreich.
3a Ich habe am 5. Juni Geburtstag.
3b Ich habe am 23. März Geburtstag.
4a Ich bin 13 Jahre alt.
4b Ich bin 14 Jahre alt.
5a Ich habe eine Gitarre, ein T-Shirt und einen Computer.
5b Ich habe ein Snowboard, eine Kamera und einen Fußball.

8 Beantworte die Fragen für dich. (AT 4/3)

2.4a/Y7

Writing. Pupils answer the questions from exercise 7 for themselves.

R Less able pupils could be provided with a simple writing frame.

+ More able pupils could write a text about themselves or a friend in the third person.

Plenary

4.6a/Y7 5.1

Aims

To consolidate dates.

To learn to work in a collaborative environment.

Ask for a volunteer to come to the board and explain to the class how to say dates in German. The volunteer can nominate two assistants to help him/her. The rest of the class can ask questions. The volunteer 'teacher' can then test the class's understanding by asking individual pupils *Wann hast du Geburtstag?*

Lernzieltest und Wiederholung

Lernzieltest `5.8`

This is a checklist of language covered in Chapter 1. Pupils can work in pairs with the checklist to check what they have learned. Points that directly address grammar and structures are marked with a G.

There is a **Lernzieltest** sheet in the Resource and Assessment File (page 11). Encourage pupils to look back at the chapter and to use the grammar section to revise what they are unclear about. You can also use the **Lernzieltest** as an end-of-unit plenary.

Wiederholung

This is a revision page to prepare pupils for the **Kontrolle** at the end of the chapter.

Resources
CD 1, tracks 22–23

1 Hör zu. Wie alt sind sie? (1–10) (AT 1/2) `1.1/Y7`

Listening. Pupils listen to the recording and write down the ages of the speakers.

1 – Hallo! Wie alt bist du, Niels?
– Ich bin vierzehn Jahre alt.
2 – Und Martina, wie alt bist du?
– Ich bin zwölf Jahre alt.
3 – Wie alt bist du, Klaus?
– Ich bin siebenundzwanzig Jahre alt.
4 – Tag, Jana, wie alt bist du?
– Ich bin dreißig Jahre alt.
5 – Paul, wie alt bist du?
– Ich bin vierundfünfzig Jahre alt.
6 – Hallo, Barbara! Wie alt bist du?
– Ich bin dreizehn Jahre alt.
7 – Wie alt bist du, Gustav?
– Ich bin fünfundvierzig Jahre alt.
8 – Und du, Kerstin, wie alt bist du?
– Ich bin siebzehn Jahre alt.
9 – Wie alt bist du, Anton?
– Ich bin achtundzwanzig Jahre alt.
10 – Steffi? Wie alt bist du?
– Ich bin dreiunddreißig Jahre alt.

`22`

> **Answers**
> 1 14 2 12 3 27 4 30 5 54 6 13 7 45 8 17
> 9 28 10 33

2 Hör zu. Welches Bild ist das? (1–8) (AT 1/2) `1.1/Y7`

Listening. Pupils listen to the recording and match the words to the pictures.

1 Ich habe ein Etui.
2 Der Kuli ist rot.
3 Hast du ein Wörterbuch für mich?
4 Wo ist der Taschenrechner?
5 Das ist ein Klebstift.
6 Hast du einen Bleistift?
7 Ich habe ein Heft.
8 Hast du ein Lineal für mich?

`23`

> **Answers**
> 1 g 2 c 3 h 4 d 5 b 6 f 7 a 8 e

3 Partnerarbeit: Mach Interviews. (AT 2/3) `1.4a/Y7 4.6a/Y7`

Speaking. Pupils work together in pairs to interview each other, using the questions and ID cards provided.

4 Lies die E-Mail. Beantworte die Fragen. (AT 3/3) `2.1/Y7 2.4a/Y7`

Reading. Pupils read the email and answer the questions.

> **Answers**
> 1 Sie heißt Silke Ahrendt.
> 2 Sie wohnt in der Schweiz.
> 3 Sie ist 13 Jahre alt.
> 4 Sie hat am 8. Februar Geburtstag.
> 5 Sie hat eine Ratte.

5 Lies die E-Mail noch mal. Schreib eine Antwort für eine Person aus Aufgabe 3. (AT 4/3) `2.4b/Y7`

Writing. Pupils write their own emails, using the one in exercise 4 as a model. They need only change the highlighted words.

Learning targets
- Learning about the euro
- Revising numbers and school items
- Revising personal information

Key framework objectives

2.2/Y7	Reading – (a) unfamiliar language
2.2/Y7	Reading – (b) text selection
3.1/Y7	Culture – aspects of everyday life
5.5	Strategies – reference materials

Grammar
- Forming questions with question words
- Regular verb *kaufen: ich kaufe, du kaufst*

Key language

Der Klebstift / Die Schere / Die CD / Das Wörterbuch kostet … Euro.
Kaufst du …
einen CD-Spieler?
eine Kamera?
ein Handy / Mountainbike / Snowboard / Skateboard?
Inline-Skates?
Ja. Nein.
Das macht … Euro.

High-frequency words

was?
brauchen
für
von
oder
natürlich
kostet
ja, nein
ich kaufe, du kaufst
das macht

Mathematics

Prices in euros

Citizenship

Currencies in other European countries

Resources

CD 1, tracks 24–25
Workbooks A and B, p.7

Starter 1   3.1/Y7

Aim
To check knowledge of the euro.

Ask pupils what currency is used in Germany; establish that it is the euro (*der Euro*), divided into cents (*der Cent*). If possible, show the class real examples of the notes and coins. Ask whether any pupils have used euros abroad, and if so, in which country or countries they used them. Establish that the euro is used in Austria also, but not in Switzerland, whose currency is the Swiss franc (*der Franken*).

1 Hör zu und lies. (AT3/3)   2.2a+b/Y7 5.5

Listening. Pupils listen to the recording and follow the story in their books. In preparation, ask the class to scan the story and decide what Valentina is doing. They should be prepared to justify their answers with reference to the text and pictures. Ask pupils how the word 'euro' is pronounced in German. Encourage pupils to use the glossed words and the glossary to look up unfamiliar vocabulary. Ask pupils for their opinion of the text. Did they enjoy reading it? Why/why not?

1 *Ich habe dreißig Euro. Was brauche ich für die Schule? … Ich brauche eine Schere, einen Klebstift und ein Wörterbuch.*   **24**

2 *Die Schere kostet sieben Euro. Der Klebstift kostet drei Euro. Das macht zehn Euro.*

3 *Das Wörterbuch kostet achtzehn Euro. Das macht achtundzwanzig Euro. Ich habe dreißig Euro.*

4 *Die neue CD von „Rammstein"! Zwanzig Euro!*

5 *Das Wörterbuch oder die CD? … Ich habe eine Idee!*

6 *Vati, hast du zwanzig Euro für mich? Ich brauche ein Wörterbuch.*
Für die Schule? Ja, natürlich!

2 Lies den Text noch mal. Was passt zusammen? (AT 3/4)   2.1/Y7

Reading. Pupils read the story again and match the items to the price tags. Pupils could check their answers in pairs: provide them with *Was kostet der/die/das … ?* and *Der/Die/Das … kostet … Euro* to enable them to go through the answers verbally.

> **Answers**
> **1** b   **2** a   **3** d   **4** c

Starter 2 4.2/Y7

Aims

To consolidate numbers 0–99.
To introduce mental arithmetic in German.

Prepare an OHT with six to ten simple addition and subtraction sums at the top, and the solutions at the bottom in jumbled order. The solutions should all be in the range 0–99. Introduce and chorus the German way of reading out a sum, e.g. *Eins plus zwei gleich drei. Zwei minus eins gleich eins.*

Read out one of the solutions. Ask for a volunteer to read out the sum which matches the solution. Read out another solution, waiting until most pupils have their hands up before choosing a pupil to read out the sum. Continue until all the sums and solutions have been read.

3 Hör zu. Was kaufen sie? Was macht das? (1–5) (AT 1/3) 1.1/Y7 3.1/Y7

Listening. Pupils listen to the recording and decide what each speaker wants to buy. Using the web page, they add up what the items cost. Draw pupils' attention to *das Handy* – it looks like an English word, but actually the English word for 'mobile phone' is totally different.

1 Oh, toll! Snowboards – ich kaufe ein Snowboard, und was noch? Hmm … ach ja! Ein Handy! Ich kaufe ein Snowboard und ein Handy!

 25

2 Ein Mountainbike – alt, aber billig! Ja, ich kaufe ein Mountainbike. Und noch etwas … ja, eine Kamera. Ich kaufe eine Kamera und ein Mountainbike.

3 Ein Skateboard für neunzehn Euro?? Das ist sehr billig. OK … ich kaufe ein Skateboard – und einen CD-Spieler.

4 Was kaufe ich heute im Web-Markt? Hmm … ich kaufe Inline-Skates. Das ist alles!

5 Ein Handy für sechsundvierzig Euro? Das ist wirklich gut! OK … ich kaufe ein Handy … und auch einen CD-Spieler!

4 Partnerarbeit: Was kaufst du? Wähle zwei Sachen aus. (AT 2/3) 1.4b/Y7

Speaking. Pupils work together in pairs to create dialogues, using the web page as a stimulus. Each pupil selects two items from the web page without telling the other, and his/her partner must guess which items. In preparation, refer pupils to the Key Language panel. Encourage pupils to focus on using *einen, eine* and *ein* correctly.

5 Was kaufst du? Schreib Sätze. (AT 4/3) 4.4/Y7

Writing. Pupils write what they would buy from the web page.

Plenary 1.4a/Y7

Aim

To develop fluency in spontaneous talk.

Elicit from pupils the subjects they have learned to talk about in Chapter 1. The **Lernzieltest** on page 16 could be used as a prompt. Write the subjects up on the board.

Divide pupils into pairs. Pairs try to keep a conversation going in German for one minute, using questions and answers learned in Chapter 1. After a minute, pupils find another partner and try again.

SELF-ACCESS READING AND WRITING AT TWO LEVELS

A Reinforcement

1 Wie alt sind sie? (AT4/2) `4.4/Y7`

Writing. Pupils identify the correct age for each person, and write out the sentences.

> **Answers**
> 1 Ich bin vier Jahre alt.
> 2 Ich bin zehn Jahre alt.
> 3 Ich bin sieben Jahre alt.
> 4 Ich bin zwölf Jahre alt.
> 5 Ich bin zwei Jahre alt.
> 6 Ich bin dreizehn Jahre alt.

2 Was passt zusammen? (AT3/2) `4.2/Y7`

Reading. Pupils match pictures of classroom equipment to sentences.

> **Answers**
> 1 a   2 e   3 c   4 b, d   5 f

3 Was passt zusammen? (AT3/2) `4.6a/Y7`

Reading. Pupils match each question to the correct answer. They could then copy both out.

> **Answers**
> 1 d   2 b   3 f   4 a   5 e   6 c

B Extension

1 Ordne die Buchstaben. (AT4/1) `4.2/Y7`

Writing. Pupils solve the anagrams and write out the expressions.

> **Answers**
> 1 Hallo
> 2 Nicht schlecht
> 3 Wie geht's?
> 4 Gut, danke
> 5 Wie heißt du?
> 6 Nicht so gut

2 Welcher Satz ist anders? Warum? (AT3/2) `2.1/Y7`

Reading. Pupils identify a sentence that they consider to be the odd-one-out, and explain why. There are various possibilities – you could tell them to find and list as many as they can.

> **Suggested answers**
> 1 a (it does not contain the word *Geburtstag* / it uses *sein* rather than *haben*)
>   c (it is a question / it does not start with *ich* / it does not contain the number *neun*)
> 2 b (it is a question, it uses *du* rather than *ich*)
>   c (a country rather than a city)
> 3 a (neuter noun)
>   b (it uses *ich* rather than *du*)
>   c (it is a question)
> 4 a (colour does not start with 'g' / noun is a cognate)
>   b (feminine noun)
>   c (colour does not rhyme with the others)

3 Was hat Viktor in seiner Schultasche? Zeichne es in deinem Heft. (AT3/3) `2.1/Y7`

Reading. Pupils read the text about Viktor's school bag, and show their comprehension of it by drawing and colouring the contents in their book.

4 Was sagen sie? (AT4/4) `2.4a/Y7`

Writing. Pupils write short texts about each of the pets, based on the illustrations.

> **Answers**
> 1 Ich heiße Josef. Ich bin vierzehn Jahre alt. Ich habe am zweiten Mai Geburtstag. Ich wohne in Deutschland.
> 2 Ich heiße Bryn. Ich bin zwei Jahre alt. Ich habe am dreißigsten Oktober Geburtstag. Ich wohne in Wales.
> 3 Ich heiße Pierre. Ich bin dreiundzwanzig Jahre alt. Ich habe am sechzehnten Januar Geburtstag. Ich wohne in Frankreich.

Übungsheft A, Seite 2

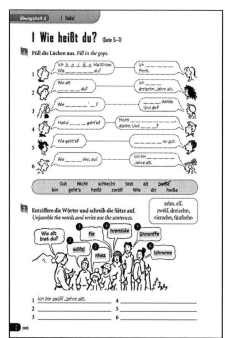

Übungsheft B, Seite 2

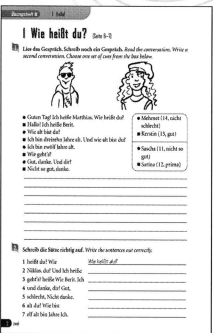

1 (AT3 Level 1, AT4 Level 1) 1 Ich heiße Matthias. Wie heißt du? – Ich heiße Berit. **2** Wie alt bist du? – Ich bin dreizehn Jahre alt. **3** Wie geht's? – Gut danke. Und dir? **4** Hallo! Wie geht's? – Nicht schlecht, danke. Und dir? **5** Wie geht's? – Nicht so gut. **6** Wie alt bist du? – Ich bin zwölf Jahre alt.

2 (AT4 Level 2) 1 Ich bin zwölf Jahre alt. **2** Ich bin zehn Jahre alt. **3** Ich bin elf Jahre alt. **4** Ich bin dreizehn Jahre alt. **5** Ich bin fünfzehn Jahre alt. **6** Ich bin vierzehn Jahre alt.

1 (AT4 Level 3)
Either of these conversations:

● Guten Tag! Ich heiße Mehmet. Wie heißt du?
■ Hallo! Ich heiße Kerstin.
● Wie alt bist du?
■ Ich bin dreizehn Jahre alt. Und wie alt bist du?
● Ich bin vierzehn Jahre alt.
■ Wie geht's?
● Nicht schlecht, danke. Und dir?
■ Gut, danke.

● Guten Tag! Ich heiße Sascha. Wie heißt du?
■ Hallo! Ich heiße Sarina.
● Wie alt bist du?
■ Ich bin zwölf Jahre alt. Und wie alt bist du?
● Ich bin elf Jahre alt.
■ Wie geht's?
● Nicht so gut, danke. Und dir?
■ Prima, danke.

2 (AT4 Level 2) 1 Wie heißt du? **2** Ich heiße Niklas. Und du? **3** Ich heiße Berit. Wie geht's? **4** Gut, danke, und dir? **5** Nicht schlecht, danke. **6** Wie alt bist du? **7** Ich bin elf Jahre alt.

Übungsheft A, Seite 3

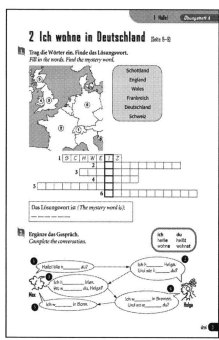

Übungsheft B, Seite 3

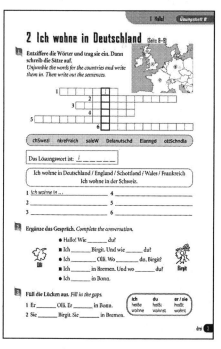

1 (AT3 Level 1, AT4 Level 1) 1 Schweiz **2** Frankreich **3** England **4** Wales **5** Schottland **6** Deutschland

Das Lösungswort ist Irland.

2 (AT4 Level 1) 1 Hallo! Wie heißt du? **2** Ich heiße Helga. Und wie heißt du? **3** Ich heiße Max. Wo wohnst du, Helga? **4** Ich wohne in Bremen. Und wo wohnst du? **5** Ich wohne in Bonn.

1 (AT4 Level 2) 1 Ich wohne in der **Schweiz**. **2** Ich wohne in **Frankreich**. **3** Ich wohne in **England**. **4** Ich wohne in **Wales**. **5** Ich wohne in **Schottland**. **6** Ich wohne in **Deutschland**.

Das Lösungswort ist Irland.

2 (AT4 Level 1)

● Hallo! Wie **heißt** du?
■ Ich **heiße** Birgit. Und wie **heißt** du?
● Ich **heiße** Olli. Wo **wohnst** du, Birgit?
■ Ich **wohne** in Bremen. Und wo **wohnst** du?
● Ich **wohne** in Bonn.

3 (AT4 Level 1) 1 Er heißt Olli. Er wohnt in Bonn. **2** Sie heißt Birgit. Sie wohnt in Bremen.

**Übungsheft A,
Seite 4**

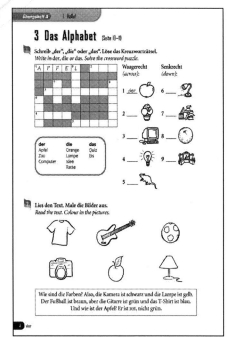

**Übungsheft B,
Seite 4**

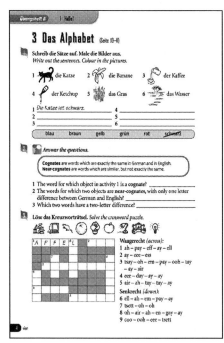

1 (AT3 Level 1, AT4 Level 1) 1 der Apfel **2** das Eis **3** der
Computer **4** die Idee **5** die Ratte **6** die Lampe **7** der Zoo **8** die
Orange **9** das Quiz

2 (AT4 Level 2) blue T-shirt, green guitar, brown football, black
camera, red apple, yellow lamp

1 (AT4 Level 2) 1 Die Katze ist schwarz. **2** Die Banane ist gelb.
3 Der Kaffee ist braun. **4** Der Ketchup ist rot. **5** Das Gras ist
grün. **6** Das Wasser ist blau.

2 1 Ketchup **2** Banane, Gras **3** Kaffee, Wasser

3 (AT4 Level 1) 1 Apfel **2** Eis **3** Computer **4** Idee **5** Ratte **6**
Lampe **7** Zoo **8** Orange **9** Quiz

**Übungsheft A,
Seite 5**

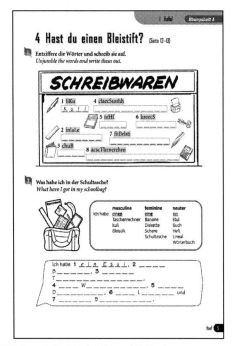

**Übungsheft B,
Seite 5**

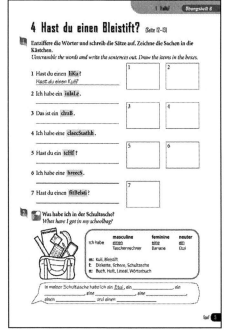

1 (AT3 Level 1, AT4 Level 1) 1 Kuli **2** Lineal **3** Buch
4 Schultasche **5** Heft **6** Schere **7** Bleistift **8** Taschenrechner

2 (AT3 Level 2, AT4 Level 2) Ich habe **1** ein Etui, **2** eine
Banane, **3** einen Taschenrechner, **4** ein Wörterbuch, **5** eine
Diskette, **6** ein Lineal und **7** einen Bleistift.

1 (AT3 Level 2, AT4 Level 2) 1 Hast du einen **Kuli**? **2** Ich habe
ein **Lineal**. **3** Das ist ein **Buch**. **4** Ich habe eine **Schultasche**.
5 Hast du ein **Heft**? **6** Ich habe eine **Schere**. **7** Hast du einen
Bleistift?

2 (AT4 Level 2-3) In meiner Schultasche habe ich ein **Etui**, ein
Wörterbuch, ein **Lineal**, eine **Diskette**, eine **Banane**, einen
Taschenrechner und einen **Bleistift**.

Übungsheft A, Seite 6

1 (AT4 Level 2) 1 Clemens: Ich habe am zwanzigsten Mai Geburtstag. **2** Maria: Ich habe am vierzehnten Februar Geburtstag. **3** Klaus: Ich habe am sechsundzwanzigsten August Geburtstag. **4** Claudia: Ich habe am neunzehnten Dezember Geburtstag. **5** Kevin: Ich habe am sechsten Juni Geburtstag. **6** Hamad:Ich habe am elften Oktober Geburtstag.

2 (AT3 Level 3, AT4 Level 2) 1● Wie heißt du? ■ Ich heiße **Marius**. ● **Wie alt** bist du? ■ Ich **bin** sechzehn. ● **Wo** wohnst du? ■ Ich **wohne** in Berlin. ● **Wann** hast du Geburtstag? ■ Ich **habe** am 21. Juni Geburtstag. ● **Was** hast du? ■ Ich **habe** einen Computer.

2 ● **Wie** heißt du? ■ Ich heiße **Hamit**. ● **Wie** alt bist du? ■ Ich **bin** dreizehn. ● **Wo** wohnst du? ■ Ich **wohne** in Essen. ● **Wann** hast du Geburtstag? ■ Ich **habe** am 11. Mai Geburtstag. ● **Was** hast du? ■ Ich **habe** eine Gitarre.

Übungsheft A, Seite 7

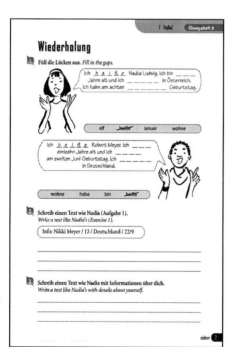

1 (AT 3 Level 3, AT4 Level 1) Ich **heiße** Nadia Ludwig. Ich bin **elf** Jahre alt und ich **wohne** in Österreich. Ich habe am achten **Januar** Geburtstag.

Ich **heiße** Robert Meyer. Ich **bin** dreizehn Jahre alt und ich **habe** am zweiten Juni Geburtstag. Ich **wohne** in Deutschland.

2 (AT4 Level 3) Ich heiße Nikki Meyer. Ich bin dreizehn Jahre alt und ich wohne in Deutschland. Ich habe am zweiundzwanzigsten September Geburtstag.

3 (AT4 Level 3)

Übungsheft B, Seite 6

1 (AT4 Level 2) 1 Clemens: Ich habe am zwanzigsten Mai Geburtstag. **2** Maria: Ich habe am vierten Februar Geburtstag. **3** Klaus: Ich habe am sechsundzwanzigsten August Geburtstag. **4** Claudia: Ich habe am neunzehnten Dezember Geburtstag. **5** Kevin: Ich habe am sechsten Juni Geburtstag. **6** Hamad: Ich habe am ersten Oktober Geburtstag.

2 (AT4 Level 3)

1● Wie heißt du? ■ Ich **heiße Marius**. ● **Wie** alt bist du? ■ Ich **bin sechzehn Jahre alt**. ● **Wo** wohnst du? ■ Ich **wohne in Berlin**. ● **Wann** hast du Geburtstag? ■ Ich **habe am einundzwanzigsten Juni Geburtstag**. ● **Was** hast du? ■ Ich **habe einen Computer**.

2● Wie heißt du? ■ Ich **heiße Hamit**. ● **Wie** alt bist du? ■ Ich **bin dreizehn Jahre alt**. ● **Wo** wohnst du? ■ Ich **wohne in Essen**. ● **Wann** hast du Geburtstag? ■ Ich **habe am elften Mai Geburtstag**. ● **Was** hast du? ■ Ich **habe eine Gitarre**.

Übungsheft B, Seite 7

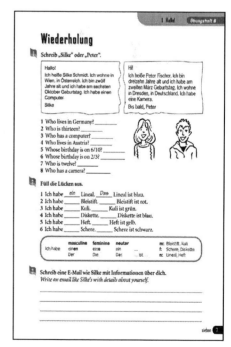

1 (AT3 Level 3)
1 Peter **2** Peter
3 Silke **4** Silke **5** Silke **6** Peter **7** Silke **8** Peter

2 (AT3 Level 2, AT4 Level 1) 1 Ich habe **ein** Lineal. **Das** Lineal ist blau. **2** Ich habe **einen** Bleistift. **Der** Bleistift ist rot. **3** Ich habe **einen** Kuli. **Der** Kuli ist grün. **4** Ich habe **eine** Diskette. **Die** Diskette ist blau. **5** Ich habe **ein** Heft. **Das** Heft ist gelb. **6** Ich habe **eine** Schere. **Die** Schere ist schwarz.

3 (AT4 Level 3)

**Übungsheft A,
Seite 8**

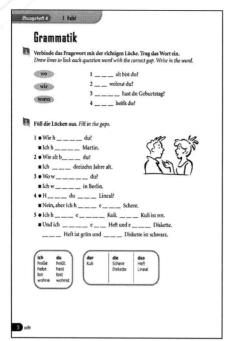

**Übungsheft B,
Seite 8**

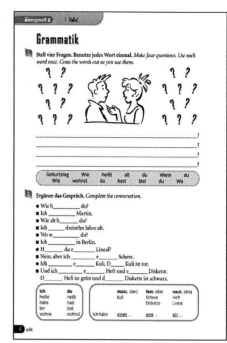

1 (AT3 Level 2) 1 Wie alt bist du? **2 Wo** wohnst du? **3 Wann** hast du Geburtstag? **4 Wie** heißt du?

2 (AT3 Level 2, AT4 Level 1) 1 Wie **heißt** du? – Ich **heiße** Martin. **2** Wie alt **bist** du? – Ich **bin** dreizehn Jahre alt. **3** Wo **wohnst** du? – Ich **wohne** in Berlin. **4 Hast** du **ein** Lineal? – Nein, aber ich **habe eine** Schere. **5** Ich **habe einen** Kuli. **Der** Kuli ist rot. – Und ich **habe ein** Heft und **eine** Diskette. **Das** Heft ist grün und **die** Diskette ist schwarz.

1 (AT4 Level 3) 1 Wie heißt du? **2** Wie alt bist du? **3** Wo wohnst du? **4** Wann hast du Geburtstag?

2 (AT3 Level 3, AT4 Level 1)
● Wie **heißt** du?
■ Ich **heiße** Martin.
● Wie alt **bist** du?
■ Ich **bin** dreizehn Jahre alt.
● Wo **wohnst** du?
■ Ich **wohne** in Berlin.
● **Hast** du **ein** Lineal?
■ Nein, aber ich **habe eine** Schere.
● Ich **habe einen** Kuli. **Der** Kuli ist rot.
■ Und ich **habe ein** Heft und **eine** Diskette. **Das** Heft ist grün und **die** Diskette ist schwarz.

Arbeitsblatt 1.1

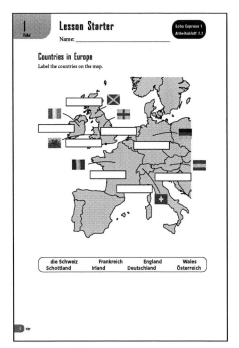

Schottland, Irland, England, Wales, Deutschland, Frankreich, Österreich, die Schweiz

Arbeitsblatt 1.2

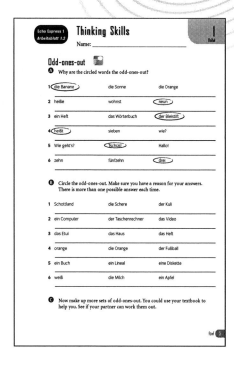

A

Accept any reasonable alternative explanations.

1 The others are round. **2** The others are verbs. **3** *Der Bleistift* is masculine, the others are neuter. Or: the others are books. **4** The others contain *ie* not *ei*. **5** The others are greetings. **6** The others are multiples of five. Or: the others have *zehn* in them.

B

Various possible answers

Arbeitsblatt 1.3

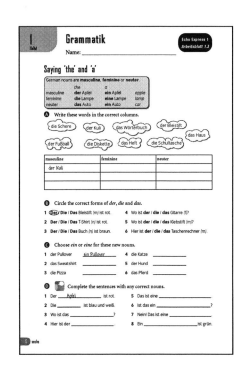

A

Masculine: Kuli, Bleistift, Fußball. *Feminine:* Schere, Diskette, Schultasche. *Neuter:* Wörterbuch, Haus, Heft.

B

1 der **2** das **3** das **4** die **5** der **6** der

C

1 ein Pullover **2** ein Sweatshirt **3** eine Pizza **4** eine Katze **5** ein Hund **6** ein Pferd

Arbeitsblatt 1.4

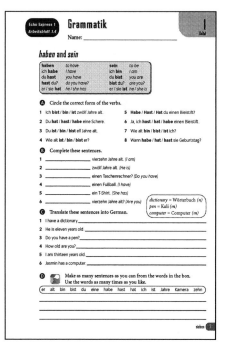

A

1 bin **2** hast **3** bist **4** ist **5** Hast **6** habe **7** bin **8** hat

B

1 Ich bin **2** Er ist **3** Hast du **4** Ich habe **5** Sie hat **6** Bist du

C

1 Ich habe ein Wörterbuch. **2** Er ist elf Jahre alt. **3** Hast du einen Kuli? **4** Wie alt bist du? **5** Ich bin dreizehn Jahre alt. **6** Jasmin hat einen Computer.

D

Possible answers

Ich habe eine Kamera. Du hast eine Kamera. Er hat eine Kamera. Ich bin zehn Jahre alt. Du bist zehn Jahre alt. Er ist zehn Jahre alt.

Habe ich eine Kamera? Hast du eine Kamera? Hat er eine Kamera? Bin ich zehn Jahre alt? Bist du zehn Jahre alt? Ist er zehn Jahre alt?

Arbeitsblatt
1.5

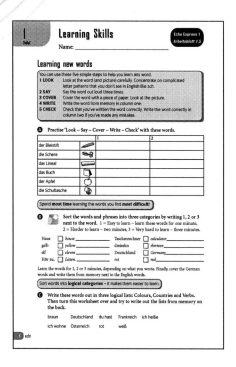

Unit Learning targets	Key framework objectives	NC levels and PoS coverage	Grammar and key language	Skills
1 Was ist dein Lieblingsfach? (pp. 22–23) • Giving your opinion about school subjects • Using *und* and *aber* to make longer sentences	1.3/Y7 Listening – (a) interpreting intonation and tone 1.3/Y7 Speaking – (b) using intonation and tone 5.4 Strategies – working out meaning	NC levels 1–4 2.1a identify patterns 2.1b memorising 2.1c knowledge of language 2.2a listen for gist 2.2d pronunciation and intonation 2.2e ask and answer questions 2.2f initiate / sustain conversations 2.2k deal with unfamiliar language 3b sounds and writing 3c apply grammar 3d use a range of vocab / structures 4b communicate in pairs etc. 4d make links with English	Possessive adjectives *mein* and *dein* Regular verb *finden: ich finde, du findest* Making longer sentence with *und* and *aber* *Was ist dein Lieblingsfach?* *Mein Lieblingsfach ist …* *Deutsch* *Englisch* *Französisch* *Religion* *Informatik* *Mathe* *Naturwissenschaften* *Werken* *Kunst* *Musik* *Theater* *Erdkunde* *Geschichte* *Sport* *Wie findest du Deutsch* (etc.)? *Ich finde Deutsch* (etc.) *gut, schlecht, interessant, langweilig, einfach, schwierig, toll, furchtbar.* *Ich finde Geschichte gut und interessant.* *Ich finde Deutsch einfach, aber langweilig.*	Pronunciation: *ei/ie* Expressing opinions
2 Wie viel Uhr ist es? (pp. 24–25) • Talking about the school timetable • Telling the time	1.1/Y7 Listening – gist and detail 1.4/Y7 Speaking – (a) social and classroom language 5.8 Strategies – evaluating and improving	NC levels 1–3 2.1a identify patterns 2.1b memorising 2.2a listen for gist 2.2e ask and answer questions 3b sounds and writing 3c apply grammar 3f compare experiences 4b communicate in pairs etc.	Irregular verb *haben: ich habe, du hast, er/sie hat* *Montag, Dienstag, Mittwoch, Donnerstag, Freitag, Samstag, Sonntag* *Was hast du am Montag* (etc.)? *Ich habe am Montag* (etc.) *Deutsch* (etc.). *Wie viel Uhr ist es?* *Es ist … Uhr …* *Wann beginnt/endet Deutsch* (etc.)? *Um … Uhr …*	Telling the time Pronunciation: *v/w*
3 Pausenbrot (pp. 26–27) • Talking about what you eat and drink at break • Checking verb endings	3.1/Y7 Culture – aspects of everyday life 4.5/Y7 Language – (a) present tense verbs	NC levels 2–3 2.1b memorising 2.1c knowledge of language 2.2a listen for gist 2.2b skim and scan 2.2e ask and answer questions 2.2f initiate / sustain conversations 3b sounds and writing 3c apply grammar 3d use a range of vocab / structures 4b communicate in pairs etc 4g language for a range of purposes	Review of regular and irregular verbs: *ich trinke, du trinkst, er/sie trinkt* *ich wohne, du wohnst, er/sie wohnt* *ich esse, du isst, er/sie isst* *ich habe, du hast, er/sie hat* *ich bin, du bist, er/sie ist* *die Kekse (der Keks), die Chips (der Chip), der Apfel, die Orange, die Banane, die Schokolade, die Bonbons (das Bonbon), das Brötchen, die Cola, der Orangensaft, das Wasser, der Kuchen* *Was isst/trinkst du in der Pause?* *Ich esse einen Apfel, einen Kuchen, eine Orange, eine Banane, ein Brötchen, Schokolade, Kekse, Chips, Bonbons, nichts.* *Ich trinke Cola, Orangensaft, Wasser, nichts.* *Ja, bitte?* *Ein Brötchen, bitte.* *Das macht fünfzig Cent.* *Bitte. Danke.*	Polite expressions Reviewing progress

Unit Learning targets	Key framework objectives	NC levels and PoS coverage	Grammar and key language	Skills
4 Was trägst du in der Schule? (pp. 28–29) ● Describing what you wear to school ● Revising *einen/eine/ein*	1.4/Y7 Speaking – (b) using prompts 2.4/Y7 Writing – (a) sentences and texts as models 4.3/Y7 Language – plurals 5.1 Strategies – patterns	**NC levels 1–3** 2.1b memorising 2.1c knowledge of language 2.2a listen for gist 2.2e ask and answer questions 2.2f initiate / sustain conversations 2.2b skim and scan 3f compare experiences 3b sounds and writing 3c apply grammar 3d use a range of vocab / structures	Indefinite article, accusative Irregular verbs *sein* and *tragen*: *es ist, sie sind* *ich trage, du trägst* *die* + plural nouns *die Jacke, die Hose, das Hemd, der Pullover, die Krawatte, die Schuhe (der Schuh), der Rock, die Socken (die Socke), das Sweatshirt, das T-Shirt, die Jeans, die Stiefel (der Stiefel)* *Der Rock (etc.) ist …* *Die Schuhe (etc.) sind …* *blau, braun, gelb, grau, grün, lila, orange, rot, schwarz, weiß.* *Was trägst du in der Schule?* *Ich trage einen Rock, Jeansrock, Pulli, eine Hose, Bluse, Jeans, Jacke, ein Hemd, T-Shirt, Sweatshirt, Schuhe, Stiefel, Sportschuhe.* *Ich finde das cool, bequem, schick.*	Expressing opinions
5 Meine Schule (pp. 30–31) ● Learning about school life in German-speaking countries ● Understanding a longer text	2.5/Y7 Writing – different text types 3.2/Y7 Culture – (a) young people: interests/ opinions 3.2/Y7 Culture – (b) challenging stereotypes 4.6/Y7 Language – (b) negatives 5.6 Strategies – reading aloud 5.7 Strategies – planning and preparing	**NC levels 3–4** 2.2a listen for gist 2.2b skim and scan 2.2c respond appropriately 2.2g write clearly and coherently 2.2k deal with unfamiliar language 3b sounds and writing 3c apply grammar 3d use a range of vocab / structures 3e different countries' cultures 3f compare experiences 4e use a range of resources 4f language of interest / enjoyment 4g language for a range of purposes	Negative article, accusative *Ich heiße / Sie heißt … .* *Ich bin / Sie ist … Jahre alt.* *Ich wohne / Sie wohnt in …* *Ich bin / Sie ist in der Klasse … .* *Die Schule beginnt um … .* *In der Pause esse / trinke ich … .* *Mein / Ninas Lieblingsfach ist …* *Ich finde … schwierig (etc.).* *Ich trage … in der Schule.* *Ich habe keine Schuluniform.*	Planning a longer text (webpage) Reading a text aloud
Lernzieltest und Wiederholung (pp. 32–33) ● Pupils' checklist and practice test		**NC levels 2–4** 3b sounds and writing 2.2a listen for gist 2.2e ask and answer questions 2.2f initiate / sustain conversations 2.2b skim and scan 4b communicate in pairs etc.		

Unit Learning targets	Key framework objectives	NC levels and PoS coverage	Grammar and key language	Skills
Mehr (pp. 34–35) • Extension material	2.2/Y7 Reading – (a) unfamiliar language 2.2/Y7 Reading – (b) text selection 2.3/Y7 Reading – text features	NC levels 3–4 **2.1d** previous knowledge **2.1e** use reference materials **2.2b** skim and scan **2.2c** respond appropriately **2.2d** pronunciation and intonation **2.2j** adapt previously-learnt language **3b** sounds and writing **3c** apply grammar **3d** use a range of vocab / structures	*Die Schule beginnt um …* *In der Pause esse/trinke ich …* *Um … Uhr habe ich Englisch* (etc.).	Reading a longer text for gist Using reference materials Reading aloud (singing)
Extra (pp. 102–103) • Self-access reading and writing at two levels		NC levels 1–4 **2.2e** ask and answer questions **2.2b** skim and scan **3c** apply grammar **3d** use a range of vocab / structures		

Learning targets

- Giving your opinion about school subjects
- Using *und* and *aber* to make longer sentences

Key framework objectives

1.3/Y7 Listening – (a) interpreting intonation and tone

1.3/Y7 Speaking – (b) using intonation and tone

5.4 Strategies – working out meaning

Grammar

- Possessive adjectives: *mein / dein*
- Connectives: *und* and *aber*
- Regular verb *finden*: *ich finde, du findest*

Key language

Was ist dein Lieblingsfach?
Mein Lieblingsfach ist …
Deutsch
Englisch
Französisch
Religion
Informatik
Mathe
Naturwissenschaften
Werken
Kunst
Musik
Theater
Erdkunde
Geschichte
Sport
Wie findest du …?
Ich finde es gut / schlecht / interessant / langweilig / einfach / schwierig / toll / furchtbar
Ich finde Geschichte gut und interessant.
Ich finde Deutsch einfach, aber langweilig.

High-frequency words

mein
dein
was?
wie?
ist
ich habe
und
aber
es
na ja

Pronunciation

ei/ie

Mathematics

Quantifying survey results

ICT

Using a spreadsheet application to show survey results

Resources

CD 1, tracks 26–28
Workbooks A and B, p.12
Flashcards 21–34
Echo Elektro 1 TPP, Express Mod 2 1.1–1.8

Starter 1

5.4 5.5

Aims

To encourage recognition of cognates. To develop strategies for finding out the meanings of unfamiliar words.

Present the German names of the school subjects from exercise 1 on an OHT, numbered 1–14. Collect ideas about what sort of words these might be.

Pupils work in pairs. They categorise the words into two groups: words whose meaning they can guess, and those whose meaning they cannot guess. Follow up by choosing two which the class cannot guess, and ask for ideas about where to find the meanings. Pupils then race to see who can find the meanings quickest in the wordlist at the end of the chapter, or the **Wortschatz** at the back of the book.

1 Wie heißt das auf Englisch? (AT 3/1)

5.4 5.5

Reading. Pupils write down the English names of the school subjects. Tell pupils that they should use the visual clues and their knowledge of English to work out as many of the words as possible, then use the **Wortschatz** at the back of the book to look up any they are not sure about. With words such as *Sport* and *Theater* which are cognates, encourage pupils to reflect, and write 'PE' and 'drama' rather than 'sport' and 'theatre'.

Answers
1 German
2 ICT
3 design and technology
4 geography
5 English
6 maths
7 art
8 history
9 French
10 science
11 music
12 PE
13 religion
14 drama

2 Hör zu. Welches Fach ist das? (1–14) (AT 1/2)   `1.1/Y7`

Listening. Pupils listen to people talking about their favourite subjects, and write down the correct German word for each. Suggest to weaker pupils that they note the first two letters of the subject heard, and perhaps write out the complete word later or when listening again.

1 – Hallo. Was ist dein Lieblingsfach?
– Mein Lieblingsfach ist Musik.   `26`

2 – Und du, was ist dein Lieblingsfach?
– Mein Lieblingsfach? Also … mein Lieblingsfach ist Sport.

3 – Hast du ein Lieblingsfach?
– Ähm … mein Lieblingsfach ist Theater.

4 – Und was ist dein Lieblingsfach?
– Mein Lieblingsfach ist … ähm… Erdkunde.

5 – Was ist dein Lieblingsfach?
– Mein Lieblingsfach ist Werken.

6 – Ist dein Lieblingsfach auch Werken?
– Nein. Mein Lieblingsfach ist Religion.

7 – Und du. Was ist dein Lieblingsfach?
– Ähm … Mein Lieblingsfach ist Mathe.

8 – Hallo. Was ist dein Lieblingsfach?
– Englisch ist super. Mein Lieblingsfach ist Englisch.

9 – Und was ist dein Lieblingsfach?
– Ähm, mein Lieblingsfach ist Geschichte.

10 – Hast du ein Lieblingsfach?
– Ja. Mein Lieblingsfach ist Deutsch.

11 – Was ist dein Lieblingsfach?
– Mein Lieblingsfach ist Kunst.

12 – Und was ist dein Lieblingsfach?
– Mein Lieblingsfach ist Informatik.

13 – Hast du ein Lieblingsfach?
– Ja. Mein Lieblingsfach ist Französisch.

14 – Und was ist dein Lieblingsfach?
– Ähm … Mein Lieblingsfach ist Naturwissenschaften.

Answers
1 Musik	2 Sport	3 Theater
4 Erdkunde	5 Werken	6 Religion
7 Mathe	8 Englisch	9 Geschichte
10 Deutsch	11 Kunst	12 Informatik
13 Französisch	14 Naturwissenschaften	

3 Wer sagt das? (AT3/2)   `2.1/Y7`

Reading. Pupils read the speech bubbles and look at the pictures. They match each speech bubble to the appropriate picture.

Answers
1 Hamit	4 Niklas
2 Marie	5 Alexander
3 Valentina	6 Lea

4 Umfrage. (AT 2/2)   `1.4a/Y7`

Speaking. Pupils move around the class asking each other what their favourite subject is and keeping a tally of how many people liked each subject. Before pupils start the exercise, you could demonstrate that they only need to change one word in the sentence to convey personally relevant information. Stress that adapting sentences is an important language-learning skill.

Suggestion

ICT Pupils could present their results as pie or bar charts using a spreadsheet application.

Aussprache: ei/ie   `4.1/Y7`

Listening. This panel explains the difference between *ei* and *ie*. Pupils attempt to pronounce the words containing *ei* and *ie* correctly, then listen to the recording and finally repeat the correct pronunciation.

drei, langweilig, einfach
vier, schwierig, Lieblingsfach   27

Starter 2   1.3a/Y7 1.3b/Y7

Aim

To develop confidence in using context (gesture, tone of voice, visual cues) in inferring meaning.

Introduce the following sentences on an OHT. Read them out with the appropriate gestures and tone of voice.

Ich finde Deutsch gut.	(one thumb up)
Ich finde Deutsch schlecht.	(one thumb down)
Ich finde Deutsch interessant.	(wide open eyes, reading textbook avidly)
Ich finde Deutsch langweilig.	(yawning, eyes half closed)
Ich finde Deutsch einfach.	(hands folded behind head, relaxed)
Ich finde Deutsch schwierig.	(mopping sweat from brow)
Ich finde Deutsch toll.	(both thumbs up)
Ich finde Deutsch furchtbar.	(both thumbs down)

Pupils confer in pairs and then write down on paper or mini-white boards what they think the adjective means.

Suggestion

As a follow up to Starter 2, read the sentences through a second time, this time asking the class to copy your gestures. Finally, they provide the gestures themselves. Now ask the class to stand, and read out the sentences in random order. Pupils mime the opinions when they hear the opinion word; pupils who mime the wrong word or fail to mime must sit down. Further mime activities can be found in the Introduction on page 10.

5 Hör zu. Wie findet Julia die Fächer? (1–8) (AT 1/2)   1.3a/Y7 1.1/Y7

Listening. Pupils listen to the recording and identify Julia's opinions about the subjects. They could listen once for the subject and then a second time to note the opinion of that subject.

1 – Wie findest du Geschichte?
– Ich finde Geschichte gut.
2 – Wie findest du … Englisch?
– Englisch? Ich finde Englisch schwierig!

28

3 – Und wie findest du Sport?
– Ich finde Sport schlecht.
4 – Aha. Wie findest du Musik?
– Na ja … Ich finde Musik furchtbar!
5 – Julia, wie findest du Deutsch?
– Ach, ich finde Deutsch einfach.
6 – Und Mathe? Wie findest du Mathe?
– Ich finde Mathe langweilig.
7 – Wie findest du … Erdkunde?
– Ich finde Erdkunde interessant.
8 – Und wie findest du Kunst?
– Ich finde Kunst toll!

Answers
1 a	2 f	3 b	4 h	5 e	6 d	7 c	8 g

6 Partnerarbeit. (AT 2/3)   1.3b/Y7

Speaking. Pupils work together in pairs to interview each other about their opinions of school subjects. To emphasise the language they should be using, go over the set phrase *Ich finde es …* and possible endings they could add to form the different opinions.

R Pairs record their interviews, then play and review them, then re-record, aiming to improve pronunciation and fluency.

+ Pairs record an interview using a greater variety of questions (*Wie heißt du?*, *Wie alt bist du?*, *Was ist dein Lieblingsfach?*, etc.) and answers. Provide 'stalling' expressions which pupils can use to give themselves time to think, e.g. *Ach …, Na ja …, Tja …, Also …, Weißt du …*

7 Lies Viktors E-Mail. Mach auf Englisch Notizen über die Fächer. (AT 3/4)   2.1/Y7 5.5

Reading. Pupils read the email and note Viktor's opinion of each subject in English. In preparation, ask the class to scan the text quickly for gist (What is it about?) and words they recognise (e.g. names of subjects; opinions). With weaker pupils, go through the text first picking out the subjects, then go through it again to look for the corresponding opinions.

Answers
science – difficult; history – bad; maths – easy but boring; English – interesting; art – great

+ Pupils re-read the text and list any unknown language. They first try to work out meanings from the context, then use the **Wortschatz** at the back of their books to check meanings. As a further task or for homework, they could write a reply to the email.

> ### ECHO-TIPP
> 4.4/Y7
>
> This shows how *aber* and *und* can be used to increase sentence length.

8 Schreib Sätze. (AT 4/3)
4.4/Y7

Writing. Pupils write sentences about the subjects, using the visual cues. In preparation, go through the **ECHO-Tipp** panel on using the connectives *und* and *aber*. Ask pupils to spot examples in Viktor's email (exercise 7).

> **Answers**
> 1 Ich finde Erdkunde einfach, aber langweilig.
> 2 Ich finde Englisch toll und interessant.
> 3 Ich finde Mathe schwierig, aber gut.
> 4 Ich finde Kunst schlecht und langweilig.

Plenary
1.1/Y7 1.3a/Y7

Aim
To develop strategies for improving listening skills.

Play the recording from exercise 5 again, while the class listens with books closed. Ask for opinions about whether the recording is easy or difficult to understand. Ask pupils who say 'easy' to support this with information they have gleaned from the recording. Why did they find it easy or difficult (e.g. slow/fast, clear/unclear, repetition, too much material, known/unknown language)?

Point out that the more you listen to German, the easier it gets to understand. Did they find the recording from exercise 5 easier this time? Suggest or elicit strategies for improving listening (relax, and don't try to understand every word; listen to tone of voice for clues; focus on the important language; prepare before you listen, e.g. by looking for clues in the book, thinking about what the listening will be about and what words you are likely to hear).

2 Wie viel Uhr ist es?

Learning targets
- Talking about the school timetable
- Telling the time

Key framework objectives
1.1/Y7 Listening – gist and detail
1.4/Y7 Speaking – (a) social and classroom language
5.8 Strategies – evaluating and improving

Grammar
- *haben: ich habe, du hast, er/sie hat*
- Question words: *wie viel? was? wann?*

Key language
Was hast du am Montag / Dienstag / Mittwoch / Donnerstag / Freitag?
Ich habe am (Montag) (Deutsch).
Wie viel Uhr ist es?
Es ist … Uhr …
Wann beginnt/endet (Deutsch)?
Um … Uhr …

High-frequency words
wie viel?
wann?
was?
es ist
ich habe, du hast, er/sie hat
am
um

Cardinal numbers 1–60
beginnt
endet

Pronunciation
w/v

Mathematics
Using the 24-hour clock

Citizenship
School routine in German-speaking countries

Resources
CD 1, tracks 29–34
Workbooks A and B, p.13
Arbeitsblatt 2.1, p. 20
Echo Elektro 1 TPP, Express Mod 2 2.1–2.10

Starter 1 — 1.4a/Y7

Aims
To reinforce school subject vocabulary.
To promote fluency of speech.

Either:

Divide the class into two teams and do a quickfire quiz on names of subjects in German: *Was heißt … auf Deutsch?*

Or:

Ask the class to stand. Each pupil in turn says a sentence beginning *Mein Lieblingsfach ist … .* They nominate another pupil to take the next turn, e.g.

Paul: *Mein Lieblingsfach ist Sport. Mary!*

Mary: *Mein Lieblingsfach ist Englisch. Sarah!*

If the pupil says the sentence correctly and names a new subject, he/she can sit down. If he/she makes a mistake, stumbles or repeats what the previous speaker said, he/she remains standing. Continue until most pupils are sitting.

1 Hör zu. Was passt zusammen? (1–7) (AT 1/1) — 4.2/Y7

Listening. Pupils listen to the recording and put the days of the week in the correct order.

1 Montag
2 Dienstag
3 Mittwoch
4 Donnerstag
5 Freitag
6 Samstag
7 Sonntag

🔘 29

Answers
1 e 2 a 3 d 4 b 5 c 6 f 7 g

2 Hör zu. Welcher Tag ist das? (1–5) (AT 1/2) — 4.2/Y7

Listening. Pupils listen to the recording and understand on which day each lesson is taking place. In preparation for listening, look at the photos and their labels with the class and establish what each of the subjects is in English: *Wie heißt „Werken" auf Englisch?*, etc. Ask pupils to study the instructions and elicit what they will be listening for (days of the week).

1 – Was hast du am Donnerstag?
– Ich habe am Donnerstag Werken.
2 – Und was hast du am Dienstag?
– Ich habe am Dienstag ... Informatik.
3 – OK ... Was hast du am Montag?
– Ähh ... ich habe am Montag Naturwissenschaften.
4 – Und am Mittwoch? Was hast du am Mittwoch?
– Ich habe am Mittwoch Französisch.
5 – Und was hast du am Freitag?
– Kunst – ich habe am Freitag Kunst.

30

Answers
1 Donnerstag
2 Dienstag
3 Montag
4 Mittwoch
5 Freitag

3 Partnerarbeit. (AT 2/3)

1.4a/Y7

Speaking. Pupils work together in pairs to interview each other about their timetables. They could have their timetables in front of them to help with the exercise. In preparation, elicit how to say 'on Monday', etc., in German: *Wie heißt "on Monday" auf Deutsch?*. They have already met a similar use of *am* with dates. Focus pupils' attention on the form of the question and answer in the Key Language panel. With a lower-ability class, gather suggestions for each day and write the subjects on the board or an OHT for pupils to refer to.

Starter 2

4.2/Y7

Aims
To revise numbers 1–24.

Either present **Arbeitsblatt 2.1** as an OHT for the whole class to work through, or photocopy it for individual pupils or pairs to work through quietly. The exercise revises numbers 1–24 (pupils join the dots to reveal a picture of an object).

You may wish to explain that the 24-hour clock is used a lot more in German-speaking countries than in the UK, e.g. for timetables (school, bus, cinema).

4 Wie viel Uhr ist es? Hör zu und überprüfe es. (AT 3/2, 1/2)

4.2/Y7

Reading/Listening. Pupils match the clock faces to the sentences. They listen to the recording to check their answers.

1 – Wie viel Uhr ist es?
– Es ist acht Uhr.
2 – Wie viel Uhr ist es?
– Es ist elf Uhr.
3 – Wie viel Uhr ist es?
– Es ist dreiundzwanzig Uhr.
4 – Wie viel Uhr ist es?
– Es ist vierzehn Uhr dreißig.
5 – Wie viel Uhr ist es?
– Es ist neun Uhr vierzig.
6 – Wie viel Uhr ist es?
– Es ist elf Uhr fünfzehn.

31

Answers
1 e   **2** c   **3** a   **4** b   **5** d   **6** f

5 Hör zu. Wie viel Uhr ist es? (1–10) (AT 1/2)

1.1/Y7

Listening. Pupils listen and note the clock times numerically. Encourage them to focus on the actual numbers heard.

1 – Wie viel Uhr ist es?
– Es ist sieben Uhr fünf.
2 – Wie viel Uhr ist es bitte?
– Es ist zehn Uhr dreißig.
3 – Wie viel Uhr ist es?
– Ähm ... es ist zwei Uhr fünfzehn.
4 – Wie viel Uhr ist es?
– Es ist acht Uhr.
5 – Wie viel Uhr ist es bitte?
– Es ist neun Uhr zwanzig.
6 – Wie viel Uhr ist es?
– Ähm ... es ist zwölf Uhr vier.
7 – Wie viel Uhr ist es?
– Es ist fünfzehn Uhr.
8 – Wie viel Uhr ist es bitte?
– Es ist achtzehn Uhr fünfzehn.
9 – Wie viel Uhr ist es?
– Es ist zwanzig Uhr.
10 – Wie viel Uhr ist es?
– Ähm ... Es ist zweiundzwanzig Uhr.

32

Answers

1 07.05	**4** 08.00	**7** 15.00	**9** 20.00
2 10.30	**5** 09.20	**8** 18.15	**10** 22.00
3 02.15	**6** 12.04		

Aussprache: w/v

Listening. This panel explains the difference in pronunciation between *w* (covered in Chapter 1, Unit 1, page 6) and *v*. Pupils listen to the recording and repeat the tongue twister three times, to practise *w* and *v*. After chorusing with the whole class, pupils could work in pairs to see who can repeat the tongue twister more times in 30 seconds. You could take this opportunity to emphasise the importance of monitoring one's own pronunciation and not pronouncing German in an 'English' way.

Wie **v**iel Uhr ist es, **V**olker?
Es ist **v**ier Uhr **v**ierzig, **W**ilfried.   **33**

6 Partnerarbeit. (AT 2/2)   1.4a/Y7

Speaking. Pupils work in pairs to practise clock times. Look at the intonation associated with asking the question before they start. Partner A asks the time and partner B responds with any time. Partner A writes down the time and partner B confirms whether this is correct. Then the roles are reversed.

7 Hör zu und lies. Was hat Viktor heute? (AT 3/3)   1.1/Y7

Listening. Pupils listen to the recording and follow the text in their books. They identify Viktor's subjects.

– *Heute habe ich Kunst … Ach Julia!*
  Wann beginnt Kunst?   **34**
– *Um zehn Uhr fünfundvierzig.*
– *O.K. … Wann endet Kunst?*
– *Um elf Uhr dreißig.*
– *Hmm … Und wann beginnt Mathe?*
– *Um zehn Uhr.*
– *O nein!*
– *Was?*
– *Es ist zehn Uhr fünf!*

> **Answers**
> Kunst, Mathe

8 Lies noch mal. Was ist nicht im Dialog? (AT 3/3)   2.1/Y7

Reading. Pupils read the dialogue again and identify the clock times which are not mentioned.

> **Answers**
> 3 and 5

R Less able pupils write out the clock times shown in exercise 7.

+ More able pupils work in pairs to write and act out their own dialogues, based on the one in the book. They could include opinions such as *O nein! Deutsch ist furchtbar!*. To support middle-ability pupils, copy the dialogue onto an OHT with certain words blanked out to be filled in by the pupils.

ECHO-Detektiv   4.5a/Y7

This panel presents *haben* in the first, second and third person singular. To check understanding, ask pupils to spot and read out sentences containing examples of *haben* from this unit. Pupils can be referred to the **Grammatik** on page 120, where they will find further practice with *haben*.

9 Lies Julias Stundenplan. Korrigiere die Sätze. (AT 3/2)   4.4/Y7

Reading. Pupils study Julia's timetable and correct the German sentences. Tell pupils that there is more than one possible answer to 5 and 6. Ask more able pupils to try to find all the possible answers.

> **Answers**
> 1 Geschichte endet um **dreizehn Uhr zehn**.
> 2 Julia hat um acht Uhr **zehn** Deutsch.
> 3 Julia hat um neun Uhr **vierzig** Englisch.
> 4 Julia hat um **zehn** Uhr Mathe.
> 5 Religion beginnt um **elf Uhr vierzig**.
>   or: Religion **endet** um zwölf Uhr fünfundzwanzig.
>   or: **Geschichte** beginnt um zwölf Uhr fünfundzwanzig.
> 6 Die Schule beginnt um **acht Uhr zehn**.
>   or: Die Schule **endet** um dreizehn Uhr zehn.

Suggestion   3.1/Y7

Elicit differences between Julia's school day and the pupils' own. Explain that Julia's school day is fairly typical of schools in German-speaking countries: most schools start at 8am and finish at around 1pm, and pupils go home for lunch. You could elicit opinions (in German), e.g. *Ich finde es gut / schlecht / toll / furchtbar*.

Plenary

5.8

Aim

To encourage pupils to improve their pronunciation.

Collect ideas for improving pronunciation, e.g.

- read aloud
- check partner's pronunciation in pairwork exercises
- record and listen
- listen and repeat
- make a note of sound patterns like German v = English f
- listen to German native speakers.

Write them on the board for pupils to copy. Discuss why good pronunciation is important (e.g. without it, you won't be understood). To emphasise the point, you could read an English sentence in an exaggerated German accent and ask pupils to write down what you said!

Learning targets
- Talking about what you eat and drink at break
- Checking verb endings

Key framework objectives
3.1/Y7 Culture – aspects of everyday life
4.5/Y7 Language – (a) present tense verbs

Grammar
- Regular verbs (*ich, du, er/sie*)
- Irregular verbs: *sein, essen* (*ich, du, er/sie*)

Key language
die Kekse
die Chips
der Apfel
die Orange
die Banane
die Schokolade
die Bonbons
das Brötchen
die Cola
der Orangensaft
das Wasser
der Kuchen
Was isst / trinkst du in der Pause?
Ich esse …
Er/Sie isst …
einen Apfel / Kuchen, eine Orange / Banane, ein Brötchen, Schokolade / Kekse / Chips / Bonbons / nichts.
Ich trinke …
Er/Sie trinkt …
Cola / Orangensaft / Wasser /
nichts.
Ja, bitte?
Ein Brötchen, bitte.
Das macht fünfzig Cent.
Bitte. Danke.

High-frequency words
ich, du
in
bitte, danke
das macht
nichts

Mathematics
Prices in euros

Resources
CD 1, tracks 35–37
Workbooks A and B, p.14
Arbeitsblatt 2.2, p. 21
Arbeitsblatt 2.3, p. 22
Flashcards 35–46
Echo Elektro 1 TPP, Express Mod 2 3.1–3.9

Starter 1   4.1/Y7

Aim
To focus on sound patterns (vowels) in German.

Display the following gapped nouns on an OHT or the board as pupils come into the class:

Apf_l   Schokolad_
K_chen   Keks_
Banan_   W_sser
Br_tchen

Tell the class that a vowel is missing from each word. Can they guess what it is? (Stress that meaning is not important at this stage.) Working in pairs, pupils write out the words, guessing what the missing vowels will be. Now read the new words slowly several times. Pupils review their guesses, and alter as necessary. Finally, collect answers around the class and complete the words on the OHT/board.

Suggestion
Use the flashcards to introduce the new vocabulary. (See the Introduction on page 9 for general suggestions for using flashcards.) You could then stick the flashcards on the board using removable adhesive. Two pupils come to the board and arrange the cards into groups, using principles of their own choosing. The rest of the class guesses what the principle is (e.g. gender, colour, shape, eat/drink, like/dislike). The pupil who guesses correctly chooses a partner to help him/her rearrange the cards, etc.

Hör zu. Was passt zusammen? (1–12) (AT 1/2)   1.1/Y7 3.1/Y7

Listening. Pupils listen to the recording and find the letter to match the items they hear.

> **1** Ich esse Schokolade … mmm!
> **2** Ich esse eine Banane … mmm!
> **3** Ich esse ein Brötchen … mmm!
> **4** Ich trinke Wasser … ahh!
> **5** Ich esse einen Apfel … mmm!
> **6** Ich trinke Cola … ahh!

35

7 *Ich trinke Orangensaft ... ahh!*
8 *Ich esse Kuchen ... mmm!*
9 *Ich esse Bonbons ... mmm! Lecker!*
10 *Ich esse eine Orange ... mmm!*
11 *Ich esse Kekse ... mmm!*
12 *Ich esse Chips ... mmm!*

Answers
1 l   **2** h   **3** e   **4** d   **5** f   **6** a   **7** b   **8** i
9 k   **10** g   **11** j   **12** c

2 Hör zu. Was essen / trinken sie in der Pause? (1–5) (AT 1/3)   1.1/Y7 3.1/Y7

Listening. Pupils listen to the recording and find in the photograph the items mentioned by each speaker. They may find it easier to complete the exercise in two stages: making shorthand notes while listening, then finding the items in the picture afterwards.

1 – *Peter, was isst du in der Pause?*
– *Ich esse ein Brötchen und einen Apfel oder eine Orange.*
– *Und was trinkst du?*
– *Ich trinke Cola.*

2 – *Stefanie, was isst du in der Pause?*
– *Ich esse nichts.*
– *Oh! Und was trinkst du?*
– *Ich trinke Orangensaft.*

3 – *Viktor, was isst du in der Pause?*
– *Ähm ... Ich esse Schokolade oder Bonbons.*
– *Und was trinkst du?*
– *Ich trinke Cola.*

4 – *Und Julia, was isst du in der Pause?*
– *Ich esse eine Banane und eine Orange.*
– *Trinkst du auch Cola?*
– *Nein. Ich trinke Orangensaft.*

5 – *Und Nina. Was isst du in der Pause?*
– *Ich esse Kekse und Chips.*
– *Und was trinkst du?*
– *Ich trinke Wasser.*

Answers
1 e, f, g   **2** b   **3** l, k, a   **4** h, g, b
5 j, c, d

3 Umfrage. (AT 2/3)   1.4a/Y7

Speaking. Pupils conduct a class survey about what their classmates eat and drink at break, and record the results, e.g. as tally marks. Prepare by looking at the form of the question and answer in detail, using the Key Language panel, and getting pupils to practise the dialogue with a partner.

4 Pausenbrot: Wähle jeden Tag etwas anderes. (AT 4/3)   4.4/Y7

Writing. Pupils write about what they eat and drink at break, choosing different items or combinations for each day. Assist less able pupils by showing them how the sentences in the example can be adapted.

More able pupils can be given extra items of food and drink to look up in their dictionaries.

Starter 2   3.1/Y7 4.2/Y7

Aims
To revise numbers to 99.
To introduce prices in euros.

Use **Arbeitsblatt 2.2** either as an OHT for whole-class use or photocopied as worksheets for individual work or pairwork. With a higher-ability class, you could reverse the OHT to increase the level of difficulty. If using photocopies, the coins could be cut out to enable pairs of pupils to practise further. For example: partner A picks a coin while partner B looks away; partner B says the value of the coin that is missing.

5 Hör zu. Was essen sie? Was kostet das? (1–4) (AT 1/3)   1.1/Y7

Listening. Pupils listen to the recording. They first identify the items each speaker asks for using letters from exercise 1, then note down how much it costs. After completing the exercise, draw pupils' attention to the polite use of *Danke* and *Bitte*.

1 – *Ja, bitte?*
– *Ein Brötchen, bitte.*
– *Das macht fünfzig Cent.*
– *Fünfzig Cent. Bitte.*
– *Danke.*
– *Bitte.*

2 – *Ja, bitte?*
– *Bonbons, bitte.*
– *Das macht neununddreißig Cent.*
– *Neununddreißig Cent. Bitte.*
– *Danke.*
– *Bitte.*

3 – *Ja, bitte?*
– *Cola, bitte.*
– *Das macht sechzig Cent.*
– *Sechzig Cent. Bitte.*
– *Danke.*
– *Bitte.*

4 – *Ja, bitte?*
– *Eine Banane, bitte.*
– *Das macht fünfundvierzig Cent.*
– *Fünfundvierzig Cent. Bitte.*
– *Danke.*
– *Bitte.*

Answers
1 Brötchen – 65 Cent
2 Bonbons – 39 Cent
3 Cola – 60 Cent
4 Banane – 45 Cent

Suggestion
To prepare for exercise 6, write the full menu on the board, getting pupils to read out the items and prices for you to write down.

6 Partnerarbeit. (AT 2/3) `1.4b/Y7`
Speaking. Pupils work in pairs to create tuck shop roleplays. Encourage them to buy at least three food items and one drink each. Higher-ability pupils could work on dialogues where they buy more than one item at a time and add up the prices.

ICT Pupils could create their own tuck shop price lists, decorated with clipart. More able pupils could be encouraged to look up their favourite items of food and drink in their dictionaries.

ECHO-Tipp
This points out how useful the high-frequency word *bitte* is. It can be used in several different situations.

7 Lies die Texte. Korrigiere die Sätze. (AT 3/3) `2.1/Y7 4.5a/Y7`
Reading. Pupils read the texts, then spot and correct the deliberate mistake in each statement about the texts. Follow-up reading, translation and writing activities can be found in the Introduction on pages 9–10.

Answers
1 Anke isst eine Orange, **einen Apfel** und eine Banane.
2 Ulli isst Kuchen, Kekse und **Schokolade**.
3 Judith trinkt Cola und isst ein Brötchen, Bonbons und **einen Apfel**.
4 Robert isst eine Banane, Chips und ein Brötchen und er trinkt **Orangensaft**.
5 Anke trinkt Wasser, aber Ulli trinkt **Cola**.

R Pupils could practise reading the texts aloud in pairs.

ECHO-Detektiv: Verb endings
`4.5a/Y7`
This panel reviews regular and irregular verbs, *trinken* and *essen*. Ask for a volunteer to explain the concept of regular verbs (i.e. they all follow the same rules). Elicit the pattern of *ich, du, er* and *sie* forms from *trinken*. Pupils could then go on to look at elements of *sein* and *essen* that are irregular.

Plenary `5.8`

Aim
To review language learned to date and identify areas for improvement.

Pupils work in pairs to check the language they have learned so far in this chapter, using the **Mini-Test** checklist. Ask pupils which points their partners found most difficult. Give pupils the task of improving those points by next lesson. Partners could then test them again.

Learning targets
- Describing what you wear to school
- Revising *einen, eine, ein*

Key framework objectives
1.4/Y7 Speaking – (b) using prompts
2.4/Y7 Writing – (a) sentences and texts as models
4.3/Y7 Language – plurals
5.1 Strategies – patterns

Grammar
- indefinite article (acc.): *einen / eine / ein*
- *sein: sie sind*
- *tragen: ich trage, du trägst*
- *die* + plural nouns

Key language
die Jacke
die Hose
das Hemd
der Pullover
die Krawatte
die Schuhe
der Rock
die Socken
das Sweatshirt
das T-Shirt
die Jeans
die Stiefel
die Bluse
die Sportschuhe
das Kleid
Der Rock (etc.) *ist …*
Die Schuhe (etc.) *sind …*
blau / braun / gelb / grau / grün / lila / orange / rot / schwarz / weiß
Was trägst du in der Schule?
Ich trage …
einen Rock / Jeansrock / Pullover
eine Hose / Bluse / Jacke
ein Hemd / T-Shirt / Sweatshirt / Kleid
Jeans / Schuhe / Stiefel / Sportschuhe
Ich finde das cool / bequem / schick.

High-frequency words
was?
es ist
sie sind
ich trage, du trägst
ich finde das

Citizenship
Differing school culture/rules in other countries

Resources
CD 1, tracks 38–39
Workbooks A and B, p.15
Arbeitsblatt 2.4, p. 23
Arbeitsblatt 2.6, p. 25
Echo Elektro 1 TPP, Express Mod 2 4.1–4.6

Starter 1
4.2/Y7

Aim
To revise colours.

Call out the colours which pupils encountered in Chapter 1 (*blau, braun, gelb, grau, grün, orange, rot, schwarz, weiß*) in random order. Pupils race to touch or hold up something of the correct colour. After you have run through each of the colours once, individual pupils can start to take over calling out the colours. The first pupil to touch the correct colour calls out the next one, and so on.

Suggestion
Use people's clothes in the classroom to introduce the new vocabulary. Decide with the class how many of the items are cognates.

1 Hör zu. Was ist die richtige Reihenfolge? (AT 1/1)
1.1/Y7

Listening. Pupils listen to the recording and note the letters of the items of clothing from the picture in the order in which they are mentioned.

der Pullover
die Krawatte
die Schuhe
die Jacke
die Hose
der Rock
das Hemd
das Sweatshirt
das T-Shirt
die Stiefel
die Bluse
das Kleid
die Jeans
die Socken
die Sportschuhe

38

Answers
j, i, n, a, d, b, f, l, e, o, h, k, g, m, c

2 Sieh dir das Bild in Aufgabe 1 an. Richtig oder falsch? (AT 3/2) `2.1/Y7`

Reading. Pupils study the picture again and decide whether the statements are true or false.

+ More able pupils can also write correct statements. Draw attention to the fact that they should use *sind* instead of *ist* for items where there is more than one. You may wish to point out at this point that *die Hose* is singular, even though its equivalent in English is plural.

Answers
1 falsch (Die Jacke ist blau.)
2 falsch (Der Rock ist braun.)
3 richtig
4 falsch (Die Jeans sind blau.)
5 richtig
6 falsch (Das Hemd ist weiß.)

ECHO-Detektiv: *the* + plural nouns
`4.3/Y7`

This panel reminds pupils about the plural form of the definitive article.

ECHO-Detektiv   `4.5a/Y7`

Pupils are reminded again about the 3rd person plural form of the verb *sein*.

3 Partnerarbeit. (AT 2/3) `1.4b/Y7`

Speaking. Pupils work in pairs to create dialogues. Partner A makes a statement about the colour of an item in the picture, and partner B decides whether the statement is true or false. Then the roles are reversed. Remind pupils to listen carefully to what their partner says, especially the item and the colour. Point out that they can ask for repetition using *Wie bitte?*. Encourage them to speak clearly and attempt good pronunciation.

Starter 2   `4.2/Y7`

Aims
To improve understanding of speech.
To consolidate clothing vocabulary and colours.

Play 'true/false sentences': make statements such as *Ich trage eine Jacke* and *Der Rock ist rot*. (For greater variety than allowed for by the school uniform, you could base the questions on pictures cut from fashion magazines/ advertisements.) Pupils stand up if the statement is true and remain sitting if it is false. Alternatively, mini-white boards could be marked with True and False. After a few examples, pupils can take over making the statements. This could be a game between two teams, with each team scoring points according to how many members of the opposing team respond incorrectly.

4 Schreib acht Sätze über die Kleidung in Aufgabe 1. (AT 4/3) `4.4/Y7`

Writing. Pupils write a sentence about eight of the items in exercise 1.

5 Hör zu und lies. Sieh dir die Bilder an. Wo ist der Fehler? (AT 3/3)
`1.1/Y7  2.1/Y7  3.1/Y7`

Listening. Pupils compare the texts with the pictures and identify the deliberate error in each text. Before starting the exercise, elicit from pupils what the task will involve. On a scale of 1–10, how hard do they feel it will be? Why? After checking answers, you could elicit reactions to the fact that pupils in German-speaking countries do not have school uniform: *Ich finde das cool / toll / gut / schlecht*, etc.

Was trägst du in der Schule?   39

Ich trage einen Jeansrock und einen Pullover. Der Pullover ist rot und der Jeansrock ist blau. Ich trage Schuhe, das finde ich schick!

Ich trage eine Hose und einen Pullover. Die Hose ist grün und der Pullover ist blau. Ich trage Stiefel. Ich finde das cool!

Ich trage eine Bluse und eine Hose. Die Hose ist grün. Ich trage auch Sportschuhe. Ich finde das bequem.

Answers

1 Der Pullover ist grün.
2 Ich trage Sportschuhe.
3 Ich trage eine Jacke und ein T-Shirt.

ECHO-Detektiv   4.3/Y7 5.1

This panel reminds pupils of the accusative forms of the indefinite article. Pupils could be referred to the **Grammatik** on page 114 for more information and practice. You could also refer them back to where they have seen this before in Chapter 1 (page 13).

6 Gedächtnisspiel: Was trägst du in der Schule? (AT 2/3)   1.4a/Y7 5.1

Speaking. Pupils play a 'chain game' about clothing. Each player adds an item of clothing to the sentence until a mistake is made. Focus more able pupils on the accurate use of *einen / eine / ein* and on the forms of the verb: *ich trage* and *du trägst*. A variation on pairwork can additionally be found in the Introduction on page 11.

7 Deine Traumuniform. (AT 4/3)   2.4a/Y7

Writing. Pupils write about their own ideal school uniform. You could use this exercise to show pupils how to build short texts from notes, e.g.

Sweatshirt – blau; Hose – schwarz; toll
becomes:

Ich trage ein Sweatshirt. Das Sweatshirt ist blau. Ich trage eine Hose. Die Hose ist schwarz. Ich finde das toll!

Plenary   4.2/Y7

Aim

To get used to revising and recycling language.

Ask pupils to work in pairs. They should make three lists of German words:

1 school subjects
2 snack items
3 clothes.

Set a time limit of about three minutes. Then combine pairs of pairs into groups of four: the groups put their ideas together, crossing out any duplicates. Again, set a time limit of about two minutes. Finally, one group reads out its lists to the class. Each subsequent group adds any additional items it has noted. List the items on the board.

Discuss the idea that language has to be revised and recycled. Just because you have learnt it once, doesn't mean it's not useful to go over it again!

Learning targets

- Learning about school life in German-speaking countries
- Understanding a longer text

Key framework objectives

2.5/Y7 Writing – different text types

3.2/Y7 Culture – (a) young people: interests/opinions

3.2/Y7 Culture – (b) challenging stereotypes

4.6/Y7 Language – (b) negatives

5.6 Strategies – reading aloud

5.7 Strategies – planning and preparing

Grammar

- *kein (acc.): keinen / keine / kein*

Key language

Ich heiße / Sie heißt … .
Ich bin / Sie ist … Jahre alt.
Ich wohne / Sie wohnt in …
Ich bin / Sie ist in der Klasse …
Die Schule beginnt um … .
In der Pause esse / trinke ich …
Mein / Ninas Lieblingsfach ist …
Ich finde … schwierig (etc.).
Ich trage … in der Schule.
Ich habe keine Schuluniform.

High-frequency words

kein, keine, keinen
ich heiße
ich wohne
ich bin, sie ist
ich esse, sie isst
ich trinke
ich finde, sie findet
ich trage
ich habe
in, um, zur

Pronunciation

Reading aloud

English

Reading and understanding a webpage

Citizenship

School routine in German-speaking countries

ICT

Planning and writing a webpage

Resources

CD 1, track 40
Workbooks A and B, p.16
Arbeitsblatt 2.5, p. 24
Echo Elektro 1 TPP, Express Mod 2 5.1–5.5

Starter 1   5.7

Aims

To consolidate school vocabulary.
To start planning a website in German.

Write in the centre of an OHT: *eine Website für die Schule.* Gather ideas around the class for useful items of language, encouraging use of the target language. Develop a network of ideas on the OHT. Provide categories, e.g. *Schuluniform, Schulfächer, Pausenbrot, Stundenplan, Schultag* to prompt and guide pupils' ideas. The OHT can be used at the end of the unit to assist in planning exercise 6.

Ask pupils to open their books and scan Nina's webpage. Which of their ideas are mentioned?

Hör zu und lies.   3.2a+b/Y7

Listening. Pupils listen to the recording and read the webpage in their books. Ask pupils to compare details of Nina's school life with their own.

40

> *Hallo!*
> *Ich heiße Nina Bukowski. Ich bin dreizehn Jahre alt. Ich wohne in Salzburg in Österreich.*
> *Meine Schule heißt das Musische Gymnasium. Ich bin in der Klasse 8a.*
> *Die Schule beginnt um acht Uhr und endet um dreizehn Uhr zehn. In der Pause esse ich ein Brötchen und ich trinke Orangensaft oder Cola.*
> *Mein Lieblingsfach ist Musik. Ich finde Englisch schwierig und Französisch ist furchtbar!*
> *Ich trage ein Sweatshirt und Jeans in der Schule – ich habe keine Schuluniform.*

Suggestion

Write the following sentences on the board or an OHT:

1 N. introduces her school.
2 N. introduces herself.
3 N. talks about food and drink.
4 N. talks about her school routine.
5 N. talks about her subjects.
6 N. talks about what she wears.

Uncover them one at a time. Working in pairs, pupils scan the webpage in exercise 1 to find the sentence or sentences which match these descriptions. When pupils think they have found the matching section of the text, they put their hands up and read it out when asked.

ECHO-Tipp: Understanding a text

5.4

This gives advice about preparing to read a text – looking for clues to help with meaning – and about reading for gist.

2 Partnerarbeit. Lies den Text vor.

5.6

Speaking. Pupils practise reading the webpage text aloud in pairs. Able pupils could be encouraged to correct each other's pronunciation. In preparation, play the recording again and ask all pupils to read along under their breath. Ask which words/passages they find particularly difficult to pronounce, and chorus these with the class. For further ideas on reading texts, see pages 9–10 of the Introduction to this guide.

3 Lies den Text noch mal und ordne die Bilder. (Vier Bilder sind nicht im Text.) (AT 3/4)

2.1/Y7

Reading. Pupils read the text again and put the pictures in the order in which the items occur in the text. In preparation, discuss how best to approach this exercise and help pupils to draw up a sequence of steps to take. For example:

1 Identify chunks of information (e.g. *acht Uhr*).
2 Scan pictures for one that matches.
3 Write down the letter of any matching picture.
4 Double-check at the end that there are only four letters left over.

Answers
d, b, f, i, j, k, h (not in text: a, c, e, g)

R Read out sentences or partial sentences from the text, translated into English, e.g.

I'm thirteen years old.
I'm in class 8a.
At break I eat a roll …

Pupils must identify and read out the German text. For further reinforcement ideas, see page 10 of the Introduction.

ECHO-Detektiv: keinen / keine / kein

4.6b/Y7

This panel explains the formation and usage of the negative article *kein*. Pupils could refer to the **Grammatik** on page 115 for detailed explanation and practice. Draw pupils' attention to the fact that this is another word that they will see a lot and can also use often in order to talk about what they don't have.

Starter 2

4.6b/Y7

Aims

To improve pupils' capacity to follow speech.
To reinforce *keinen / keine / kein*.

Make a list of eight to ten sentences containing *einen / eine / ein* or *keinen / keine / kein*, and known language from Chapters 1 and 2. For example:

Ich habe einen Bleistift.
Ich trage keine Schuluniform.
Es gibt eine Pause um zehn Uhr dreißig.
Ich habe kein Wörterbuch.
Ich esse keine Kekse.
Es gibt keine Pause um elf Uhr.
Ich habe keinen Kuli.
Ich esse einen Kuchen.
Hast du ein Wörterbuch?

Do not show the list to the class at this point. (However, you may find it useful to write the list on an OHT for discussion at the end of the starter.) Pupils work in pairs. They write a large tick on one mini-whiteboard or piece of paper, and a large cross on another. They place these in front of them on the desk. Read out the sentences one at a time, clearly but at close to normal speed. When pupils hear *einen*, *eine* or *ein* they must hold up the tick; when they hear *keinen*, *keine* or *kein* they must hold up the cross. Pupils can compete with their partners to grab the correct answer and hold it up. Finally, you could display the sentences on an OHT and elicit English translations from the class.

4 Schreib acht Sätze. (AT 4/3) `4.4/Y7`

Writing. Pupils use the words in the three boxes to write eight sentences about Nina and her school, using the third person.

> **Answers**
> Sie heißt Nina Bukowski.
> Sie ist dreizehn Jahre alt.
> Sie ist in der Klasse 8a.
> Sie isst ein Brötchen in der Pause.
> Sie findet Französisch furchtbar.
> Die Schule beginnt um acht Uhr.
> Ninas Lieblingsfach ist Musik.
> Sie hat keine Schuluniform.

5 Schreib eine Webseite über deine Schule. (AT 4/4) `2.5/Y7 5.7`

ICT *Writing.* Pupils plan and write a webpage about their own school. Brainstorm with them what they feel should be in it and how to structure the material. For pupils in need of more support, Nina's webpage could be adapted as a writing frame.

This exercise could be the starting point for a collaborative ICT project, with individual pupils responsible for paragraphs about timetable, subjects, uniform, etc. If practicable, the resulting pages, or a selection of work from them, could be uploaded to the school website as an example of pupils' work. Alternatively pupils could present their work in a PowerPoint presentation. Planning the webpage could be your **plenary**. Refer pupils back to the mindmap created for the starter, and add any refinements or additional ideas prompted by this unit.

You could show a few bookmarked examples of German school homepages, using a computer or digital projector.

Plenary `4.6b/Y7`

Aim

To reinforce *keinen / keine / kein.*

Ask for a volunteer to come to the front of the class and explain what he/she has learned about *keinen / keine / kein* in this unit (e.g. meaning, how to to use it, examples). He/She can nominate an 'assistant' to help. The volunteers can then test the class by asking questions.

Lernzieltest

5.8

This is a checklist of language covered in Chapter 2. Pupils can work with the checklist in pairs to check what they have learned. Points which directly address grammar and structures are marked with a G. There is a **Lernzieltest** sheet in the Resource and Assessment File (page 28). Encourage pupils to look back at the chapter and to use the grammar section to revise what they are unclear about.

You can also use the **Lernzieltest** as an end-of-unit plenary.

Wiederholung

This is a revision page to prepare pupils for the **Kontrolle** at the end of the chapter.

Resources

CD 1, track 41

1 Hör zu. Welches Fach ist das? (1–6) (AT 1/2)

1.1/Y7

Listening. Pupils listen to the recording and match the pictures to the subjects mentioned by the speakers.

1 – Was hast du um zehn Uhr?
  – Um zehn Uhr habe ich Französisch. Das ist mein Lieblingsfach. 41
2 – Was hast du um elf Uhr vierzig?
  – Ich habe Religion. Das finde ich super langweilig!
3 – Hast du auch am Montag Werken?
  – Ja. Werken finde ich total interessant!
  – Ich auch!
4 – Wie findest du Erdkunde?
  – Uff! Erdkunde? Na ja, Erdkunde finde ich ... gut.
5 – Was hast du am Freitag um zwölf Uhr fünfundzwanzig?
  – Ich habe Deutsch. Du auch?
  – Ja, leider. Deutsch finde ich furchtbar!
6 – Wann hast du Theater?
  – Theater? Theater habe ich am Montag und am Mittwoch. Das finde ich toll!

Answers
1 c   2 d   3 e   4 a   5 b   6 f

2 Partnerarbeit: Mach zwei Interviews. (AT 2/3)

1.4a/Y7

Speaking. Pupils interview each other about their school subjects and school routine, using the two lists of questions provided.

3 Lies die E-Mail. Beantworte die Fragen auf Englisch. (AT 3/3)

2.1/Y7

Reading. Pupils read the email and answer the questions in English.

Answers
1 English
2 RE and science
3 1.30 p.m.
4 crisps, a roll, orange juice
5 trousers, a sweatshirt, trainers

4 Ergänze die Sätze. Schreib sie aus. (AT 4/3)

4.4/Y7

Writing. Pupils complete the sentences, using the picture cues.

Answers
1 Mein Lieblingsfach ist Sport.
2 Ich finde Mathe langweilig.
3 Ich esse eine Banane und ich trinke Cola.
4 Die Schule beginnt um neun Uhr und endet um fünfzehn Uhr dreißig.

5 Schreib eine E-Mail an Jan. Benutze die Sätze aus Aufgabe 4. (AT4/3–4)

2.4b/Y7

Writing. Pupils write an answer to Jan's email, incorporating the sentences they wrote for exercise 4.

Learning targets

- Understanding imaginative texts about an ideal school
- Finding out the meanings of unknown words

Key framework objectives

2.2/Y7	Reading – (a) unfamiliar language
2.2/Y7	Reading – (b) text selection
2.3/Y7	Reading – text features

Key language

Die Schule beginnt um …
In der Pause esse / trinke ich …
Um … Uhr habe ich Englisch (etc.).

High-frequency words

meine
ich habe
in
um
das ist
sehr
und
keine
wie?

Pronunciation

Reading aloud (singing)

English

Reading and understanding an imaginative text

Resources

CD 1, tracks 42–43
Workbooks A and B, p. 17

Starter 1   4.4/Y7

Aims

To encourage pupils to form grammatically correct sentences.
To consolidate school vocabulary.

Present three headings on the board or an OHT: *Schulfächer, Schuluniform, Pausenbrot.*
Elicit and clarify their meanings as necessary.

Divide pupils into teams and give them three minutes to write as many sentences as possible on an OHT about these three topics. The sentences must be grammatically correct (but do not penalise minor errors), be legible and make sense. After the time limit has expired, a representative from each team comes to the OHP and displays the team's sentences. Help the class to spot errors and decide whether sentences are valid. The team with the most correct sentences wins a small prize. The class could also vote for the best/most creative/most difficult/silliest sentence.

Using the sentences as a basis, pupils could then do a grammar treasure hunt (see the Introduction page 10).

1 Hör zu und lies.   2.2a+b/Y7

Listening. Pupils listen to the recording and follow the story in their books. In preparation, ask them to assess the text for visual clues, gist and level of difficulty. Ask pupils what they thought of the text. Did they enjoy reading in this format? Why/why not?

> – *Wie ist meine Traumschule?*
> – *Die Schule beginnt um zehn Uhr. Ich habe Musik – Rockmusik. Sie ist sehr laut!* **42**
> – *Um zehn Uhr fünfzig habe ich eine Pause. In der Pause esse ich im Schul-Restaurant Pasta. Lecker!*
> – *Um elf Uhr dreißig endet die Pause. Ich habe Englisch. Ich sehe eine TV-Show aus Amerika.*
> – *Um zwölf Uhr fünfzehn habe ich Informatik. Ich spiele Computerspiele. Das ist toll! Um dreizehn Uhr zwanzig endet die Schule …*
> – *Peter! Es ist sieben Uhr vierzig! Die Schule beginnt in zwanzig Minuten. Du kommst zu spät!*

2 Schreib Peters Stundenplan für die „Traumschule". (AT 3/4)   2.1/Y7

Writing. Pupils read the story again and note down the times and subjects mentioned.

> ### Answers
> 10.00 – Rockmusik
> 10.50 – Pause
> 11.30 – Englisch
> 12.15 – Informatik
> 13.20 – Die Schule endet

3 Rate mal: Wie heißt das auf Englisch? (AT 3/4) `5.4`

Reading. Pupils attempt to work out the meanings of unknown words from the story, using context and other clues. Look at each of the words with the whole class. Discuss ideas for working out and checking the meanings.

> **Answers**
> 1 tasty, delicious
> 2 the computer game
> 3 you arrive, come
> 4 too late

Starter 2 `4.4/Y7`

Aims
To improve fluency of speech.
To revise language about school.

Divide up an A4 sheet into cards of approximately the size of a business card. (You need enough cards for half of your class.) On each card, write a unique cue such as *Lieblingsfach: Englisch, Pause: Brötchen* or *Jeans und T-Shirt.* Make a photocopy of the sheet, then cut out the cards. (Each card now has an identical 'twin' and there is one card for each pupil in the class.) Mix up the cards and put them in a bag. Pupils draw a card from the bag as they come into the class. They must conceal it from other pupils. If there are cards left in the bag, give an extra card to each of the most able pupils.

Pupils circulate in the class, saying sentences such as *Mein Lieblingsfach ist Englisch* to find their 'twin'. Twins sit down together, until finally all pupils are seated.

4 Deine Meinung: Traumschule oder Realität? (AT 3/3) `2.2a/Y7`

Reading. Pupils read the speech bubbles and decide which, in their opinion, belong to 'dream school' and which belong to 'real school'. They identify and look up unknown words.

The most able pupils could go on to write their own sentences for *Traumschule* and *Realität*.

5 Hör zu und sing mit. `2.2a+b/Y7 2.3/Y7 5.4`

Listening. Pupils listen to the song, then sing along. Further ideas for exploitation of songs can be found in the Introduction on page 10. Ask pupils to look for particular features which are used. For example, the use of actions and questions within the song. Pupils could write their own verse using similar features.

Ich trage eine Hose.
Wie ist die Hose?
Sie ist bequem und grün.
Ich trage einen Rock.
Wie ist der Rock?
Er ist rot und schön.

Die Schuluniform ist doof, doof, doof!
Die Schuluniform ist toll, toll, toll!

Ich trage eine Jacke.
Wie ist die Jacke?
Sie ist praktisch und blau.
Ich trage einen Pulli.
Wie ist der Pulli?
Er ist hässlich und grau!

Die Schuluniform ist doof, doof, doof!
Die Schuluniform ist toll, toll, toll!

Ich trage ein Hemd
Wie ist das Hemd?
Es ist cool und weiß.
Ich trage schwarze Socken.
Wie sind die Socken?
Sie sind bequem, aber heiß.

Die Schuluniform ist doof, doof, doof!
Die Schuluniform ist toll, toll, toll!

6 Wie ist deine Traumschule? Schreib Sätze. (AT 4/3–4) `2.4a/Y7 5.5`

Writing. Pupils write sentences about their own 'dream school'. Discuss the use of dictionaries and other resources to look up unknown words.

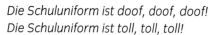 Pupils write sentences based on their 'dream school' timetables.

Plenary `1.4a+b/Y7`

Aim
To develop fluency in spontaneous talk.

Pupils work in groups of three. They take it in turns to attempt to speak without pause on the subject of *die Schule*. The first pupil talks for 20 seconds, the second for 40 seconds and the third for a minute.

SELF-ACCESS READING AND WRITING AT TWO LEVELS

A Reinforcement

1 Welches Fach ist das? Schreib das Wort auf. (AT4/1)   `4.2/Y7`

Writing. Pupils copy and complete the words for school subjects, using the picture clues for support.

> **Answers**
> 1 Englisch   2 Erdkunde   3 Geschichte   4 Mathe
> 5 Religion   6 Deutsch

2 Positiv oder negativ? (AT3/2)   `2.1/Y7`

Reading. Pupils read each sentence, and decide whether the opinion expressed is positive or negative.

> **Answers**
> 1 positiv   2 negativ   3 negativ   4 positiv
> 5 negativ   6 negativ

3 Wie findest du das? (AT4/2)   `2.4a/Y7`

Writing. Pupils write out the sentences from exercise 2, changing the coloured words to reflect their own opinions. They can find ideas in the original versions of the sentences.

4 Lies die Sätze und finde die richtigen Bilder. (AT3/2)   `2.1/Y7`

Reading. Pupils read the sentences, and find the correct two pictures for each one.

> **Answers**
> 1 f, b   2 e,i   3 g, d   4 a,j   5 h, c

B Extension

1 Lies Valentinas Stundenplan. Richtig oder falsch? Schreib die Sätze richtig auf. (AT 3/2)   `2.1/Y7`

Reading. Pupils use the school timetable to work out if each sentence is true or false. They write out the false sentences correctly.

> **Answers**
> 1 Falsch. Deutsch beginnt um acht Uhr *zehn*.
> 2 Richtig
> 3 Falsch. Sport endet um dreizehn Uhr *zehn*.
> 4 Falsch. Die erste Pause endet um *zehn Uhr*.
> 5 Richtig
> 6 Falsch. Die zweite Pause beginnt um elf Uhr *dreißig*.

2 Was sagt Valentina über die Schulfächer? Schreib sechs Sätze. (AT4/3)   `2.4a/Y7`

Writing. Pupils write six sentences to show what Valentina thinks of the subjects, based on the pictures drawn on his timetable. Accept any suitable adjectives.

> **Answers**
> 1 Ich finde Deutsch toll.
> 2 Ich finde Englisch gut.
> 3 Ich finde Mathe schlecht.
> 4 Ich finde Erdkunde langweilig.
> 5 Ich finde Kunst schwierig.
> 6 Ich finde Sport toll.

3 Lies die Texte und sieh dir das Bild an. Wer ist das? (AT3/4)   `2.1/Y7`

Reading. Pupils read the two texts about school uniform, and decide to whom each item of clothing pictured belongs. As an extra task, they could draw, colour and label pictures of Lea and Marie, using lines from the texts as labels.

> **Answers**
> 1 Marie
> 2 Marie
> 3 Lea
> 4 Lea
> 5 Marie
> 6 Lea

Übungsheft A, Seite 12

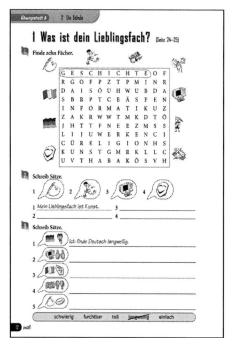

1 (AT3 Level 1) Geschichte, Informatik, Werken, Religion, Kunst, Sport, Theater, Musik, Deutsch, Französisch

2 (AT4 Level 2) 1 Mein Lieblingsfach ist Kunst. **2** Mein Lieblingsfach ist Sport. **3** Mein Lieblingsfach ist Informatik. **4** Mein Lieblingsfach ist Theater.

3 (AT4 Level 2) 1 Ich finde Deutsch langweilig. **2** Ich finde Informatik toll. **3** Ich finde Französisch schwierig. **4** Ich finde Englisch furchtbar. **5** Ich finde Kunst einfach.

Übungsheft B, Seite 12

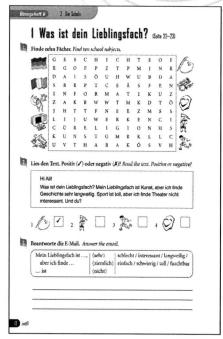

1 (AT3 Level 1) Geschichte, Informatik, Werken, Religion, Kunst, Sport, Theater, Musik, Deutsch, Französisch

2 (AT3 Level 3) 1 ✓ **2** ✗ **3** ✓ **4** ✗

3 (AT4 Level 3)

Übungsheft A, Seite 13

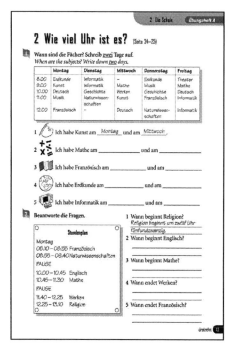

1 (AT3 Level 1, AT4 Level 1) 1 Ich habe Kunst am **Montag** und am **Mittwoch**. **2** Ich habe Mathe am **Mittwoch** und am **Freitag**. **3** Ich habe Französisch am **Montag** und am **Donnerstag**. **4** Ich habe Erdkunde am **Montag** und am **Donnerstag**. **5** Ich habe Informatik am **Dienstag** und am **Freitag**.

2 (AT3 Level 2, AT4 Level 2) 1 Religion beginnt um zwölf Uhr fünfundzwanzig. **2** Englisch beginnt um zehn Uhr. **3** Mathe beginnt um zehn Uhr fünfundvierzig. **4** Werken endet um zwölf Uhr fünfundzwanzig. **5** Französisch endet um acht Uhr fünfundfünfzig.

Übungsheft B, Seite 13

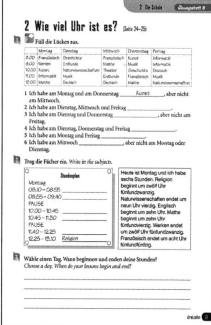

1 (AT3 Level 2, AT4 Level 1) 1 Ich habe am Montag und am Donnerstag **Kunst**, aber nicht am Mittwoch. **2** Ich habe am Dienstag, Mittwoch und Freitag **Deutsch**. **3** Ich habe am Dienstag und Donnerstag **Geschichte**, aber nicht am Freitag. **4** Ich habe am Dienstag, Donnerstag und Freitag **Musik**. **5** Ich habe am Montag und Freitag **Informatik**. **6** Ich habe am Mittwoch **Theater**, aber nicht am Montag oder Dienstag.

2 (AT3 Level 3)

08.10–08.55	Französisch
08.55–09.40	Naturwissenschaften
10.00–10.45	Englisch
10.45–11.30	Mathe
11.40–12.25	Werken
12.25–13.10	Religion

3 (AT4 Level 3)

**Übungsheft A,
Seite 14**

1 (AT3 Levels 2, AT4 Level 1) 1 Bonbons **2** Wasser **3** Orange
4 Apfel **5** Kuchen **6** Kekse

Das Lösungswort ist Banane.

2 (AT4 Level 2) 1 Ich **esse** ein **Brötchen**. **2** Ich **trinke**
Orangensaft. **3** Ich **trinke Wasser**. **4** Ich **esse** einen **Apfel**. **5**
Ich **esse Kekse**. **6** Ich **trinke Cola**.

**Übungsheft B,
Seite 14**

**1 (AT3 Level 3,
AT4 Level 1)** In der
Pause esse ich **1**
Bonbons und ich
trinke **2 Wasser**.
Olaf isst eine **3**
Orange oder einen
4 Apfel und Sonja
isst **5 Kuchen** oder
6 Kekse.

Das Lösungswort
ist Banane.

2 (AT3 Level 3) Hallo Mehmet! Ich heiße Peter. In der
Schulpause **esse** ich ein Brötchen und Kekse. Ich **trinke**
Orangensaft. Ich **finde** das super. Meine Freundin Raifa **trinkt**
Wasser und sie **isst** einen Apfel. Sie **findet** das lecker. Und du?
Was **isst** du und was **trinkst** du?

3 (AT4 Level 3)

**Übungsheft A,
Seite 15**

1 (AT4 Level 1) 1 Jacke **2** Rock **3** Krawatte **4** Pullover **5** Jeans
6 Hose **7** Sweatshirt **8** Schuhe

2 (AT3 Level 3, AT4 Level 1) Ich trage eine Bluse, **1 einen**
Rock, **2 eine** Jacke und **3 Stiefel**. Und was trägst du?

Ich trage **4 eine** Hose, **5 ein** Hemd, **6 einen** Pullover und
7 Sportschuhe. Tschüs!

**Übungsheft B,
Seite 15**

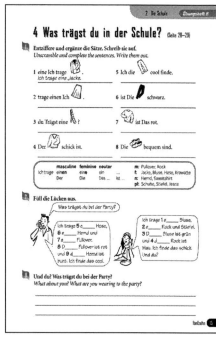

1 (AT4 Level 2) 1 Ich trage eine Jacke. **2** Ich trage einen Rock.
3 Trägst du eine Krawatte? **4** Der Pullover ist schick. **5** Ich finde
die Jeans cool. **6** Die Hose ist schwarz. **7** Das Sweatshirt ist rot.
8 Die Schuhe sind bequem.

2 (AT3 Level 3, AT4 Level 1) Ich trage **1 eine** Bluse, **2 einen**
Rock und Stiefel. **3 Die** Bluse ist grün und **4 der** Rock ist blau.
Ich finde das schick. Und du? – Ich trage **5 eine** Hose, **6 ein**
Hemd und **7 einen** Pullover. **8 Der** Pullover ist rot und **9 das**
Hemd ist bunt. Ich finde das cool.

3 (AT4 Level 3)

Übungsheft A, Seite 16

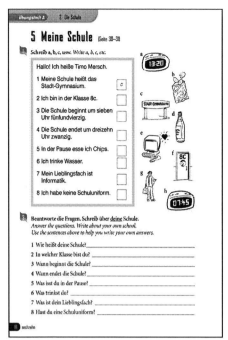

1 (AT3 Level 2) 1c 2f 3h 4a 5b 6d 7e 8g

2 (AT3 Level 2, AT4 Level 3)

Übungsheft B, Seite 16

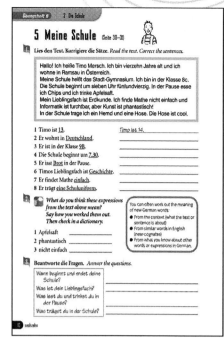

1 (AT3 Level 4, AT4 Level 3) 1 Timo ist 14. 2 Er wohnt in Österreich. 3 Er ist in der Klasse 8c. 4 Die Schule beginnt um 7.45. 5 Er isst Chips in der Pause. 6 Timos Lieblingsfach ist Erdkunde. 7 Er findet Mathe nicht einfach. 8 Er trägt keine Schuluniform.

2 (AT3 Level 3) 1 apple juice 2 fantastic 3 not easy

3 (AT4 Level 4)

Übungsheft A, Seite 17

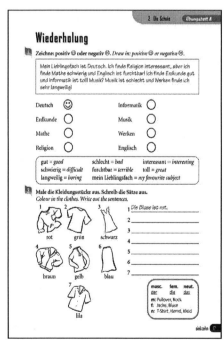

1 (AT3 Level 3) Deutsch ☺, Erdkunde ☺, Mathe ☹, Religion ☺, Informatik ☺, Musik ☹, Werken ☹, Englisch ☹

2 (AT4 Level 2) 1 Die Bluse ist rot. *(red)* 2 Das T-Shirt ist grün. *(green)* 3 Das Kleid ist schwarz. *(black)* 4 Die Jacke ist braun. *(brown)* 5 Der Pullover ist gelb. *(yellow)* 6 Der Rock ist blau. *(blue)* 7 Das Hemd ist lila. *(mauve)*

Übungsheft B, Seite 17

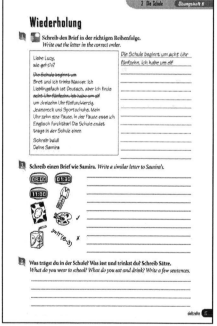

1 (AT3 Level 4, AT4 Level 3) Liebe Lucy, wie geht's? Die Schule beginnt um acht Uhr fünfzehn. Ich habe um elf Uhr zehn eine Pause. In der Pause esse ich Brot und ich trinke Wasser. Ich trage in der Schule einen Jeansrock und Sportschuhe. Mein Lieblingsfach ist Deutsch, aber ich finde Englisch furchtbar! Die Schule endet um dreizehn Uhr fünfundvierzig. Schreib bald! Deine Samira

(Order could vary, as long as the letter makes sense.)

2 (AT4 Level 4) Die Schule beginnt um acht Uhr. Ich habe um elf Uhr eine Pause. In der Pause esse ich Chips und ich trinke Orangensaft. Die Schule endet um dreizehn Uhr dreißig. Ich trage in der Schule eine Hose und einen Pullover. Mein Lieblingsfach ist Kunst, aber ich finde Mathe furchtbar.

3 (AT4 Level 3–4)

**Übungsheft A,
Seite 18**

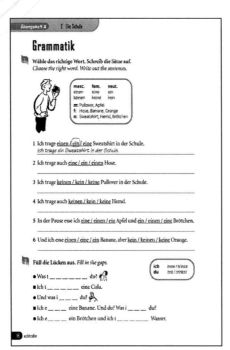

**Übungsheft B,
Seite 18**

1 (AT3 Level 2) 1 Ich trage **ein** Sweatshirt in der Schule. **2** Ich trage auch **eine** Hose. **3** Ich trage **keinen** Pullover in der Schule. **4** Ich trage auch **kein** Hemd. **5** In der Pause esse ich **einen** Apfel und **ein** Brötchen. **6** Und ich esse **eine** Banane, aber **keine** Orange.

2 (AT3 Level 2)

- Was **trinkst** du?
- Ich **trinke** eine Cola.
- Und was **isst** du?
- Ich **esse** eine Banane. Und du? Was **isst** du?
- Ich **esse** ein Brötchen und ich **trinke** Wasser.

1 (AT4 Level 2)

- Was **trinkst** du?
- Ich **trinke** eine Cola.
- Und was **isst** du?
- Ich **esse** eine Banane. Und du? Was **isst** du?
- Ich **esse** ein Brötchen und ich **trinke** Wasser.
- Was **trinkt** Matthias?
- Er **trinkt** Orangensaft.
- Und was **isst** Julia?
- Sie **isst** Kekse.

2 (AT3 Level 3) 1 Ich trage **einen** Pullover und **einen** Jeansrock, aber **keine** Hose. Ich esse **einen** Apfel. **2** Ich trage **ein** T-Shirt und Jeans, aber natürlich **keinen** Rock. Ich esse **eine** Banane.

Arbeitsblatt 2.1

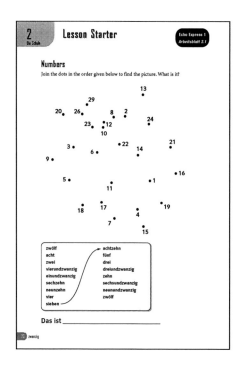

Das ist ein Apfel

Arbeitsblatt 2.2

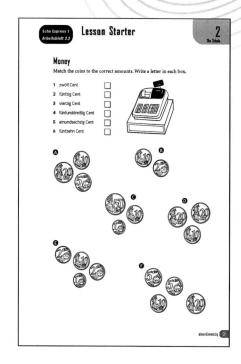

1 B **2** D **3** F **4** A **5** C **6** E

Arbeitsblatt 2.3

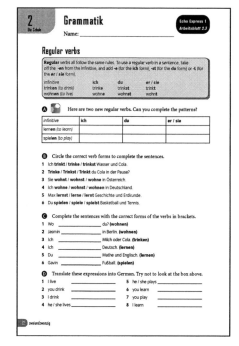

A
lerne, lernst, lernt, spiele, spielst, spielt

B
1 trinke **2** Trinkst **3** wohnt **4** wohne **5** lernt **6** spielst

C
1 wohnst **2** wohnt **3** trinke **4** lerne **5** lernst **6** spielt

D
1 ich wohne **2** du trinkst **3** ich trinke **4** er / sie wohnt **5** er / sie spielt **6** du lernst **7** du spielst **8** ich lerne

Arbeitsblatt 2.4

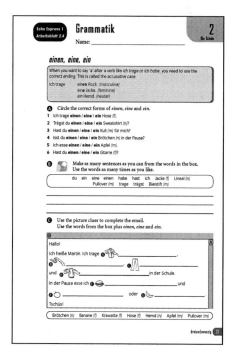

A
1 eine **2** ein **3** einen **4** ein **5** einen **6** eine

B
Possible answers

Ich trage eine Jacke. Ich trage einen Pullover. Du trägst eine Jacke. Du trägst einen Pullover. Ich habe ein Lineal. Ich habe einen Bleistift. Du hast ein Lineal. Du hast einen Bleistift.

C
A ein Hemd **B** eine Krawatte **C** eine Hose **D** einen Pullover **E** ein Brötchen **F** einen Apfel **G** eine Banane

2 Resource and assessment file

Arbeitsblatt 2.5

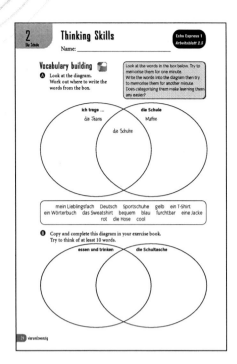

Arbeitsblatt 2.6

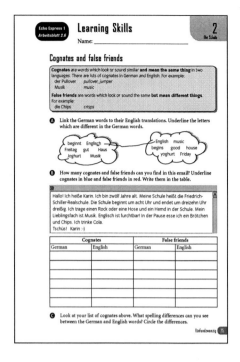

A
Possible answers

ich trage die Jeans, Sportschuhe, ein T-Shirt, bequem, cool, gelb, rot, blau

die Schule Mathe, Deutsch, mein Lieblingsfach, ein Wörterbuch, furchtbar

could apply to both: die Schuhe, eine Jacke, die Hose, das Sweatshirt

A
beginnt – begins, Englisch – English, Freitag – Friday, gut – good, Haus – house, Joghurt – yoghurt, Musik – music

B
Possible answers. Allow any plausible alternatives or additions.

Cognates		False friends	
German	**English**	**German**	**English**
Hallo!	*Hello! Hi!*	bin	*am*
Schule	*school*	Hose	*trousers*
beginnt	*begins*	Chips	*crisps*
endet	*ends*	Pause	*break*
in	*in*	die	*the*
Musik	*music*	Rock	*skirt*
Englisch	*English*		
trinke	*drink*		
Cola	*cola*		

C
Many possible answers. Help pupils to spot these key differences.

German	English	
alt	*old*	t = d
trinke	*drink*	
Schule	*school*	u = oo
beginnt	*begins*	*different endings on verbs*
endet	*ends*	
Musik	*music*	k = c
Englisch	*English*	sch = sh

3 Familie und Freunde

Unit Learning targets	Key framework objectives	NC levels and PoS coverage	Grammar and key language	Skills
1 Das ist meine Familie (pp. 38–39) • Giving information about family members • Using the possessive adjectives *mein* and *dein* ('my' and 'your')	**1.4/Y7** Speaking – (b) using prompts **2.4/Y7** Writing – (b) building text **4.6/Y7** Language – (a) questions	**NC levels** 1–4 **3b** sounds and writing **3c** apply grammar **2.2a** listen for gist **2.2d** pronunciation and intonation **2.2e** ask and answer questions **4b** communicate in pairs etc.	Plural nouns: *Brüder / Schwestern* Possessive adjectives *mein(e) / dein(e)* *Ich habe einen / eine …* (revisited) *Er / Sie ist …* (revisited) *Er / Sie heißt …* (revisited) *Hast du ?* *Ich habe …* *einen Bruder / Halbbruder / Stiefbruder* *eine Schwester / Halbschwester / Stiefschwester* *zwei Brüder / Schwestern* *Ich bin Einzelkind.* *Wie heißt er / sie?* *Wie alt ist er / sie?* *Er / Sie heißt …* *Er / Sie ist … Jahre alt.* *Mein Vater / Stiefvater / Großvater / Onkel / Cousin* *Das ist mein …* *Meine Mutter / Stiefmutter / Großmutter / Tante / Cousine* *Das ist meine …* Numbers 1–100	Pronunciation: *u/ü* Appreciating the importance of high-frequency words
2 Wie sieht sie aus? (pp. 40–41) • Describing people's appearance • Using adjectives with nouns	**2.4/Y7** Writing – (a) sentences and texts as models **4.4/Y7** Language – sentence formation	**NC levels** 2–4 **2.2a** listen for gist **2.2d** pronunciation and intonation **2.2j** adapt previously-learnt language **3b** sounds and writing **3c** apply grammar	Adjectival endings before noun (*lange, braune,* etc.) *haben* and *sein: ich / du / er / sie / es* *braune / blonde / rote / schwarze / lange / kurze / glatte / lockige Haare* *grüne / braune / blaue / graue Augen* *groß / mittelgroß / klein / schlank / kräftig / dick*	Pronunciation: *au*
3 Er ist lustig (pp. 42–43) • Talking about people's characteristics • Making sentences more interesting	**1.2/Y7** Listening – unfamiliar language **1.3/Y7** Listening – (a) interpreting intonation and tone **1.3/Y7** Speaking – (b) using intonation and tone **2.3/Y7** Reading – text features **4.6/Y7** Language – (b) negatives	**NC levels** 1–4 **2.2a** listen for gist **2.2d** pronunciation and intonation **2.2j** adapt previously-learnt language **3b** sounds and writing **3c** apply grammar **3d** use a range of vocab / structures	Connectives: *und, aber, auch* Qualifiers: *sehr, ziemlich* *nicht* *auch* *Wie bist du?* *Wie ist … ?* *Ich bin / Du bist / Er/Sie ist freundlich / lustig / laut / schüchtern / intelligent / sportlich / musikalisch / kreativ / faul / launisch / unpünktlich.* *Herr / Frau*	Using connectives and qualifiers to make sentences longer / more interesting

Unit Learning targets	Key framework objectives	NC levels and PoS coverage	Grammar and key language	Skills
4 Haustiere (pp. 44–45) • Talking about pets • Using plural forms of nouns	2.4/Y7 Writing – (b) building text 4.3/Y7 Language – plurals 5.1 Strategies – patterns	NC levels 2–4 2.1b memorising 2.1d previous knowledge 2.1e use reference materials 2.2a listen for gist 2.2b skim and scan 2.2c respond appropriately 2.2e ask and answer questions 2.2g write clearly and coherently 2.2h redraft to improve writing 3c apply grammar 3d use a range of vocab / structures 4b communicate in pairs etc.	*Ich habe einen / eine / ein …* (revisited) Plural forms of nouns (pets) *Hast du ein Haustier?* *Ich habe einen Goldfisch(e) / Hamster(-) / Hund(e) / Wellensittich(e).* *Ich habe eine Katze(n) / Schlange(n) / Schildkröte(n).* *Ich habe ein Kaninchen(-) / Meerschweinchen(-) / Pferd(e).* *Ich habe zwei / drei,* etc. + plural forms *Ich habe keine Haustiere.* *Er / Sie / Es ist … / heißt …* Colours, descriptions (revisited)	Finding out plural forms of nouns
5 E-Mails (pp. 46–47) • Understanding a longer email and writing a reply • Finding out the meanings of new words	1.5/Y7 Speaking – (a) presenting 1.5/Y7 Speaking – (b) expression/ non-verbal techniques 3.2/Y7 Culture – (a) young people: interests/ opinions 3.2/Y7 Culture – (b) challenging stereotypes	NC levels 3–4 2.1d previous knowledge 2.2b skim and scan 2.2c respond approriately 2.2e ask and answer questions 2.2j adapt previously-learnt language 3b sounds and writing 3d use a range of vocab / structures 4b communicate in pairs etc. 4g language for a range of purposes	*Hallo!* *Ich heiße* *Ich bin / Er/Sie ist … Jahre alt.* *Ich habe am … Geburtstag.* *Ich wohne in …* *Das ist in …* *Ich habe …* (family and pets) *Ich habe …* (appearance) *Ich bin / Er/Sie ist …* (character) *Mein(e) … ist …* *Wie geht's?* *Hast du Geschwister?* *Hast du ein Haustier?* *Wie siehst du aus?* *Schreib bald! dein /deine*	Reading/ listening to a longer text for gist Deducing the meanings of new words Composing an email in German
Lernzieltest und Wiederholung (pp. 48–49) • Pupils' checklist and practice test		NC levels 2–4 3c apply grammar 3d use a range of vocab / structures 4b communicate in pairs etc.		
Mehr (pp. 50–51) • Understanding and giving information about a famous person	1.2/Y7 Listening – unfamiliar language 1.5/Y7 Speaking – (a) presenting 1.5/Y7 Speaking – (b) expression/ non-verbal techniques 5.7 Strategies – planning and preparing	NC levels 3–4 3c apply grammar 3d use a range of vocab / structures 2.2e ask and answer questions 2.2j adapt previously-learnt language 2.2b skim and scan 4e use a range of resources 4f language of interest / enjoyment 4g language for a range of purposes 2.2c respond appropriately	Third person singular verb forms (revisited) Profile of a famous person: *Name* *Alter* *Geburtstag* *Wohnort* *Freundin* *Geschwister* *Haustiere* *Größe* *Haare* *Augen* *Persönlichkeit* *Er / Sie ist / heißt / hat / wohnt / isst / trinkt*	
Extra (pp. 104–105) • Self-access reading and writing at two levels		NC levels 1–4 3c apply grammar 3d use a range of vocab / structures 2.2e ask and answer questions		

Learning targets
- Giving information about family members
- Using the possessive adjectives *mein* and *dein* ('my' and 'your')

Key framework objectives
1.4/Y7 Speaking – (b) using prompts
2.4/Y7 Writing – (b) building text
4.6/Y7 Language – (a) questions

Grammar
- Plurals: *Brüder / Schwestern*
- Possessive adjectives *mein(e) / dein(e)*

- *haben + einen / eine* (revisited)
- *Er / Sie ist…* (revisited)
- *Er / Sie heißt …* (revisited)

Key language
Hast du Geschwister?
Ich habe …
einen Bruder / Halbbruder / Stiefbruder
eine Schwester / Halbschwester / Stiefschwester
zwei Brüder / Schwestern
Ich bin Einzelkind.
Wie heißt er / sie?
Er / Sie heißt …
Wie alt ist er / sie?
Er / Sie ist … Jahre alt.
mein Vater / Stiefvater / Großvater / Onkel / Cousin
meine Mutter / Stiefmutter / Großmutter / Tante / Cousine
Das ist mein / meine …
Numbers 1–100

High-frequency words
hast du?
ich habe
einen / eine
ich bin
er / sie ist
wie?
und
mein(e)
dein(e)
das ist

Pronunciation
u/ü

Mathematics
Using numbers to give ages
Simple arithmetic

Resources
CD 2, tracks 2–4
Workbooks A and B, p.22
Echo Elektro 1 TPP, Express Mod 3 1.1–1.8

Starter 1
4.6a/Y7

Aim
To recap question forms encountered in Chapters 1 and 2.

Reveal the following list of English questions on the board or an OHT. You may wish to use just the first five with a less confident class. Pupils work in pairs, and race to find and write down the correct German equivalents, using their textbooks for reference. You may then wish to discuss the question words found, and the *hast du?* question form.

Further translation activities can be found in the Introduction on page 10.

What are you called?
How old are you?
Where do you live?
Have you got a ruler?
What is your favourite subject?
How do you find German?
When does geography start?
What do you eat at break?

Suggestion
Before starting exercise 1, get pupils to look at the pictures and speech bubbles for the task for 30 seconds before shutting their books. Ask them what they think they will be learning this lesson. How did they work it out? (e.g. clues in the pictures, prior knowledge of the high frequency words *ich, habe, ein*; similarity to English; links between words.)

Hör zu. Was passt zusammen? (1–7) (AT 1/2)
4.3/Y7

Listening. Pupils listen to the recording and match each speaker to the correct picture. Briefly discuss the reason for *einen / eine* (already encountered in Chapters 1 and 2) and ask what the difference is between *Bruder* and *Brüder, Schwester* and *Schwestern* – plural forms are looked at in more detail in Unit 4 of this chapter.

1 – *Hallo! Hast du Geschwister?*
  – *Nein! Ich bin Einzelkind.*
2 – *Und hast du Geschwister?*
  – *Ja. Ich habe zwei Brüder.*
3 – *Und du, hast du Geschwister?*
  – *Ja. Ich habe zwei Schwestern.*

4 – *Hast du Geschwister?*
– *Ja. Ich habe einen Stiefbruder.*

5 – *Und hast du Geschwister?*
– *Ja. Ich habe eine Schwester.*

6 – *Hast du auch Geschwister?*
– *Ja. Ich habe eine Halbschwester.*

7 – *Und du? Hast du Geschwister?*
– *Ja. Ich habe einen Bruder.*

Answers

1 g	2 b	3 e	4 c	5 d	6 f	7 a

Aussprache: u / ü   4.1/Y7

Listening: Pupils listen to and repeat the question and answer illustrating the difference in sound between *u* and *ü*. Pairs could then practise pronouncing the question and answer, competing to see how many times they can repeat them correctly in ten seconds.

> *Hast du einen Bruder?*
> *Ja, ich habe fünf Brüder!*   **3**

2 Klassenumfrage. (AT 2/2) 1.4a/Y7 4.6a/Y7

Speaking. Pupils conduct a survey about brothers and sisters and note their findings as shown. Set a time limit, so that all pupils finish at the same time.

  Afterwards, pupils could write sentences showing what some of their interviewees said (using first or third person verb forms, depending on level). Encourage them to focus on accuracy.

3 Lies den text. Wer ist das? Kopiere die Tabelle und füll sie aus. (AT 3/3) 2.1/Y7

Reading. Pupils read the text and write details of each person mentioned into a copy of the grid.

Answers

	Wer?	Name	Alter	Details
a	Ich	Sabine	16	Zürich, Schweiz
b	Schwester	Lulu	12	trinkt Cola
c	Bruder	Zaki	13	super doof
d	Halbschwester	Anabel	4	Lieblingsfarbe rot
e	Halbbruder	Max	1	toll

Starter 2   4.2/Y7

Aim

To practise numbers 1–100, prior to saying and understanding ages of family members.

Before starting the game, you may wish to quickly revise key numbers with the class. Then ask for a volunteer 'searcher', who leaves the room briefly while another pupil hides a soft toy or other object somewhere in the classroom. As the volunteer begins to search, the rest of the class count aloud from one upwards in German, getting louder or quieter to assist the searcher, depending on how close he/she is getting to the hidden object. Write the name of the volunteer, and the number the class had reached, on the board when the object is found, and play again with another searcher.

4 Hör zu. Wer ist das? (1–10) (AT 1/2) 1.1/Y7

Listening. Pupils listen and identify which family members Michael is talking about. Weaker pupils could first note the relevant letter, then later, or when listening again, copy the correct word from the Key Language box.

Suggestion

Before or after listening, elicit the English words for the family members. You could also ask pupils to pretend they are Michael, and to identify who each of the family members is, using the words in the Key Language box, as a whole class or pairwork activity. For example: *a? das ist mein Großvater* or *Wer ist Jochen? Jochen ist mein Vater.* Additionally, to practise numbers, pupils could work in pairs and ask each other the ages of the family members: *Wie alt ist Hanno?*, etc.

> **1** *Meine Großmutter heißt Hedwig. Sie ist dreiundsiebzig.*   **4**
>
> **2** *Mein Großvater heißt Wilfried. Er ist einundsiebzig Jahre alt.*
>
> **3** *Mein Vater heißt Jochen. Er ist vierzig.*
>
> **4** *Meine Mutter heißt Heike. Sie ist neununddreißig.*
>
> **5** *Mein Bruder heißt Stefan. Er ist siebzehn Jahre alt.*
>
> **6** *Mein Stiefvater heißt Rolf. Er ist einundvierzig Jahre alt.*
>
> **7** *Meine Tante heißt Birgit. Sie ist sechsunddreißig Jahre alt.*
>
> **8** *Mein Onkel heißt Lutz. Er ist dreiundvierzig Jahre alt.*
>
> **9** *Meine Cousine heißt Marlies. Sie ist nur ein Jahr alt.*
>
> **10** *Mein Cousin heißt Marc. Er ist fünfzehn Jahre alt.*

Answers
1 b – meine Großmutter
2 a – mein Großvater
3 e – mein Vater
4 f – meine Mutter
5 k – mein Bruder
6 g – mein Stiefvater
7 d – meine Tante
8 c – mein Onkel
9 i – meine Cousine
10 h – mein Cousin

ECHO-Detektiv: *mein* (my) and *dein* (your)   4.3/Y7

This panel shows pupils when to add an 'e' to *mein / dein*, i.e. before feminine nouns. Point out that the endings are the same as for *ein*. For further practice, refer pupils to page 115 of the **Grammatik** at the back of the book.

ECHO-Tipp   4.2/Y7
A reminder to pupils about *er* and *sie*.

5 Partnerarbeit: Michaels Familie. (AT 2/4)   1.4b/Y7

Speaking. Pairs of pupils follow the example dialogue given to ask about and identify members of Michael's family. Encourage pupils to be accurate in their use of *dein* or *deine*. Pupils should also try to start working without the example dialogue once they have been through it once or twice. After they have completed the task, you could discuss with them why it was important to try to do this.

6 Schreib einen Absatz über dich und deine Familie. (AT 4/1–4)   2.4b/Y7

Writing. Pupils write a paragraph about themselves and their family. Encourage them to include opinions, as well as names and ages of family members.

Weaker pupils could draw their own family tree, using Michael's as a model and the Key Language box to add *mein Vater*, etc., as well as names and ages. Most could then write sentences about family members. This could be developed into a short text about a member or members of their own family (relationship, name and age), illustrated with photos.

For additional speaking practice, pupils could give a partner information from their own family tree, e.g. *Mein Vater heißt John, er ist 39.* Partners listen and attempt to sketch the family tree. Alternatively, pupils draw an initial family tree without names and ages, using only *meine Mutter*, etc. They then swap books, and complete each other's family trees by asking and answering questions: *Wie heißt deine Mutter? Wie alt ist sie?*, etc.

Plenary   5.1

Aim
To recap what pupils know so far about different kinds of German words.

Write some or all of the following categories on the board or an OHT. Tell pupils they must work with a partner to think of at least two German words per category. Decide whether you will allow them to refer to the Pupil's Book. Afterwards, collate and discuss their answers, giving two possible marks per category, with bonus marks available for unusual correct answers.

Nouns
Plural nouns
Pronouns
Possessive adjectives
Verbs with *ich*
Verbs with *du*
Verbs with *er / sie*
Words with an Umlaut
Question words

Learning targets

- Describing people's appearance
- Using adjectives with nouns

Key framework objectives

2.4/Y7 Writing – (a) sentences and texts as models

4.4/Y7 Language – sentence formation

Grammar

- Using adjectives before nouns
- *haben: ich habe, du hast, er / sie hat* (revisited)
- *sein: ich bin, du bist, er / sie ist* (revisited)

Key language

Ich habe …
Du hast …
Er / Sie hat …
braune / blonde / rote / schwarze /
lange / kurze / glatte / lockige
Haare
grüne / braune / blaue / graue
Augen
Ich bin …
Du bist …
Er / Sie ist …
groß / mittelgroß / klein /
schlank / kräftig / dick

High-frequency words

ich habe
du hast
er/sie hat
ich bin
du bist

er/sie ist
wie
und
ist das …?

Pronunciation

au

English

Adjectives

Resources

CD 2, tracks 5–7
Workbooks A and B, p.23
Arbeitsblatt 3.1, p. 38
Echo Elektro 1 TPP, Express
Mod 3 2.1–2.5

Starter 1

5.4

Aim

To encourage use of cognates and non-linguistic clues (physical evidence) to work out unknown language items.

Write three or four sentences on the board describing members of the class. The sentences should be factually correct, e.g.

Gavin hat braune Haare.
Paula hat blonde Haare.
Ich habe blaue Augen.

Read the sentences aloud with the whole class. Draw their attention to the fact that the final 'e' of *braune* and *Haare* is pronounced. Working in pairs or small groups, pupils try to guess what the sentences mean. Set a time limit and elicit answers. Ask for a class consensus before confirming the correct answers. You could then write additional similar sentences, and give pupils further time to confer. Ask the class to guess what today's lesson will be about, before they open their books.

1 Hör zu. Wie sehen sie aus? (1–8) (AT 1/2)

1.1/Y7

Listening. Pupils listen to the descriptions, and find the 'Identikit' pictures which match them. When checking answers, you could point out that German speakers say 'hairs' rather than 'hair'.

R Pupils could reinforce the new vocabulary working in pairs: partner A reads out one of the phrases from the 'Identikit' and partner B gives the correct letter; or partner A reads out one of the phrases from the 'Identikit' and partner B (with book closed) identifies someone in the class who has that feature.

1 – Theo: Wie siehst du aus?
  – Ich habe grüne Augen.
2 – Und du, Vikki? Wie siehst du aus?
  – Ich habe graue Augen.
3 – Bastian, wie siehst du aus?
  – Ich habe kurze Haare.
4 – Und du, Lisa? Wie siehst du aus?
  – Ich habe lockige Haare.
5 – Stefanie, wie siehst du aus?
  – Ich habe blaue Augen und lange Haare.
6 – Und du, Oliver, wie siehst du aus?
  – Ich habe braune Augen und rote Haare.
7 – Wie siehst du aus, Jan?
  – Ich habe grüne Augen und glatte Haare.

8 – *Wie siehst du aus, Eva?*
– *Also, ich habe auch grüne Augen und ich habe blonde Haare.*

> **Answers**
> **1** a   **2** d   **3** e   **4** g   **5** b, f   **6** c, j
> **7** a, h   **8** a, i

2 Verbinde die Satzteile und beschreib Anja, Manja und Tanja. (AT 3/2)

4.4/Y7

Writing. Pupils look at the photos of three girls, and select the correct words from those given to form a sentence describing each of them. To find the correct solution, encourage pupils to eliminate the wrong options at the end of each stage, rather than working out each character one by one.

> **Answers**
> **Manja:** Ich habe lange, lockige braune Haare und braune Augen.
> **Anja:** Ich habe glatte, blonde Haare und graue Augen.
> **Tanja:** Ich habe kurze, glatte, schwarze Haare und braune Augen.

ECHO-Detektiv: Adjective endings

4.3/Y7

Pupils read the panel and spot the 'e' ending used with hair and eyes. At this stage, this is the only form they need to know, and you may wish to leave further explanation until later.

Aussprache: au

4.1/Y7

Listening. Pupils listen to the recording and read through the tongue twister. They then repeat it three times.

■ *Blaue Frauen haben immer graue Augen.* 6

R Pupils could chorus the colours *blau, braun, grau* for further practice of the *au* sound.

3 Wie siehst du aus? Und zwei Mitglieder deiner Familie? (AT 4/3)

2.4a/Y7

Writing. Pupils write a short description of themselves, and of two members of their family. Encourage them to use more than one adjective when describing hair.

Starter 2

4.4/Y7

Aim

To reinforce language for describing hair and eyes.

Select volunteers to be the 'caller' at the front of the class. They make up a sentence about appearance, e.g. *ich habe kurze Haare.* Pupils listen, and stand up if the sentence applies to them. More confident 'callers' will be able to include extra detail in their sentences. Check with the class that the correct pupils have stood up. Sentences with *er* or *sie* could also be used – pupils only standing up if they are additionally of the correct gender.

4 Hör zu und schau das Bild an. Wer ist das? (1–5) (AT 1/2)

1.1/Y7

Listening. Pupils listen to the descriptions, based on build only, and identify the correct picture. They can use the Key Language box for support. Remind weaker pupils to listen out for *er* or *sie*, in order to identify whether each description is of a man or woman.

1 – *Wie sieht er aus?*
– *Er ist groß und kräftig!*   7
2 – *Wie sieht sie aus?*
– *Sie ist mittelgroß und schlank.*
3 – *Wie sieht er aus?*
– *Er ist klein und dick.*
4 – *Wie sieht sie aus?*
– *Sie ist klein und schlank.*
5 – *Wie sieht er aus?*
– *Er ist groß und schlank.*

> **Answers**
> **1** Thor Stein   **2** Lena Lexis   **3** Ulf Brocken
> **4** Lisa Lautstark   **5** Max Maxi

5 Füll die Lücken im Text aus. (AT 3/3)

4.4/Y7

Reading. Pupils use the same pictures of the band members and select the correct word from those given for each gap in the text.

Follow-up reading, translation and writing activities can be found in the Introduction on pages 9–10.

Answers

1 schlank
2 lange
3 kräftig
4 blonde
5 ist
6 rote
7 Ulf Brocken
8 und
9 kurze
10 klein
11 hat
12 lockige

R Suggest to weaker students that they look at the context of each gap to decide what type of word it is likely to be, e.g. is it something the person is or has? Remind them to refer to the picture for help.

+ Pupils who finish quickly could write sentences describing members of the class, using just *er / sie* (no names). Partners read these and guess who is being described (writing down their guess if the activity needs to be done quietly), or the whole class could later listen and guess.

6 Gruppenarbeit. Beschreib jemand aus „Total Stark". (AT 2/3) `1.4b/Y7`

Speaking. Pupils work in pairs to ask about and identify band members, following the sample dialogue.

7 Beschreib drei berühmte Personen. (AT 4/3–4) `2.4a/Y7 4.4/Y7`

Writing. Pupils write descriptions of three famous people. Encourage them to write a short paragraph about each, using the text from exercise 5 for ideas. They could perhaps include additional information (age, where lives etc). If done as a homework task, illustrations could be added.

Plenary `4.5a/Y7 5.2`

Aim

To help pupils appreciate the importance of the familiar high-frequency verbs *haben* and *sein*.

Pupils work together briefly in pairs to write down a sentence using the verb *haben* or *sein*. Collect examples around the class and write them on the board or an OHT, correcting any mistakes. Can pupils see that these verbs are used in all sorts of different situations? What does this tell them about priorities in their language learning? (e.g. Learn them, and you'll be able to talk about lots of things.) Collect ideas around the class about how to learn verbs, e.g. chanting, testing each other, 'look say cover write check'.

Learning targets
- Talking about people's characteristics
- Making sentences more interesting

Key framework objectives
1.2/Y7 Listening – unfamiliar language
1.3/Y7 Listening – (a) interpreting intonation and tone
1.3/Y7 Speaking – (b) using intonation and tone
2.3/Y7 Reading – text features
4.6/Y7 Language – (b) negatives

Grammar
- Connectives: *und, aber, auch*
- Qualifiers: *sehr, ziemlich*
- *nicht*

Key language
Wie bist du?
Wie ist …?
Ich bin …
Du bist …
Er / Sie ist …
freundlich / lustig / laut / schüchtern / intelligent / sportlich / musikalisch / kreativ / faul / launisch / unpünktlich
und
aber
auch
nicht
sehr
ziemlich

High-frequency words
wie?

ich bin
du bist
er / sie ist
und
aber
auch
nicht
sehr
ziemlich

English
Connectives and qualifiers

Resources
CD 2, tracks 8–11
Workbooks A and B, p.24
Arbeitsblatt 3.2, p. 39
Arbeitsblatt 3.3, p. 40
Flashcards 47–57
Echo Elektro 1 TPP, Express Mod 3 3.1–3.7

Starter 1
5.4

Aim
To introduce the new personality adjectives, using prior knowledge of cognates and prefixes.

Write some or all of the new personality adjectives from this unit on the board or an OHT, scattered randomly, together with a 'plus' and a 'minus' sign. Read the words aloud (or ask pupils to try this) and ask the class to guess what sort of words they are. Pupils then sort the words into two lists, positive and negative, using their knowledge of cognates and prefixes to make guesses. Does the word 'look' positive or negative? If they can guess the meaning, do they feel it is a positive or negative characteristic? After a few minutes, elicit or give the meanings, and discuss their decisions and how they arrived at them.

1 Hör zu. Was passt zusammen? (1–11) (AT 1/1)
1.1/Y7

Listening. Pupils listen to the new language, matching numbers to letters.

1 – *Wie bist du, Amelie?*
  – *Ich bin kreativ.*
2 – *Wie bist du, Tobias?*
  – *Ich bin sportlich.*
3 – *Wie bist du, Mareike?*
  – *Ich bin lustig.*
4 – *Wie bist du, Felix?*
  – *Ich bin freundlich.*
5 – *Wie bist du, Sarah?*
  – *Ich bin intelligent.*
6 – *Wie bist du, Christian?*
  – *Ich bin musikalisch.*
7 – *Wie bist du, Hannah?*
  – *Ich bin unpünktlich.*
8 – *Wie bist du, Wolfgang?*
  – *Ich bin schüchtern.*
9 – *Wie bist du, Thomas?*
  – *Ich bin launisch.*
10 – *Wie bist du, Leon?*
  – *Ich bin faul.*
11 – *Wie bist du, Petra?*
  – *Ich bin laut.*

Answers
1 d	2 c	3 j	4 a	5 b	6 h	7 f	8 i
9 g	10 k	11 e					

Suggestion
You may wish to reinforce the new vocabulary through mime at this point. After some initial practice and guessing (in pairs or as a whole class),

divide the class into two teams to play charades. A volunteer from each team picks characteristics written on cards from a hat and mimes them – team members have to guess within a time limit using the phrase *du bist …*. See page 10 for further games ideas.

2 Partnerarbeit. (AT 2/2)   1.4a/Y7

Speaking. This could be a brief pairwork or group exercise, or it could be extended to multiple interviews with note taking, and reporting back using *er / sie ist …* orally or in writing. Start by practising the question with the class.

3 Hör zu und lies. Wie heißen die Lehrer? (AT 3/3)   1.1/Y7 2.1/Y7

Listening/Reading. Pupils listen to and read the description of teachers, and match names to pictures.

> *Frau Schütte ist freundlich, aber sie ist launisch. Herr Arendt ist kreativ, aber er ist unpünktlich. Frau Schmidt ist intelligent und musikalisch. Sie ist auch schüchtern. Wie ist Herr Heumann? Er ist laut und lustig.*   **9**

Answers
1 Herr Heumann   3 Herr Arendt
2 Frau Schütte   4 Frau Schmid

ECHO-Tipp   4.4/Y7
Refer pupils to this panel about the use of *und*, *aber* and *auch* before they do writing exercise 4.

4 Beschreib zwei deiner Lehrer. (AT 4/3–4)   4.4/Y7

Writing. Pupils write sentences about two of their own teachers. Explain the use of *Herr*, and *Frau* (used for all female teachers, regardless of marital status). Make able pupils aware that *aber* is always preceded by a comma. Encourage more confident learners to make their sentences as long as they can, using the connectives in the **ECHO-Tipp** panel.

➕ This could also be done as a speaking task, without including the teacher's name in the sentences. Partners, or the whole class, have to guess who is being described. Physical description could be revised and included here too. You may wish to insist that descriptions are positive! These extra adjectives will be useful:
nett (nice), *hilfsbereit* (helpful), *streng* (strict).

Starter 2   4.2/Y7

Aim
To revise personality words from the previous lesson.

Knock-down miming game: divide the class into two or three teams. A volunteer from the first team has one minute to guess what characteristic each of the other team members is miming – by pointing at individuals and saying *Du bist …* . If correct, that pupil sits down. Count up the number of seated team members at the end of the given time. Then the other team tries to beat the score.

Further mime activities can be found in the Introduction on page 10.

5 Lies den Text. Wie ist Bart Simpson? Mach Notizen auf Englisch. (AT 3/3)   2.1/Y7

Reading. This task introduces the concept of qualifiers. Pupils read the text about Bart Simpson and note his characteristics in English.

Answers
Very loud, fairly intelligent, not shy, fairly friendly, not very creative, not very sporty, very funny, not musical.

ECHO-Detektiv   4.2/Y7 4.6b/Y7
Use this panel to consider qualifiers. Ask pupils why they think it is useful to know them.

6 Hör zu. Füll die Tabelle aus. (AT 1/3)   1.2/Y7 1.3a/Y7 4.6b/Y7

Listening. Pupils listen to this long recording and focus on personal characteristics and qualifiers to fill in the table. Give them the names of the three Simpsons characters to add to their table before they start listening. Pupils will need to listen two or three times and make notes, in order to complete the task. Pause the recording after the character description before moving on to the physical description each time.

> *Also, Lisa Simpson ist nicht sportlich, aber sie ist sehr intelligent! Sie ist auch sehr musikalisch – sie spielt sehr gut Saxophon. Und was noch? Ach ja, sie ist ziemlich launisch. Wie sieht sie aus? Ähm, Lisa ist sehr klein, und das findet sie nicht gut. Sie hat ziemlich kurze, blonde Haare und ist sehr schlank.*   **10**

Und wie ist Lisas Mutter, Marge Simpson? Marge ist nicht musikalisch, aber sie ist ziemlich kreativ und sie ist auch freundlich. Wie Lisa, ist sie eine intelligente Frau. Und wie sieht sie aus? Sie ist ziemlich groß, aber nicht dick, und hat lange, lockige, blaue Haare. Sie findet die Farbe sehr schön.

Und jetzt, wie ist der Vater, Homer Simpson? Also, er ist ziemlich lustig und sehr laut. Er ist nicht schüchtern, aber er ist ... ähm ... sehr faul und unpünktlich. Und wie sieht Homer aus? Na ja, er ist ziemlich klein und sehr dick. Und er hat keine Haare. Das findet er ein bisschen doof.

Answers

Name	Charakter	Wie sieht er/sie aus?
1 Lisa Simpson	nicht sportlich, sehr intelligent, sehr musikalisch, ziemlich launisch	sehr klein, ziemlich kurze blonde Haare, sehr schlank
2 Marge Simpson	nicht musikalisch, ziemlich kreativ, freundlich, intelligent	ziemlich groß, nicht dick, lange lockige blaue Haare
3 Homer Simpson	ziemlich lustig, sehr laut, nicht schüchtern, sehr faul, unpünktlich	ziemlich klein, sehr dick, keine Haare

⁷ **Wie bist du? Schreib vier lange Sätze über dich. (AT 4/3)** `1.3b/Y7 4.4/Y7`

➕ *Writing.* Pupils write four sentences about themselves. Encourage them to use connectives and qualifiers to extend these. Weaker classes could start by writing simple sentences, then adding qualifiers and joining the sentences together. You could ask pupils to read their sentences aloud, using appropriate, even exaggerated, expression when they say *aber*, *sehr*, *ziemlich* or *nicht*.

Suggestion

Prepare three or four brief, positive descriptions of members of the class on an OHT (you could also include physical descriptions), using *er / sie* but not names, and including the connectives and qualifiers learnt. Reveal them one at a time, and ask pupils to write down who they think it is. Reveal the answers, and see how many they guessed correctly. This is a wonderful chance to show quieter pupils that you value their qualities!

⁸ **Hör zu und sing mit.** `2.2a/Y7 2.3/Y7`

Listening/Reading. Pupils listen and read, then sing along. Divide the class in two to sing the two voices of the conversation.

Higher-ability classes could firstly listen with their books closed, and tell you what the song is about. Alternatively, after singing the song, get them to close their books and answer your 'memory test' questions, e.g. *Wie heißt Georgs Bruder? Wie sieht er aus?*

 11

Hallo, Georg,
Hast du Geschwister?
Ja, ich habe einen Bruder
Und er heißt Frank.

Wie sieht er denn aus?
Hat er blonde Haare?
Nein. Er hat grüne Haare!
Er ist groß und sehr schlank!

Und hast du ein Haustier?
Hast du eine Katze?
Nein, ich habe eine Schlange
Und sie heißt Klaus.

Ach, eine Schlange,
Wie sieht sie denn aus?
Sie ist lang, grün und gelb,
Aber sie ist schüchtern wie eine Maus.

Ist sie ziemlich freundlich?
Ja, sie ist sehr freundlich.
Ach wie toll!
Ja, Klaus ist toll.

Plenary `5.8`

Aim

To review language learned to date and identify areas for improvement.

Pupils work in pairs to check the language they have learned so far in this chapter, using the **Mini-Test** checklist. Ask pupils which points their partners found most difficult. Give them the task of improving these points by next lesson. Partners could then test them again.

Learning targets
- Talking about pets
- Using plural forms of nouns

Key framework objectives
2.4/Y7 Writing – (b) building text
4.3/Y7 Language – plurals
5.1 Strategies – patterns

Grammar
- Plural forms of nouns
- *haben + einen / eine / ein* (revisited)
- *er / sie / es* = it

Key language
Hast du ein Haustier?
Ich habe einen …
Goldfisch
Hamster
Hund
Wellensittich
Ich habe eine …
Katze
Schlange
Schildkröte
Ich habe ein …
Kaninchen
Meerschweinchen
Pferd
Ich habe zwei / drei, etc. + plural forms
Ich habe keine Haustiere.
Er / Sie / Es heißt …
Er / Sie / Es ist…
braun / gelb / orange / schwarz
freundlich, lustig, intelligent, etc.

High-frequency words
ich habe
hast du?
du bist
und
er / sie / es
ist
heißt
einen / eine / ein

English
Learning and using plurals of nouns

ICT
Creating a poster about pets

Resources
CD 2, tracks 12–14
Workbooks A and B, p.25
Arbeitsblatt 3.4, p. 41
Arbeitsblatt 3.5, p. 42
Echo Elektro 1 TPP, Express Mod 3 4.1–4.9

Starter 1   5.1

Aim
To encourage pupils to use their prior knowledge of German pronunciation to try saying 'difficult' new words.

Write these five new words on the board or OHT:

Hund	*Meerschweinchen*
Katze	*Wellensittich*
Kaninchen	

(Substitute *Schlange / Pferd* for a less able group.) Pairs (or groups) could attempt to pronounce each word, then consolidate and build confidence through whole-class chorusing (use louder/quieter, etc. to make this fun). Tell them to look for parts of words that they already know how to pronounce, to get them started (e.g. *und, ich*), and remind them that there are no 'silent letters' in German.

At this stage they will not understand the words. Ask if anyone knows what type of words they are (nouns, pets), how they know, and whether they can guess the meanings of any of the words.

Suggestion
Before embarking on exercise 1, you may wish to present the pet words with flashcards from your department (easily guessed ones could be omitted). Present them in gender groups, allowing plenty of practice time. See the list of ideas for games with flashcards on pages 8–9.

Hör zu und wiederhole. (1–10) (AT 1)   5.1
Listening. Pupils listen to the recording and repeat.

1 *Ich habe einen Goldfisch.*
2 *Ich habe einen Hamster.*
3 *Ich habe einen Hund.*
4 *Ich habe einen Wellensittich.*
5 *Ich habe eine Katze.*
6 *Ich habe eine Schildkröte.*
7 *Ich habe eine Schlange.*
8 *Ich habe ein Kaninchen.*
9 *Ich habe ein Meerschweinchen.*
10 *Ich habe ein Pferd.*

12

2 Finde die Paare oben. (AT 3/2)

5.4

Reading. Pupils match the words for pets to pictures (this could be done as a research exercise using the vocabulary list, if no prior presentation has been used). You may wish pupils to write down the pairs of German and English words. Ask why the nouns are arranged in three coloured groups, and recap the use of *einen / eine / ein* if necessary. At this point you may want to ask pupils about their own pets (you will need to give them the phrase *Ich habe keine Haustiere*, which comes up in exercises 6 and 7, and to give vocabulary for unusual pets).

Answers

1 i	2 j	3 g	4 a	5 b	6 c	7 h	8 d
9 e	10 f						

3 Hör zu. Welche Haustiere hat er / sie? (AT 1/3)

1.1/Y7

Listening. Using the pictures from exercise 1, pupils note down the pets each person has. You might want to advise less confident pupils to note down first the German pet words they hear (or the first few letters of each for speed – using the list in the book), which they can then match to the correct picture later or when listening again. Play the recording at least twice. Alternatively, a weaker class could simply look at the list of German words in exercise 1, and write down the numbers of those heard.

1 – *Hast du ein Haustier, Viktor?*
   – *Ja, ich habe einen Hund und eine Katze.* **13**
2 – *Und du, Peter?*
   – *Ja, ich habe ein Kaninchen.*
3 – *Stefanie, hast du ein Haustier?*
   – *Ja, ich habe einen Goldfisch, einen Hund und ein Meerschweinchen.*
4 – *Und du, Julia?*
   – *Ich habe ein Pferd und eine Schildkröte.*

Answers

Viktor – g, b	Peter – d
Stefanie – i, g, e	Julia – g, f, c

4 Was sagen sie? Schreib Sätze. (AT 4/2)

4.4/Y7

Writing. Pupils write a sentence for each of the characters in exercise 3. Encourage them to copy *einen / eine / ein* and the spellings of the pet words carefully.

Answers

Viktor: Ich habe einen Hund und eine Katze.
Peter: Ich habe ein Kaninchen.
Stefanie: Ich habe einen Goldfisch, einen Hund und ein Meerschweinchen.
Julia: Ich habe ein Pferd und eine Schildkröte.

Starter 2

4.2/Y7

Aim
To recap vocabulary for pets.

Write a pet word on a piece of paper and put it out of sight, e.g. in a drawer. Start to draw that pet on the board or an OHT, one line at a time. You could start with a round circle for the pet's head, or a triangle for the nose, or a small circle for an eye – the images can be quite abstract, with no special drawing skills required! Pupils work in small teams, and, after each new line has been added to the picture, a team secretary writes down their bet on which animal it is. Ask all teams to read these out. The first team(s) to get it right wins a point (confirm this by revealing the answer you have hidden). They may guess immediately or it may take a few goes. Pupils could then take over the drawing role from you.

Suggestion
Use this starter as an opportunity to give pupils extra useful words and phrases such as *Das ist vielleicht ...*, *hoffentlich*, *keine Ahnung*. Strong teams could try to discuss their guesses using only German.

5 Gedächtnisspiel. (AT 2/2)

1.4b/Y7

Speaking. Pupils play this memory game in groups, building up a list of pets. Encourage confident pupils to focus on the accurate use of *einen / eine / ein* or on the use of plurals. Afterwards, discuss with pupils why activities like this help them to improve their fluency; could they use this technique in any other situations to help with language learning?

6 Hör zu. Wer ist das? (1–5) (AT 1/2–3)

1.1/Y7

Listening. Pupils listen to statements about pets, and match them to the correct pet owner in the picture. More able pupils could also listen for extra details.

1 – Hast du ein Haustier?
– Ja, ich habe zwei Pferde und eine Schildkröte.
2 – Und du, hast du ein Haustier?
– Ja, ich habe drei Goldfische. Sie sind toll!
3 – Hast du ein Haustier?
– Nein, ich habe keine Haustiere. Ich finde das langweilig.
4 – Und hast du Haustiere?
– Ich habe meine zwei Katzen, Franzi und Fritzi, und eine Schlange – sie heißt Susi.
5 – Hast du ein Haustier?
– Ja, ich habe drei Wellensittiche und zwei Hunde. Ludwig ist vierzehn Jahre alt und Lala ist sieben.

 14

Answers
1 c   2 d   3 e   4 a   5 b

ECHO-Detektiv: Plurals of nouns

4.3/Y7

This panel introduces three main plural noun endings. Before pupils read it, show them six of the plural forms, scattered in random order on the board or an OHT. Elicit the fact that they are plurals of pet words. Have they seen any other plurals in the book so far? (Brüder / Schwestern) Discuss how they managed to guess this correctly (knowing that words in other languages change in the plural). How do German plurals so far seem different from English ones? Do all English words have the same plural ending? Elicit examples. Then look at the grammar box together. Flashcards could be used to practise the plural forms.

+ With a more able class, ask them where they could find plurals of other pet words. You may wish them to look up some additional plural forms. You could also use **Arbeitsblatt 3.2**.

7 Partnerarbeit: Wer bist du? (AT 2/2)

4.3/Y7

Speaking. This offers oral practice of the plural forms, using the illustration from exercise 6.

+ Pupils could go on to ask and answer questions about their own pets, using plural forms where necessary. This could be a pair or group survey task. Practise the question *Hast du ein Haustier?* first. To give names and ages, many pupils will at this point simply apply *er* to male pets, and *sie* to female ones, and you might feel it is too early to give a full explanation of gender-related pronouns. With a more able group, you may wish to explain the correct use of *er / sie / es* as pronouns related to the gender of the noun.

8 Lies den Text und füll die Tabelle aus. (AT3/4)

2.1/Y7 2.2a/Y7

Reading. Pupils read the text about pets, and fill in the required details in a copy of the grid. Remind them that they may need to look up new words. Follow-up reading, translation and writing activities are in the Introduction on pages 9–10.

Answers

Tier	Name	Alter	Farbe	Persönlichkeit
Hund	Rocky	–	braun	lustig, intelligent
Schlange	Susi	2	grün, gelb	launisch, nicht freundlich
Katze	Franzi	12	schwarz	schüchtern
Pferd	Lili	5	schwarz	faul

ECHO-Detektiv: er / sie / es = *it*

You may wish to draw this to the attention of pupils before starting exercise 9.

9 Beschreibe deine Haustiere oder Traumhaustiere. (AT 4/3–4)

2.4b/Y7

Writing. Pupils write about their own pet, or a dream pet. This could be done for display work, perhaps using ICT. They can use the text from the previous exercise for ideas, and include an illustration. Weaker pupils can write short, simple sentences. More able pupils should be able to write a paragraph using compound sentences, and to build in opinions.

Plenary

4.3/Y7 5.2

Aim

To look at strategies for researching, recording and learning plural forms of nouns.

Give pupils a few minutes to revise and test each other on the three different types of plural endings seen in this unit. Then conduct a quick-fire quiz to check how many plural forms of nouns for pets the class can remember. You could use flashcards for this, and compete with the class – a point for you every time one of them makes a wrong guess. Discuss why these plurals are important, and how they can be checked – mention regular and irregular plurals in English, too. With a more able class, gather ideas for memorising and recording plural forms.

Learning targets

- Understanding a longer email and writing a reply
- Finding out the meanings of new words

Key framework objectives

1.5/Y7 Speaking – (a) presenting

1.5/Y7 Speaking – (b) expression/non-verbal techniques

3.2/Y7 Culture – (a) young people: interests/opinions

3.2/Y7 Culture – (b) challenging stereotypes

Grammar

- Formulating questions (see Starter 2)
- Using connectives and qualifiers

Key language

Hallo!
Ich heiße …
Ich bin / Er/Sie ist … Jahre alt.
Ich habe am … Geburtstag.
Ich wohne in …
Das ist in …
Ich habe … (family and pets)
Ich habe … (Haare / Augen)
Ich bin / Er/Sie ist … (character)
Wie geht's?
Hast du Geschwister?
Hast du ein Haustier?
Wie siehst du aus?
Schreib bald!
dein /deine

High-frequency words

sehr
aber
und
ich heiße
ich bin
er/sie/das ist

ich habe
hast du?
wie?
mein / meine
dein / deine

English

Structuring an email to a friend

Citizenship

Penfriend links with another country

ICT

Word process, or possibly send, an email

Resources

CD 2, track 15
Workbooks A and B, p.26
Echo Elektro 1 TPP, Express
Mod 3 5.1–5.4

Starter 1

3.2a+b/Y7

Aim

To introduce the concept, and benefits, of links with pupils in German-speaking countries.

Before looking at the book, explain that the class will be looking at an email from a German pupil looking for a penfriend. Ask pupils to predict the content of the email – what sort of things would one say? Ask pairs of pupils to think of one question and one sentence in German that might be in such an email (using language they already know). Take the opportunity to discuss any links your school has with others abroad, and what pupils might expect to gain from such links.

Suggestion

Before doing exercise 1, ask pupils to scan the page and assess what the email is about, who it is written to and why, and how difficult they think it is (if you have done Starter 1, they will have been given a head start with some of these). Direct pupils' attention to the **ECHO-Tipp** panel about reading for gist.

Hör zu und lies Julias E-Mail. (AT1/4)

3.2a/Y7 5.6

Listening/Reading. Pupils listen to the recording and follow the text in their books. They could then read the email aloud in pairs, with emphasis on getting the correct pronunciation and intonation.

Draw pupils' attention to the phrases typically used at the beginning and end of emails like this.

Hallo!

Wie geht's? Ich suche einen Brieffreund oder eine Brieffreundin! Mein Name ist Julia Döring und ich wohne in Dresden. (Das ist eine Stadt in Deutschland.) Ich bin zwölf Jahre alt und habe am ersten September Geburtstag. Ich bin jetzt in der Klasse 8C.

Meine Familie ist ziemlich normal. Ich habe eine Schwester, Tanja. Sie ist vierzehn Jahre alt. Sie ist lustig und sehr laut! Hast du Geschwister? Mein Vater heißt Jens. Er ist achtunddreißig Jahre alt. Er ist sehr groß und kräftig, aber ziemlich schüchtern. Meine Mutter, Bettina, ist toll. Sie ist nicht schüchtern, aber sehr freundlich und lustig.

Toby wohnt auch bei uns. Das ist mein Pferd! Es ist fünf Jahre alt. Es ist braun und ziemlich groß. Es ist auch sehr freundlich. Hast du ein Haustier?

Wie siehst du aus? Ich habe rote Haare und blaue Augen. Ich bin ziemlich groß und schlank. Ich bin sehr sportlich, aber sehr unpünktlich!

Schreib bald!

Deine Julia

2 Welcher Absatz ist das? (AT 3/4) `2.1/Y7`

Reading. Pupils identify the paragraph in the email that contains each type of information.

> **Answers**
> 1 b   2 c   3 d   4 a

3 Finde die richtige Antwort. (AT 3/4)
`2.1/Y7 2.2/Y7`

Reading. Pupils look at the email text in greater detail, to find the correct multiple-choice answers. Encourage them to scan for the section where they know they might find the right answer. Follow-up reading, translation and writing exercises can be found in the Introduction on pages 9–10.

> **Answers**
> 1 b   2 c   3 c   4 a   5 b   6 c   7 a

> ## ECHO-Tipp: Finding out what a new word means   `5.3 5.4`
> Read the skills box with pupils and encourage them to follow this strategy when doing exercise 4.

4 Was sind diese neuen Wörter auf Englisch? (AT 3/4)   `5.3 5.4`

Reading. Pupils work out what each new word means. Discuss their findings, and how they reached these conclusions.

> **Answers**
> *Ich suche* = I'm looking for / searching for
> *Brieffreund* = penfriend
> *Schreib bald* = write soon

Starter 2   `4.6a/Y7`

Aim
To practise the formation of questions, in preparation for a writing task.

Divide the class into teams of roughly equal size and ability, seated together. Copy the following words onto slips of paper and put them, folded, into a bag, hat or similar object. Volunteers pick a word out of the hat, and show it to the class. Each team must write down a question beginning with that word, before you say stop. Listen to each team's answer, and check the spelling of the written version, awarding a point for each correct question – two points if the question has not been used by anybody else. A more able class could see how many questions they can come up with using the word in the time given.

Wie (x 2)
Was (x 2)
Wo
Wann
Hast

5 Partnerarbeit: Sprich 30 Sekunden lang über deine Familie und Haustiere. (AT 2/3–4)   `1.5a+b/Y7`

Speaking. Pupils time each other to see if they can speak about their family and pets in German for a minimum of 30 seconds. Suggest that they prepare by making a few notes (perhaps with some pointers on the board), but discourage them from reading a script aloud. Encourage pupils to use facial and verbal expression and also to use non-verbal techniques. More able pupils could assess each other's language – giving credit for fluency, pronunciation, use of connectives, opinions etc.

6 Schreib eine Antwort an Julia. Beantworte ihre Fragen. (AT 4/4)

2.4a/Y7 2.5/Y7

Writing. Pupils use the writing frame, and Julia's own email as a model, to write a reply to her. Point out that they must find the questions she asks, and include their own answers to them in the reply. Encourage them to ask questions of their own.

R For lower ability pupils, you could write up the beginnings of the sentences in the writing frame on the board or an OHT. Brainstorm ideas that pupils could use in each paragraph and model the writing process, including checking use of capital letters for nouns and other issues that they might need to be reminded about.

+ Encourage more able pupils to include extra information and questions, and to make use of connectives and qualifiers to lengthen their sentences. Refer them back to the earlier pages of this chapter for ideas. They could also think about questions to add to make the letter sound more natural.

ICT Their 'emails' should ideally be word-processed for authenticity. You may even be able to send them to a partner school as real emails.

Plenary

4.4/Y7

Aims

To reinforce the language of this chapter.
To practise the use of connectives and qualifiers.

At this stage of the course, most pupils should be able to build long sentences successfully, using connectives and qualifiers. Select one pupil after another (choose according to how difficult a stage the sentence is at) to add a word to the chain and build sentences around the class. Write the sentence up on the board as it develops. By dividing the class into two teams, and selecting from one team then the other, make it into a competition by awarding a point to the opposing team when someone is unable to take a sentence further.

Lernzieltest 5.8

This is a checklist of language covered in Chapter 3. Pupils can work with the checklist in pairs to check what they have learned. Points which directly address grammar and structures are marked with a G. There is a **Lernzieltest** sheet in the Resource and Assessment File (page 45). Encourage pupils to look back at the chapter and to use the grammar section to revise what they are unclear about.

You can also use this as an end-of-unit plenary.

Wiederholung

A confidence-building revision test to prepare pupils for the **Kontrolle** at the end of the chapter.

Resources
CD 2, track 16

1 Hör zu. Theos Familie. Wie ist die richtige Reihenfolge? (AT 1/3) 1.1/Y7

Listening. Pupils listen and select the pictures in the correct order.

> *Also, hier sind meine Photos. So, das bin ich. Ich heiße Theo. Ich bin dreizehn Jahre alt – ich werde vierzehn im April. Und das ist mein Wellensittich, Willi, er ist süß. Das hier ist mein Vater. Er heißt Volker. Und das ist meine Mutter. Sie ist vierzig Jahre alt. Sie ist sehr freundlich. Hier ist meine Katze, Fifi. Sie ist toll, aber ziemlich schüchtern.Und, zuletzt, das ist meine Schwester, Susi.* 16

Answers
e, c, b, d, a, f

2 Partnerarbeit: Mach Interviews. (AT 2/3–4) 1.4a/Y7

Speaking. Pupils select five relevant questions from those given, to ask their partners. More able pupils can of course make up other similar questions of their own, and give more extended answers.

3 Was denkst du? Richtig oder falsch? (AT 3/2) 2.1/Y7

Reading. Pupils use the pictures to determine whether each statement about appearance is true or false. They could correct the two false statements.

Answers
1 falsch 2 richtig 3 richtig 4 richtig
5 falsch 6 richtig

4 Schreib die E-Mail ab und füll die Lücken aus. (AT 3 & 4/3) 4.4/Y7

Reading/Writing. Pupils copy out the email and fill each numbered gap with the correct word from those given in the box.

Answers
1 Hallo
2 habe
3 ist
4 aber
5 laut
6 nicht
7 bin
8 du
9 mein
10 heißt
11 er
12 Schreib

5 Beautworte die E-mail aus Aufgabe 4. (AT 4/4) 2.4b/Y7

Writing. Pupils write their own reply to Olive's email.

Learning targets
- Understanding and giving information about a famous person
- Finding out about famous people from German-speaking countries

Key framework objectives

1.2/Y7	Listening – unfamiliar language
1.5/Y7	Speaking – (a) presenting
1.5/Y7	Speaking – (b) expression/non-verbal techniques
5.7	Strategies – planning and preparing

Grammar
- Further practice of third person present tense verb forms

Key language
Name
Alter
Geburtstag
Wohnort
Freundin
Geschwister
Haustiere
Größe
Haare
Augen
Persönlichkeit

High-frequency words
er / sie
nicht
sehr
wie?
wann?
wo?
wer?
ja, richtig
nein, falsch

Pronunciation
German names

English
Assessing a text for gist, intended audience, and difficulty

Citizenship
Finding out about people who are well known in sport, entertainment and other areas

ICT
Preparing visual material for an oral mini-presentation
Preparing display material

Resources
CD 2, track 17
Workbooks A and B, p. 27

Starter 1   4.5a/Y7 4.6a/Y7

Aim
To recap how to ask questions using verb forms in the third person singular.

Display a picture of a person of interest. This could be a German-speaking politician, pop star or sportsperson, possibly unknown to pupils. Volunteers ask questions, e.g. *Wie heißt er?, Wie alt ist er?*. Answers can be supplied by you or by members of the class if known. Get a confident pupil to note the answers on the board. Finish by getting the class to tell you facts about the person, in German, using *er* or *sie*. If you have a recording or video clip of the person to quickly show at the end of the activity, it would help to bring the topic of famous people alive for pupils.

Suggestion
Before doing exercise 1, look at the *Steckbrief* with the class. Encourage pupils to assess the text for gist, intended audience and difficulty.

1 Hör zu. Finde im Steckbrief fünf Fehler. (AT 1/3, AT 3/3)   1.2/Y7 2.2b/Y7

Listening/Reading. Pupils listen to the recording and look at the information about the fictional teenage film star Benjamin Braun. They identify the differences between the recording and the text in their books. They should use the printed version as the basis for their writing in exercise 2.

> *Filmstar Benjamin Braun ist 19 Jahre alt und er wohnt in der Hauptstadt von Deutschland, in Berlin. Benjamins Geburtstag ist am vierzehnten März, dann hat er immer eine große Party.*
>
> *Seine Freundin heißt Katharina, sie ist sechzehn Jahre alt und wohnt auch in Berlin. Benjamins Familie ist ziemlich groß: Benjamin, seine Eltern, zwei Schwestern und zwei Brüder. Bei ihm wohnt auch eine kleine Katze mit dem Namen Lili.*
>
> *Benjamin sieht sehr gut aus: Er ist groß und schlank und er hat blonde Haare und braune Augen. Sein Charakter ist ziemlich interessant: Er ist lustig, sehr laut, aber gar nicht launisch und nicht faul.*

🔘 17

Answers
Geburtstag: 14.03
Freundin: 16 Jahre alt
Geschwister: zwei Schwester und zwei Brüder
Haare: blond
Charakter: launisch

2 Beantworte die Fragen über Benjamin. Schreib einen Absatz. (AT 3/3, AT 4/3)   `2.4b/Y7` `4.4/Y7`

Writing. Pupils answer these comprehension questions about the *Steckbrief*, in full sentences to give practice in using third person singular forms. They should form a paragraph with their answers. The questions and answers are useful preparation for the speaking and writing activities which follow.

Answers
(accept alternative correct wording)
1. Er ist neunzehn Jahre alt.
2. Er hat am 24. März Geburtstag.
3. Er wohnt in Berlin, in Deutschland.
4. Ja, er hat eine Freundin. Sie heißt Katharina und sie ist 17 Jahre alt.
5. Ja, er hat eine Schwester und zwei Brüder.
6. Ja, er hat eine Katze, Lili.
7. Er ist 1,80m groß. Er hat braune Haare und braune Augen.
8. Er ist lustig, laut, nicht launisch und sehr faul.

3 Partnerarbeit: berühmte Leute. Wer ist das? (AT 2/3–4)   `1.4b/Y7`

Speaking. Pupils choose any famous person, and answer their partner's questions about him or her until the identity has been correctly guessed. You may wish to demonstrate with the whole class first – perhaps revealing a picture of the person when they guess correctly. Pupils could select from the questions in the previous task. This could be played competitively, by counting the number of questions needed to guess correctly. Weaker pupils can participate by giving short answers, perhaps paired with a more able pupil to help them.

Suggestion
Look at the **ECHO-Tipp** panel about famous people. Discuss the categories of famous person with the class, brainstorming ideas. Aim to use at least some German while doing this (*Ja, er kommt aus Deutschland,* etc.). If they don't know current musicians or film stars, you could discuss why that is the case.

Aim
To recap language for giving information about a famous person, in preparation for creative speaking and writing tasks.

Give pupils one minute to study again the *Steckbrief* of Benjamin Braun in their textbooks, telling them that you will be testing them on how many details they can remember. They then close their books, and work in pairs to write as many sentences as they can about him in German (although you may prefer weaker pupils to write in English), in three minutes. Either collate answers immediately, awarding a point for every factually correct sentence (ignoring minor errors), or collect them in and look through them later in the lesson while pupils are preparing their creative work.

ECHO-Tipp   `4.1/Y7`
This reminder that nouns are always written with a capital letter in German will be helpful to pupils when doing exercise 4.

4 Lies den Text und füll die Tabelle aus. (AT 3/4)   `2.1/Y7` `2.2b/Y7`

Reading. Pupils read the text about an Austrian ski champion and extract different types of words in order to complete the grid. Encourage them to find as many examples of each as they can.

Answers
Accept any correct answers.

 Pupils who finish quickly could also translate the text into English.

5 Minivortrag: eine berühmte Person. (AT 2/4)   `1.5 a+b/Y7` `5.7`

Speaking. This talk will need to be prepared carefully by pupils. Some should be able to learn their talk, rather than simply reading from a script, or perhaps to use brief prompts only. Encourage able pupils to extend their sentences and to use a wide range of previously learnt vocabulary. Presentations could include illustrative material, and could be done to a partner or small group, or to the whole class, as your plenary. Weaker pupils could simply read out a *Steckbrief* (as in the example about Benjamin Braun).

ICT Numerous images of famous people are available on the Internet for downloading. Pupils could use PowerPoint for their presentation, or make use of ICT for their poster.

6 Schreib einen Absatz über eine berühmte Person. (AT 4/4)

2.4b/Y7 2.5/Y7

Writing. Pupils write a paragraph about a famous person of their choice. This could be based on the person who is the subject of their presentation.

Plenary

1.5a+b/Y7

Aim

To give a short presentation in German.

Volunteers perform their presentation about a famous person to the class or in groups, making use of illustrative material for added interest. Encourage pupils to use expression and non-verbal techniques. Encourage positive feedback and appreciation from the audience.

SELF-ACCESS READING AND WRITING AT TWO LEVELS

A Reinforcement

Was passt zusammen? (AT 3/2)
2.1/Y7

Reading. Pupils match the statements about family members to the pictures.

> **Answers**
> 1 d   2 e   3 a   4 b   5 c

Verbinde die Worthälften. (AT 4/1)
4.2/Y7

Writing. Pupils match the word halves to copy words for pets.

> **Answers**
> Wellensittich, Meerschweinchen, Schildkröte, Kaninchen, Goldfisch, Schlange, Hamster, Katze

Richtig oder falsch? (AT 3/3)
2.1/Y7

Reading. Pupils decide whether the sentences are true or false in describing the pictures. Pupils could then write out the false sentences correctly.

> **Answers**
> 1 richtig   2 falsch   3 richtig
> 4 falsch   5 falsch   6 falsch

Schreib den Text ab und füll die Lücken aus. Zeichne Boris. (AT 4/2)
4.4/Y7

Writing. Pupils write out the text, filling in each gap with the correct word from those given. They then use the information to draw a picture of Boris.

> **Answers**
> Hallo! Ich bin **groß** und kräftig. Ich habe **blonde**, lockige **Haare**. Ich habe kurze Haare. Ich habe **grüne** Augen. Ich bin sehr **musikalisch** und sportlich. Ich bin **freundlich**.

B Extension

Was passt zusammen? Füll die Lücken aus. (AT 4/2)
4.4/Y7

Reading. Pupils match each sentence to a picture, then complete the sentence based on the picture.

> **Answers**
> 1   c   Ich habe **zwei** Katzen.
> 2   d   Ich habe eine **Schlange** und ein Kaninchen.
> 3   a   Ich habe **drei** Schildkröten.
> 4   b   Ich habe einen Wellensittich und ein **Pferd**.
> 5   f   Ich habe einen **Hund**.
> 6   e   Ich habe **zwei** Goldfische und eine **Katze**.

Lies Annas Brief und beantworte die Fragen. Benutze „er" oder „sie". (AT 3&4/3)
4.4/Y7

Reading/Writing. Pupils write answers to questions in full sentences, using *er* or *sie*.

> **Answers**
> 1 Sie wohnt in Hamburg, in Deutschland.
> 2 Sie ist ziemlich klein und schlank.
> 3 Er heißt Andreas.
> 4 Er ist sehr launisch.
> 5 Er hat am vierten April Geburtstag.
> 6 Er wohnt in Amerika.

Schreib den Text ab und füll die Lücken aus. (AT 4/3)
4.4/Y7

Writing. Pupils copy the text and fill in the missing words, checking meanings as necessary.

> **Answers**
> Stefan ist **zehn** Jahre alt. Er hat am **zwanzigsten Mai** Geburtstag. Er ist **groß** und **schlank**. Er hat **blaue Augen**. Er hat **kurze, schwarze** Haare. Er ist sehr **intelligent** und ziemlich **sportlich**. Er ist auch **musikalisch**. Er hat einen **Hund**, Albi. Albi ist **braun** und **freundlich**.

Beschreib einen Freund / eine Freundin. (AT 4/3–4)
2.4a/Y7

Writing. Pupils write their own text about a friend, using the one in exercise 3 as a model. Give credit for accuracy, range of vocabulary, and use of connectives and qualifiers to vary structure.

Übungsheft A, Seite 22

1 (AT3 Level 2)
1 Ich habe einen Bruder. **2** Ich habe zwei Schwestern. **3** Ich habe zwei Stiefbrüder. **4** Ich bin Einzelkind. **5** Ich habe eine Halbschwester.

2 (AT4 Level 3) 1 Das ist meine Schwester. Sie heißt Anni. Sie ist dreizehn Jahre alt. **2** Das ist meine Tante. Sie heißt Petra. Sie ist siebenunddreißig Jahre alt. **3** Das ist mein Stiefbruder. Er heißt Karl. Er ist zwölf Jahre alt. **4** Das ist mein Bruder. Er heißt Dieter. Er ist fünfzehn Jahre alt. **5** Das ist mein Vater. Er heißt Jochen. Er ist neununddreißig Jahre alt. **6** Das ist meine Großmutter. Sie heißt Helga. Sie ist siebzig Jahre alt.

Übungsheft B, Seite 22

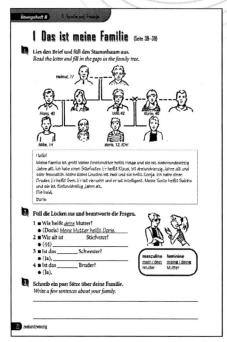

1 (AT3 Level 4) *Top line:* Helmut, 77 and **Helga, 77**. *Second line:* Hans, 40, *and* **Sabine, 35**; Udo, 42, Karin, 40, *and* **Klaus, 43**. *Bottom line:* Mike, 14, *and* **Sonja, 2**; Boris, 12, (ICH!) *and* **Sven, 14**.

2 (AT4 Level 3) 1 Wie heißt **deine** Mutter? – **Meine Mutter heißt Doris. 2** Wie alt ist **dein** Stiefvater? – **Mein Stiefvater ist vierundvierzig Jahre alt. 3** Ist das **deine** Schwester? – **Ja, das ist meine Schwester. 4** Ist das **dein** Bruder? – **Ja, das ist mein Bruder.**

3 (AT4 Level 3)

Übungsheft A, Seite 23

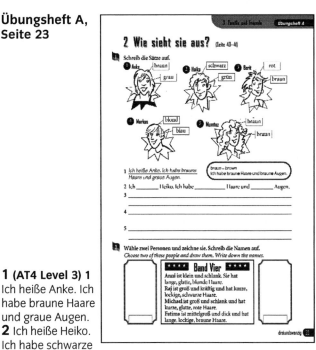

1 (AT4 Level 3) 1 Ich heiße Anke. Ich habe braune Haare und graue Augen. **2** Ich heiße Heiko. Ich habe schwarze Haare und grüne Augen. **3** Ich heiße Berit. Ich habe rote Haare und braune Augen. **4** Ich heiße Markus. Ich habe blonde Haare und blaue Augen. **5** Ich heiß Mumtaz. Ich habe braune Haare und braune Augen.

2 (AT3 Level 3) *Pupils choose two of these to draw:* **Anni:** small and slim, with long, blond straight hair. **Raj:** big and strong, with short, black curly hair. **Michael:** tall and slim, with short, red straight hair. **Fatima:** medium height and fat, with long, curly brown hair.

Übungsheft B, Seite 23

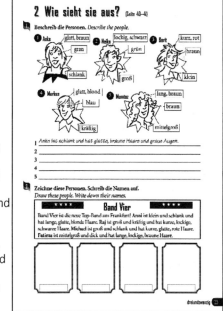

1 (AT4 Level 4)
1 Anke ist schlank und hat glatte, braune Haare und graue Augen. **2** Heiko ist groß und hat lockige, schwarze Haare und grüne Augen. **3** Berit ist klein und hat kurze, rote Haare und braune Augen. **4** Markus ist kräftig und hat glatte, blonde Haare und blaue Augen. **5** Mumtaz ist mittelgroß und hat lange, braune Haare und braune Augen.

2 (AT3 Level 4) Anni: short and slim, with long, straight blond hair. **Raj:** tall and strong, with short, curly black hair. **Michael:** tall and slim, with short, straight red hair. **Fatima:** medium height and fat, with long, curly brown hair.

Übungsheft A, Seite 24

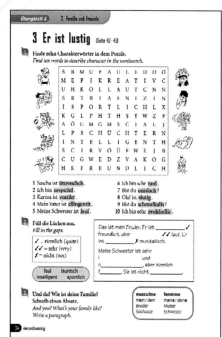

1 (AT3 Level 2) 1 schüchtern **2** sportlich **3** kreativ **4** intelligent **5** faul **6** laut **7** launisch **8** lustig **9** musikalisch **10** freundlich

2 (AT3 Level 3, AT4 Level 2) Das ist mein Bruder. Er ist **ziemlich** freundlich, aber **sehr** laut. Er ist **nicht** musikalisch.

Meine Schwester ist sehr **intelligent** und **sportlich**, aber ziemlich **faul**. Sie ist nicht **launisch**.

3 (AT4 Level 0)

Übungsheft B, Seite 24

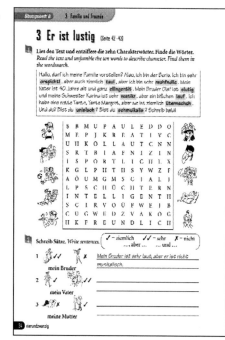

1 (AT3 Level 4) sportlich, laut, freundlich, intelligent, lustig, kreativ, faul, schüchtern, launisch, musikalisch

2 (AT4 Level 3) 1 Mein Bruder ist sehr laut, aber er ist nicht musikalisch. **2** Mein Vater ist ziemlich sportlich und sehr intelligent. **3** Meine Mutter ist nicht faul, aber / und sie ist ziemlich kreativ.

Übungsheft A, Seite 25

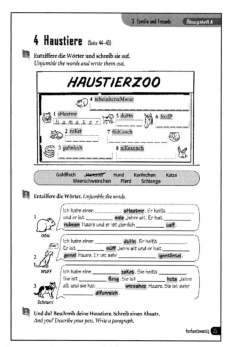

1 (AT4 Level 1) 1 Hamster **2** Katze **3** Schlange **4** Meerschweinchen **5** Hund **6** Pferd **7** Goldfisch **8** Kaninchen

2 (AT3 Level 3) 1 Ich habe einen **Hamster**. Er heißt **Dösi** und er ist **zwei** Jahre alt. Er hat **braune** Haare und er ist ziemlich **faul**. **2** Ich habe einen **Hund**. Er heißt **Wuff**. Er ist **fünf** Jahre alt und er hat **lange** Haare. Er ist sehr **intelligent**. **3** Ich habe eine **Katze**. Sie heiß **Schnurri**. Sie ist **groß**. Sie ist **acht** Jahre alt und sie hat **schwarze** Haare. Sie ist sehr **freundlich**.

3 (AT4 Level 3–4)

Übungsheft B, Seite 25

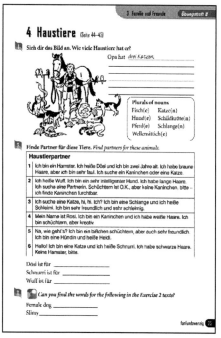

1 (AT4 Level 3) Opa hat drei Katzen, sechs Wellensittiche, ein Pferd, fünf Schlangen, zwei Fische, fünf Schildkröten und einen Hund.

2 (AT3 Level 3) Dösi ist für Rosi. Schnurri ist für Schleimi. Wuff ist für Heidi.

3 (AT3 Level 3) *female dog* = Hündin; *slimy* = schleimig

**Übungsheft A,
Seite 26**

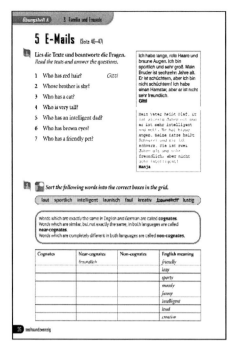

**Übungsheft B,
Seite 26**

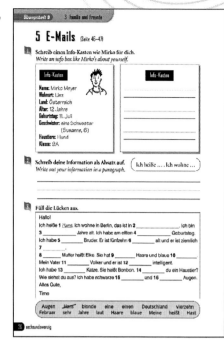

1 (AT3 Level 3) 1 Gitti **2** Gitti **3** Manja **4** Gitti **5** Manja **6** Gitti
7 Manja

2 (AT3 Level 3) Cognates: intelligent *(intelligent)*. **Near-cognates:** freundlich *(friendly)*, sportlich *(sporty)*, laut *(loud)*, kreativ *(creative)*. **Non-cognates:** faul *(lazy)*, launisch *(moody)*, lustig *(funny)*.

1 (AT3 Level 2, AT4 Level 2)

2 (AT4 Level 3–4)

3 (AT3 Level 4) 1 Hans **2** Deutschland **3** vierzehn **4** Februar **5** einen **6** Jahre **7** laut **8** Meine **9** blonde **10** Augen **11** heißt **12** sehr **13** eine **14** Hast **15** Haare **16** blaue

**Übungsheft A,
Seite 27**

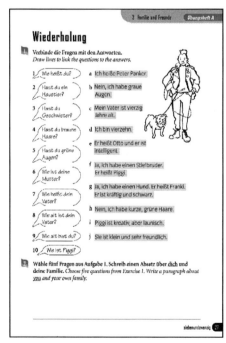

**Übungsheft B,
Seite 27**

1 (AT3 Level 2) 1a **2**g **3**f **4**h **5**b **6**j **7**e **8**c **9**d **10**i

2 (AT4 Level 4)

1 (AT3 Level 4) 1 ✗ **2** ✓ **3** ✗ **4** ✓ **5** ✗ **6** ✓ **7** ✗ **8** ✓ **9** ✓ **10** ✗

2 (AT4 Level 4)

**Übungsheft A,
Seite 28**

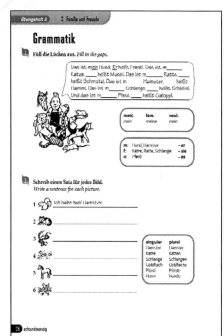

**Übungsheft B,
Seite 28**

1 (AT3 Level 3) Das ist **mein** Hund. **Er** heißt Franki. Das ist **meine** Katze. **Sie** heißt Muesli. Das ist **meine** Ratte. **Sie** heißt Schmutzi. Das ist **mein** Hamster. **Er** heißt Hammi. Das ist **meine** Schlange. **Sie** heißt Schleimi. Und das ist **mein** Pferd. **Es** heißt Galoppi.

2 (AT4 Level 2) Ich habe … **1** zwei Hamster **2** eine Katze **3** drei Schlangen **4** fünf Goldfische **5** ein Pferd **6** vier Hunde.

1 (AT3 Level 3) Ich habe viele Haustiere. Das ist **mein** Hund. **Er** heißt Franki. Das ist **meine** Katze. **Sie** heißt Muesli. Das ist **meine** Ratte. **Sie** heißt Schmutzi, und das ist **mein** Hamster. **Er** heißt Hammi. Ich habe auch **eine** Schlange (**sie** heißt Schleimi) und ich habe **ein** Pferd. **Es** heißt Galoppi.

2 (AT3 Level 3) Hast du ein Haustier? – Ja, ich **habe** einen Hamster und mein Bruder **hat** eine Katze. Der Hamster **ist** klein und **hat** schwarze Haare, aber die Katze **ist** groß und **hat** weiße Haare. Und du? **Hast** du ein Haustier? – Ich **habe** einen Hund. Er **ist** sehr groß, aber ich **bin** klein!

Arbeitsblatt 3.1

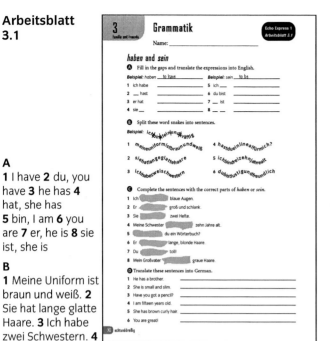

A

1 I have **2** du, you have **3** he has **4** hat, she has **5** bin, I am **6** you are **7** er, he is **8** sie ist, she is

B

1 Meine Uniform ist braun und weiß. **2** Sie hat lange glatte Haare. **3** Ich habe zwei Schwestern. **4** Hast du ein Lineal für mich? **5** Ich bin dreizehn Jahre alt. **6** Du bist lustig und freundlich.

C

1 habe **2** ist **3** hat **4** ist **5** Hast **6** hat **7** bist **8** hat

D

1 Er hat einen Bruder. **2** Sie ist klein und schlank. **3** Hast du einen Bleistift? **4** Ich bin fünfzehn Jahre alt. **5** Sie hat lockige, braune Haare. **6** Du bist toll!

Arbeitsblatt 3.2

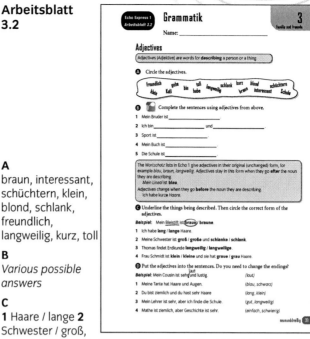

A

braun, interessant, schüchtern, klein, blond, schlank, freundlich, langweilig, kurz, toll

B

Various possible answers

C

1 Haare / lange **2** Schwester / groß, schlank **3** Erdkunde / langweilig **4** Frau Schmidt / klein, Haare / graue

D

1 Meine Tante hat schwarze Haare und blaue Augen. **2** Du bist ziemlich klein und du hast sehr lange Haare. **3** Mein Lehrer ist sehr gut / langweilig, aber ich finde die Schule gut / langweilig. **4** Mathe ist ziemlich einfach / schwierig, aber Geschichte ist sehr einfach / schwierig.

Arbeitsblatt 3.3

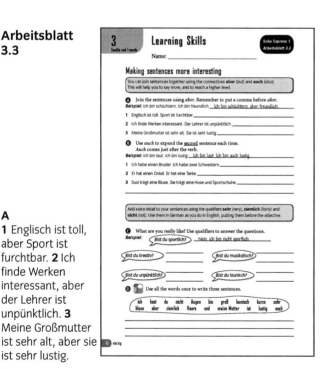

A

1 Englisch ist toll, aber Sport ist furchtbar. **2** Ich finde Werken interessant, aber der Lehrer ist unpünktlich. **3** Meine Großmutter ist sehr alt, aber sie ist sehr lustig.

B

1 Ich habe einen Bruder. Ich habe auch zwei Schwestern. **2** Er hat einen Onkel. Er hat auch eine Tante. **3** Susi trägt eine Bluse. Sie trägt auch eine Hose und Sportschuhe.

D

Possible answer

Ich bin nicht groß.

Du hast blaue Augen und kurze Haare.

Meine Mutter ist ziemlich launisch, aber auch sehr lustig.

Arbeitsblatt 3.4

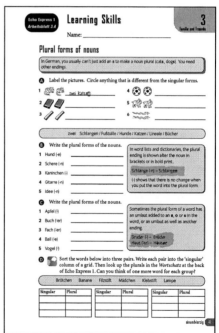

A

1 zwei Katzen **2** zwei Bücher **3** zwei Lineale **4** zwei Fußbälle **5** zwei Hunde **6** zwei Schlangen

B

1 Hunde **2** Scheren **3** Kaninchen **4** Gitarren **5** Ideen

C

1 Äpfel **2** Bücher **3** Fächer **4** Bälle **5** Vögel

D

Lampe / Lampen, Banane / Bananen; Brötchen / Brötchen, Mädchen / Mädchen; Klebstift / Klebstifte, Filzstift / Filzstifte

Other possible words to add:
Katze, Kaninchen, Bleistift

Arbeitsblatt 3.5

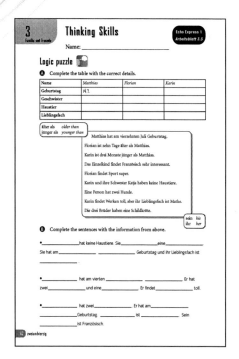

3 Thinking Skills

Echo Express 1
Arbeitsblatt 3.5

Name: _____

Logic puzzle

A Complete the table with the correct details.

Name	Matthias	Florian	Karin
Geburtstag	14.7.		
Geschwister			
Haustier			
Lieblingsfach			

älter als   older than
jünger als   younger than

Matthias hat am vierzehnten Juli Geburtstag.

Florian ist zehn Tage älter als Matthias.

Karin ist drei Monate jünger als Matthias.

Das Einzelkind findet Französisch sehr interessant.

Florian findet Sport super.

Karin und ihre Schwester Katja haben keine Haustiere.

Eine Person hat zwei Hunde.

Karin findet Werken toll, aber ihr Lieblingsfach ist Mathe.

Die drei Brüder haben eine Schildkröte.

sein   his
ihr   her

B Complete the sentences with the information from above.

• _____ hat keine Haustiere. Sie_____ eine_____
Sie hat am_____ _____ Geburtstag und ihr Lieblingsfach ist
_____ .

• _____ hat am vierten _____ Er hat
zwei_____ und eine_____ Er findet_____ toll.

• _____ hat zwei_____ Er hat am_____
_____ Geburtstag _____ ist _____ Sein
_____ ist Französisch.

zweiundvierzig

A

Name	Matthias	Florian	Karin
Geburtstag	14.7	4.7	14.10
Geschwister	–	2 Brüder	1 Schwester
Haustier	2 Hunde	1 Schildkröte	–
Lieblingsfach	Französisch	Sport	Mathe

B

Karin / hat / Schwester / vierzehnten / Oktober / Mathe.

Florian / Juli / Geburtstag / Brüder / Schildkröte / Sport.

Matthias / Hunde / vierzehnten / Juli / Er / Einzelkind / Lieblingsfach.

4 Freizeit

Unit Learning targets	Key framework objectives	NC levels and PoS coverage	Grammar and key language	Skills
1 Sport (pp. 54–55) • Talking about sports • Using *gern* to show what you like doing	**1.4/Y8** Speaking – (b) unscripted conversations **5.3** Strategies – English/other languages	**NC levels** 2–4 **2.1c** knowledge of language **2.2d** pronunciation and intonation **2.2e** ask and answer questions **3b** sounds and writing **3c** apply grammar **3d** use a range of vocab / structures **4b** communicate in pairs etc.	Present tense paradigms: *ich / du / er / sie* forms of *spielen / gehen / wohnen* Forming closed questions Use of *gern* *Ich spiele …* *Spielst du …?* *Er / Sie spielt* *gern / nicht gern* *Basketball* *Federball* *Fußball* *Rugby* *Tennis* *Tischtennis* *Volleyball* *Ich gehe …* *Gehst du …?* *Er / Sie geht …* *angeln* *reiten* *schwimmen* *Snowboard fahren* *wandern*	Pronunciation of cognates
2 Hobbys und Lieblingssachen (pp. 56–57) • Talking about your hobbies and favourite things • Using the present tense of regular and irregular verbs	**4.1/Y8** Language – sounds/spelling exceptions **4.6/Y8** Language – (a) range of questions	**NC levels** 2–4 **2.1c** knowledge of language **2.1d** previous knowledge **2.1e** use reference materials **2.2d** pronunciation and intonation **2.2e** ask and answer questions **2.2j** adapt previously-learnt language **3b** sounds and writing **3c** apply grammar **3d** use a range of vocab / structures **4b** communicate in pairs etc. **4d** make links with English	*Ich* and *du* forms of other verbs, including some strong verbs *sein(e) / ihr(e)* *Lieblings-* (revisited) *gern* (revisited) *Ich spiele Gitarre.* *Ich spiele am Computer.* *Ich gehe in die Stadt.* *Ich gehe in den Jugendklub.* *Ich gehe ins Kino.* *Ich tanze.* *Ich lese.* *Ich besuche meine Freunde.* *Ich höre Musik.* *Ich sehe fern.* *Ich fahre Rad.* *Ich faulenze.* *Was ist dein(e) / mein(e) / sein(e) / ihr(e) …?* *Lieblingshaustier / Lieblingsfarbe / Lieblingssport / Lieblingssendung / Lieblingsmannschaft / Lieblingsmusik / Lieblingszahl / Lieblingsauto*	Looking up the meanings of verbs Pronunciation: *a / ä* Word building

Unit Learning targets	Key framework objectives	NC levels and PoS coverage	Grammar and key language	Skills
3 Wie oft spielst du Fußball? (pp. 58–59) • Saying how often you do things • Using *wir* (we)	2.5/Y7 Writing – different text types	NC levels 2–4 2.1d previous knowledge 2.2e ask and answer questions 2.2j adapt previously-learnt language 2.2h redraft to improve writing 3b sounds and writing 3c apply grammar 3d use a range of vocab / structures 4b communicate in pairs etc.	Adverbs of frequency *wir* *Wie oft?* *jeden Tag* *(ein)mal pro Woche* *am Wochenende* *oft* *manchmal* *nie* *Liebe(r)* *Danke für deinen Brief* *Schreib bald* *Dein(e)*	Writing a letter to a penfriend
4 Möchtest du ins Kino gehen? (pp.60–61) • Arranging to go out and when to meet • Using *möchtest du … ?* (would you like … ?) with an infinitive	4.4/Y8 Language – developing sentences 4.5/Y8 Language – (b) range of modal verbs	NC levels 2–4 2.1a identify patterns 2.2d pronunciation and intonation 2.2e ask and answer questions 3b sounds and writing 3c apply grammar 3d use a range of vocab / structures 4b communicate in pairs etc.	*Möchtest du ?* + infinitive Introduction to *in* + accusative Verb as second idea *Hast du am Donnerstag / Freitag / Samstag / Sonntag Zeit?* *Möchtest du …* *Fußball / Tennis / Basketball / Cricket spielen ?* *in die Stadt / in die Disko / in den Jugendklub / ins Kino gehen?* *Ja, gern.* *Ja, das mag ich.* *Nein, das mag ich nicht.* *Nein, das ist langweilig.* *Wann treffen wir uns?* *Um … Uhr* Revision of digital time Revision of greetings *Bis dann / Bis Samstag*	Expressing wishes and opinions Pronunciation: o / ö
5 Abenteuer im Freien (pp. 62–63) • Understanding information about an adventure sports centre • Using *man kann* to say what activities there are	4.5/Y7 Language – (b) modal verbs 2.1/Y8 Reading – authentic materials 3.2/Y8 Culture – (b) customs/ traditions 5.2 Strategies – memorising	NC levels 2–4 2.1a identify patterns 2.1c knowledge of language 2.2e ask and answer questions 2.2c respond appropriately 3b sounds and writing 3c apply grammar 3d use a range of vocab / structures 4b communicate in pairs etc. 4f language of interest / enjoyment 4g language for a range of purposes	Modal verbs: *Man kann* + infinitive *Ich mag* + infinitive *Man kann …* *Kann man …?* *Ich mag … Mountainbike fahren* *Wildwasser fahren* *Kanu fahren* *klettern* *schwimmen* *segeln* *windsurfen* *Tennis spielen* *Tischtennis spielen* *Volleyball spielen* *Basketball spielen*	Writing a simple letter of enquiry Receptive introduction of *du/Sie*

Unit Learning targets	Key framework objectives	NC levels and PoS coverage	Grammar and key language	Skills
Lernzieltest und Wiederholung (pp. 64–65) • Pupils' checklist and practice test		NC levels 2–4 2.1b memorising		
Mehr (pp. 66–67) • Reading a letter about plans for next week • Making plans to go out next week	1.4/Y8 Speaking – (a) classroom exchanges 2.2/Y8 Reading – (a) longer, more complex texts 5.8 Strategies – evaluating and improving	NC levels 2–5 2.1c knowledge of language 2.2e ask and answer questions 3b sounds and writing 3c apply grammar 3d use a range of vocab / structures 4b communicate in pairs etc.	Present tense to talk about close future (receptive) Verb as second idea (revision) *Möchtest du* + infinitive? (revision) *Möchtest du am (Montag) (ins Kino gehen)?* *Nein, ich (spiele Fußball).* *Ja, gern. Wann treffen wir uns?* *Um (sechs) Uhr.* *Bis dann.*	
Extra (pp. 106–107) • Self-access reading and writing at two levels		NC levels 2–4 3c apply grammar 3d use a range of vocab / structures 2.2e ask and answer questions 2.2j adapt previously-learnt language		

Learning targets
- Talking about sports
- Using *gern* to say what you like doing

Key framework objectives
1.4/Y8 Speaking – (b) unscripted conversations
5.3 Strategies – English/other languages

Grammar
- Present tense regular verbs: 1st, 2nd, 3rd person
- Forming closed questions
- Using *(nicht) gern*

Key language
Ich spiele …
Spielst du …?
Er / Sie spielt …
gern / nicht gern
Basketball / Federball / Fußball / Rugby / Tennis / Tischtennis / Volleyball
Ich gehe …
Gehst du …?
Er / Sie geht …
angeln / reiten / schwimmen / Snowboard fahren / wandern

High-frequency words
gern
nicht gern
ich gehe
gehst du …?
er / sie geht
ich spiele
du spielst
er / sie spielt
das ist …

ich finde das …
sehr
aber
auch
und

Pronunciation
Sports cognates

English
Applying regular verb endings
Closed questions

Citizenship
Sport as an international link

Resources
CD 2, tracks 18–20
Workbooks A and B, p. 32
Arbeitsblatt 4.1, p. 58
Arbeitsblatt 4.3, p. 60
Flashcards 58–69
Echo Elektro 1 TPP, Express
Mod 4 1.1–1.7

Starter 1   5.3

Aim
To build confidence in aural recognition of cognates.

Give each pupil a copy of **Arbeitsblatt 4.1**. Explain that they will hear you read out a list of new German words, and must join the pictures shown on the worksheet in the order that they hear them. First, elicit what type of words they are going to be (evident from the pictures). Read out the following list of sports cognates, allowing time for weaker pupils to find and join the pictures. At the end, ask all pupils to hold up their completed worksheet, which should show the outline of a tennis racquet.

Tennis	*Tischtennis*
Basketball	*Snowboard fahren*
Fußball	*Volleyball*
Schwimmen	*Reiten*
Rugby	

Suggestion   5.3
Before looking at exercise 1, ask pupils why they think many of the German sports words are the same as in English, or very similar (common roots of the languages; modern sports with international names). Ask them to guess the meanings of *wandern*, *Federball*, and *angeln*.

1 Hör zu. Was passt zusammen? (1–12) (AT 1/2)   4.2/Y7

Listening. Pupils listen to the statements about sport, and identify the correct picture. After discussing the answers, check that weaker pupils are clear about the difference between *ich spiele* and *ich gehe*.

1 *Ich spiele Federball.*
2 *Ich gehe wandern.*
3 *Ich spiele Rugby.*
4 *Ich gehe schwimmen.*
5 *Ich spiele Tischtennis.*
6 *Ich spiele Fußball.*
7 *Ich gehe angeln.*
8 *Ich gehe reiten.*

9 *Ich spiele Volleyball.*
10 *Ich spiele Tennis.*
11 *Ich gehe Snowboard fahren.*
12 *Ich spiele Basketball.*

Answers

1 e	2 k	3 g	4 i	5 f	6 b	7 j	8 h
9 d	10 a	11 l	12 c				

R To practise this vocabulary, pupils could mime and guess the sports in pairs or small groups. Further mime activities can be found in the Introduction on page 10.

Aussprache: Pronouncing cognates `5.3`

Listening. This panel clarifies the fact that, although a number of words look very similar in English and German, their pronunciation is often different. Pupils listen and repeat, to practise the differences in pronunciation between these cognates and their English versions. Encourage them to start in a whisper, building to a crescendo.

Fußball, Fußball, Fußball
Basketball, Basketball, Basketball
Volleyball, Volleyball, Volleyball
Rugby, Rugby, Rugby!

 19

Suggestion

Additional activities with this recording are:
– say each line faster than the previous one
– diminish the volume
– say each line with expression depending on whether pupils like the sport or not
– halves of the class compete.

ECHO-Detektiv `4.5a/Y7`

This reminder of regular present tense verb endings will help pupils with the tasks that follow.

2 Partnerarbeit: Was machst du? (AT 2/2) `4.5a/Y7`

Speaking. Pairs form closed questions about sports to interview their partner. With less confident pupils, you may wish to practise this question formation first, emphasising how to pronounce the *du* forms of *spielen* and *gehen* and getting members of the class to ask you questions.

3 Spielen oder gehen? Schreib Sätze. (AT 4/2) `5.1/Y7`

Writing. Pupils construct simple sentences, prompted by the pronouns and illustrations given, using different forms of *spielen* or *gehen*. Encourage

them to think carefully about which of these two verbs is needed. Refer them to the **ECHO-Detektiv** on page 54 to check verb endings.

Answers
1 Er spielt Tennis.
2 Sie geht reiten.
3 Du spielst Volleyball.
4 Ich gehe angeln.
5 Sie geht wandern.

+ Pupils who finish quickly could make up their own additional sentences about sport. Alternatively, they could make the sentences they have created negative, by adding *nicht*.

Starter 2 `4.2/Y7`

Aim

To recap and consolidate spellings of sports vocabulary and verb forms.

Copy the following six sports phrases with vowels missing onto the board or an OHT. Set a time limit for pupils to write out the phrases correctly with the vowels included. Encourage the pupils to hear the phrases in their heads or to say them out loud as they work, in order to help them decide which vowels are missing. To make the task more challenging, you could flip the OHT over, so that the phrases appear backwards to pupils and become harder to decipher.

Reveal the answers, so that pairs can correct each other's work and award a mark out of six – they must focus on accuracy, including capital letters for nouns.

ch spl Fdrbll	*(Ich spiele Federball.)*
S ght rtn	*(Sie geht reiten.)*
D splst Fßbll	*(Du spielst Fußball.)*
r ght wndrn	*(Er geht wandern.)*
ch gh ngln	*(Ich gehe angeln.)*
Mn Mttr splt Tschtnns	*(Meine Mutter spielt Tischtennis.)*

4 Hör zu und lies. Schreib die richtigen Buchstaben auf. (AT 1/4, AT 3/4) `1.3a+b/Y7`

Listening/Reading. Pupils listen to and read the text about sports likes and dislikes, and select the relevant pictures for each person mentioned. Ask pupils to listen for the tone used by the speakers when talking about likes and dislikes. This can firstly be done as a 'listen and read' – ask pupils to identify the new word *gern* and to speculate as to its meaning. Stronger classes could do the matching task using the audio only, then read the text to check. Afterwards, ask pupils to read the text aloud, using appropriate expression with regard to the likes and dislikes.

> *Mein Name ist Viktor. Sport ist mein Lieblingsfach in der Schule. Ich spiele gern Federball, aber ich spiele nicht gern Basketball. Federball macht Spaß, aber Basketball ist furchtbar – der Lehrer ist doof!*
>
> *Meine Freundin Julia ist auch sehr sportlich. Sie spielt gern Federball und Fußball, aber sie geht nicht gern schwimmen. Sie findet es langweilig und kalt!*
>
> *Peter ist gar nicht sportlich und spielt nicht gern Fußball. Er findet es schwierig und ein bisschen langweilig!*
>
> *Aber Stefanie ist sehr sportlich. Sie spielt gern Fußball in der Schule und geht gern schwimmen in ihrer Freizeit. Sie findet das alles toll!*

20

Answers
Viktor – c, b
Julia – c, a, e
Peter – f
Stefanie – a, d

ECHO-Detektiv: gern   4.4/Y8

Point out to pupils how useful this 'little word' is because they can use it in many situations to give opinions on what they like doing. Ask pupils to write or say a sentence with *gern*, using language they already know, e.g. *Ich spiele gern Tennis, ich wohne gern in Manchester, ich esse gern Kekse.* They could say these to you in order to exit the room at the end of the lesson. As a more challenging alternative, ask pupils to create three sentences with *gern / nicht gern*, one of which is not true. They read them out, and partners or the rest of the class guess which one is false.

5 Partnerarbeit: Stell sechs Fragen und notier die Antworten. (AT 2/3–4)   1.4b/Y8 1.3b/Y7

Speaking. Pairs interview each other about sports likes and dislikes, responding in full sentences with an opinion. They note answers, which are then used in writing exercise 6. This speaking task could be developed into a group or class survey.

Encourage more confident learners to add 'extras' into their dialogues, e.g. greetings, agreeing or disagreeing with an opinion.

6 Was macht er / sie gern? Schreib Sätze über deinen Partner / deine Partnerin. (AT 4/3)   4.4/Y8

Writing. Pupils use notes made during the speaking task to write sentences about their partner using *gern / nicht gern* and opinions. Remind them to think carefully about their choice of verb and verb ending.

7 Verbinde deine Sätze aus Aufgabe 6 und schreib einen Text. (AT4/4)   4.4/Y8

Writing. Pupils link their sentences with *und, aber* and *auch* to write a paragraph about their partner. Firstly, direct pupils to the **ECHO-Tipp** to remind them of these useful words for linking ideas in sentences and making them longer or more interesting. They may find the text in exercise 4 a useful source of ideas.

Plenary   4.5a/Y7

Aim
To recap sports vocabulary, and present tense forms of *spielen* and *gehen*.

Quick team game miming sports: divide the class into two teams. The first team has one minute (timed by a volunteer from the opposite team), to mime and guess as many of the 14 sports as possible. As soon as a correct guess has been made, e.g. *Du spielst Tennis*, that person stands up and mimes another. Keep a tally of the number of words guessed. The opposite team then has the same amount of time to do the activity. The team guessing the most is the winner. Adjust the time limit for weaker or more able classes.

Play the game using a specific pronoun that keeps changing. Ask pupils to include *gern / nicht gern* in their sentences. Pupils could signal these by including a thumbs up / thumbs down action in the course of the mime. Take away points for using English rather than German pronunciation.

Further variations on mime activities can additionally be found in the Introduction on page 10.

Learning targets
- Talking about your hobbies and favourite things
- Using *sein* (his) and *ihr* (her)

Key framework objectives
4.1/Y8 Language – sounds/ spelling exceptions
4.6/Y8 Language – (a) range of questions

Grammar
- Regular verbs (*ich, du, er / sie*)
- Irregular verbs (*ich, du, er / sie*)
- *gern*
- Possessive adjectives: *sein(e) / ihr(e)*

Key language
Ich spiele / du spielst / er/sie spielt …
Gitarre / am Computer.
Ich gehe / du gehst / er/sie geht …
in den Jugendklub / in die Stadt / ins Kino.
Ich tanze / du tanzst / er/sie tanzt.
Ich lese / du liest / er/sie liest.
Ich besuche / du besuchst / er/sie besucht Freunde.
Ich höre / du hörst / er/sie hört Musik.
Ich sehe / du siehst / er/sie sieht fern.
Ich fahre / du fährst / er/sie fährt Rad.
Ich faulenze / du faulenzst / er/sie faulenzt.
Was ist …?
dein(e) / mein(e) / sein(e) / ihr(e)
Lieblingsauto
Lieblingsfarbe
Lieblingshaustier
Lieblingsmannschaft
Lieblingsmusik
Lieblingssendung
Lieblingssport
Lieblingszahl

High-frequency words
ich
du
er / sie
gern
nicht
am
ins
was?
ist
mein
dein
sein
ihr

Pronunciation
a / ä

English
Possessive adjectives

Resources
CD 2, tracks 21–24
Workbooks A and B, p.33
Arbeitsblatt 4.2, p.59
Arbeitsblatt 4.4, p.61
Echo Elektro 1 TPP, Express Mod 4 2.1–2.10

Starter 1 5.1

Aim
To familiarise pupils with the infinitives of verbs.
Verb race: show the class these four new infinitives on the board: *hören, lesen, tanzen, besuchen*. Get them to have a go at pronouncing these new words, based on their prior knowledge of sound-spelling links. Pupils then race to find out their meanings. The first five to arrive at the front of the class with the correct meanings (written on paper or mini-whiteboards) are the winners. Afterwards, elicit the fact that these are verbs, and remind pupils that all verbs have an infinitive – ask for other examples, e.g. *spielen, gehen, heißen, wohnen, haben*. Before starting exercise 1, make sure all pupils are clear that this is the form given in word lists and dictionaries.

Rate mal: Was sind diese Hobbys? Hör zu und überprüfe es. (1–12) (AT 1 & 3/2) 5.4

Reading/Listening. Pupils match phrases about hobbies to pictures. They will probably need to look some of them up. Answers can be checked by listening to the recording. You could then use the recording for 'listen and repeat' pronunciation practice, pausing it between items. Halves of the class could repeat the question or the answer, alternating between the two.

1 – Was machst du in deiner Freizeit?
  – Ich gehe ins Kino. **21**
2 – Und du, was machst du in deiner Freizeit?
  – Ich gehe in den Jugendklub.
3 – Gehst du in die Stadt in deiner Freizeit?
  – Ja, ich gehe in die Stadt.

4 – *Fährst du in deiner Freizeit Rad?*
   – *Ja, ich fahre Rad.*
5 – *Hallo, siehst du in deiner Freizeit fern?*
   – *Ähm … ja, ich sehe fern.*
6 – *Hallo, hörst du in deiner Freizeit Musik?*
   – *Ja, ich höre Musik.*
7 – *Liest du in deiner Freizeit?*
   – *Ja, ich lese gern.*
8 – *Tanzt du manchmal in deiner Freizeit?*
   – *Ich tanze gern.*
9 – *Besuchst du deine Freunde?*
   – *Ja, ich besuche meine Freunde.*
10 – *Und du, spielst du gern am Computer?*
   – *Ja, ich spiele am Computer.*
11 – *Was machst du in deiner Freizeit?*
   – *Ich spiele gern Gitarre.*
12 – *Hallo, was machst du in deiner Freizeit?*
   – *Ich faulenze.*

Answers
1 e Ich gehe ins Kino.
2 d Ich gehe in den Jugendklub.
3 c Ich gehe in die Stadt.
4 k Ich fahre Rad.
5 j Ich sehe fern.
6 i Ich höre Musik.
7 g Ich lese.
8 f Ich tanze.
9 h Ich besuche meine Freunde.
10 b Ich spiele am Computer.
11 a Ich spiele Gitarre.
12 l Ich faulenze.

 Partnerarbeit. (AT 2/2) 1.4b/Y8 4.6a/Y8

Speaking. In pairs, pupils practise the new vocabulary using the pictures from exercise 1. They could then ask and answer the question for real, in pairs, groups, or as a class survey activity.

 Hör zu. Was machen sie? (Bilder aus Aufgabe 1) (1–8) (AT 1/2) 1.1/Y7

Listening. Pupils note the hobbies mentioned, using the numbered pictures in exercise 1. Encourage weaker pupils to focus on the hobby words themselves, and tell them that some speakers will say more than one hobby.

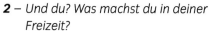 22

1 – *Was machst du in deiner Freizeit?*
   – *Ich gehe ins Kino.*
2 – *Und du? Was machst du in deiner Freizeit?*
   – *Ähm … ich faulenze!*
3 – *Hallo. Was machst du in deiner Freizeit?*
   – *Ich besuche meine Freunde.*
4 – *Besuchst du auch deine Freunde in deiner Freizeit?*
   – *Nein. Ich spiele am Computer.*
5 – *Und was machst du?*
   – *Ich höre Musik und ich lese gern.*
6 – *Hallo, was machst du in deiner Freizeit?*
   – *Ich gehe gern in die Stadt und ich fahre Rad.*
7 – *Was machst du in deiner Freizeit?*
   – *Ich spiele gern Gitarre und ich sehe fern.*
8 – *Und du? Was machst du in deiner Freizeit?*
   – *Ich gehe in den Jugendklub und ich tanze gern.*

Answers
1 1   2 12   3 9   4 10   5 6, 7   6 3, 4
7 11, 5   8 2, 8

4 Lies den Text und full die Tabelle aus (Bilder aus Aufgabe 1). (AT 3/4) 2.1/Y7

Reading. Pupils read the text and complete the grid, selecting the correct pictures from exercise 1 for each person mentioned. Draw their attention to the third person verb forms in the text. Follow-up reading, translation and writing activities can be found in the Introduction on pages 9–10.

Answers

Anja	Karl	Guido
3, 9, 12	4, 2, 8	5, 7, 11

ECHO-Detektiv: Irregular verbs
5.1

This panel shows pupils how three useful hobby-related verbs change their stem vowels in the second and third person singular forms. Ask the class to pick out examples of these from Anja's text in exercise 4. They could also write or say 'leisure' sentences about a partner to practise the three irregular verbs.

Aussprache: a / ä (AT 1/ 💬)   4.1/Y8

Listening. This panel shows the effect of an umlaut on the letter *a*. Pupils identify which of the two sounds they hear in each case. You may wish to write the words on the board without umlauts, and ask a group of pupils to come to the front and fill in an umlaut where they think they have heard one.

> **1** *fahre*
> **2** *fährst*
> **3** *Vater*
> **4** *fährt*
> **5** *Äpfel*

🔘 23

Starter 2   3.1/Y7

Aim

To find out what pupils know about some popular aspects of everyday life in German-speaking countries.

Tell the class that today's lesson will be about people's favourite things. Give small groups three minutes to brainstorm ideas of what German-speaking young people might say is their favourite in each of the categories below (i.e. what German-related names do they know in each category?). Start by eliciting the meanings of the categories, perhaps by giving examples. With a weaker class, you may prefer to give the categories in English.

Auto • Mannschaft • Sendung • Musik

Discuss their answers, and which ones are likely to be similar to their own (e.g. T.V. programme, car). If there was a category for which they could think of no ideas at all (possibly music), why do they think that is? If time allows, you may wish briefly to show examples of advertisements for German cars, posters of a team or a recording/video clip of a pop group.

5 Lies den Text. Füll die Lücken unten aus. (AT 3/3)   5.1

Reading. Pupils read through the cartoon strip about favourite things, and use the information to fill gaps in the summative text below. They use the recording in exercise 6 to check their answers. With less confident pupils you may wish firstly to read and discuss the cartoon together, then elicit the meanings of *sein* and *ihr* before they tackle the gap-filling task.

6 Hör zu und überprüfe es. (AT 1/3)   1.1/Y7

Listening. Pupils listen to the recording to check their answers.

> *Kiki findet schnelle Autos toll! Ihr Lieblingsauto ist ein Porsche. Sie ist auch Fußballfan. Ihre Lieblingsmannschaft ist Bayern München. Ihre Lieblingsfarbe ist Schwarz. Maxi Maus ist ihr Freund. Sein Lieblingssport ist Fußball. Sein Lieblingshaustier ist eine Katze, und seine Lieblingssendung ist „Tom und Jerry", natürlich!*

🔘 24

> **Answers**
> **1** Porsche
> **2** Bayern München
> **3** Schwarz
> **4** Lieblingssport
> **5** Lieblingshaustier
> **6** Lieblingssendung

ECHO-Detektiv   5.1

This panel shows the change in ending of *sein* and *ihr* in the nominative. Explain to more able pupils that this is the same as for *ein / kein / mein / dein*, which they already know. With weaker learners, you may prefer simply to focus on the meanings of these two possessive adjectives.

Suggestion

To help pupils consolidate their understanding of the possessive adjectives learnt so far, give small groups a limited time to prepare and practise a short and simple 'rap' tune, using only the line *mein, dein, sein, ihr* (with pointing and gestures to make their meanings clear). Groups then perform to the class.

7 Partnerarbeit: Interviews über Hobbys und Lieblingssachen. Mach Notizen. (AT 2/3)   1.4b/Y8

Speaking. This could be done in pairs, or as a group or whole-class survey, using perhaps a limited number of questions. Pupils need to make detailed notes of their findings, in preparation for writing about a partner in exercise 8. A further variation on pairwork can be found in the Introduction on page 11.

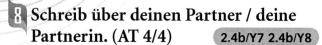

8 Schreib über deinen Partner / deine Partnerin. (AT 4/4) `2.4b/Y7 2.4b/Y8`

Writing. Pupils write an extended report about the leisure interests of a partner, using third person verb forms and the possessive adjectives *sein* and *ihr,* to include hobbies, opinions and favourite things. Remind them to include compound sentences using connectives.

R Less confident pupils could make a poster about their own favourite things, or write a report in the first person about their own leisure interests.

Plenary `4.2/Y8 4.6a/Y8`

Aim
To recap the language learnt for talking about hobbies and favourite things.

Tell pupils they are going to find out how well they know others in the class by now. Write any five questions about favourite things and leisure activities on the board (the class could choose them). Include a mixture of types of question – open questions formed with a question word, and closed questions. Compare and contrast these. Then, working with a different partner from usual, pupils write down what they think his/her answers will be to each. Pairs interview each other to see how many of these guesses are correct, and award each other marks out of five. Encourage them to add spontaneous comments and opinions during their interviews.

Learning targets
- Saying how often you do things
- Using *wir* (we)

Key framework objectives
2.5/Y7 Writing – different text types

Grammar
- Adverbs of frequency
- *wir* with regular verbs

Key language
Wie oft …
spielst du Fußball?
gehst du schwimmen?
spielst du am Computer?
siehst du fern?
liest du ein Buch?
fährst du Rad?
jeden Tag
(ein)mal pro Woche
am Wochenende
oft
manchmal
nie
Liebe(r)
Danke für deinen Brief
Schreib bald
Dein(e)

High-frequency words
wir
wie oft?
jeden

oft
manchmal
nie
einmal
zweimal
dreimal
pro
am
für
dein
spielen

English
Letter-writing conventions

ICT
Word-processing

Resources
CD 2, tracks 25–27
Workbooks A and B, p.34
Arbeitsblatt 4.5, p. 62
Echo Elektro 1 TPP, Express
Mod 4 3.1–3.7

Starter 1   4.2/Y7

Aims
To revise leisure activities in preparation for the tasks in this unit.

Play *Simon sagt*: say sports/leisure activity phrases to the class, who have to instantly mime them, as long as the instruction is prefaced with *Simon sagt*. Anybody who gets it wrong or doesn't know what to mime, sits down, until only three are left – the winners. Phrases could include *ich / du / er / sie*.

Further mime activities can be found in the Introduction on page 10.

1 Hör zu und lies.   4.2/Y8

Listening/Reading. Pupils listen to the recording and look at the pictures and text. Start by getting them to work out what the characters are talking about. Which words gave them clues about this?

1 – Wie oft spielst du Fußball, Peter?
– Ich spiele immer Fußball – jeden Tag.
2 – Und wie oft spielst du Fußball, Viktor?
– Ich spiele manchmal Fußball – einmal pro Woche.
3 – Julia, wie oft spielst du Fußball?
– Ich spiele oft Fußball – dreimal pro Woche.
4 – Und Stefanie, wie oft spielst du Fußball?
– Ich spiele am Wochenende Fußball.
5 – Nina, wie oft spielst du Fußball?
– Ich spiele nie Fußball.

25

2 Wer ist das? (AT 3/2)   4.2/Y8

Reading. Pupils look again at how often each character plays football, and identify which line of the grid represents each one.

> **Answers**
> **a** Peter   **b** Stefanie   **c** Julia   **d** Nina   **e** Viktor

3 Hör zu und mach Notizen. (1–6) (AT 1/3)   1.1/Y7 1.1/Y8

Listening. Pupils listen to the recording and make brief notes to show the hobbies and frequencies mentioned. Make sure weaker learners focus specifically on the hobbies mentioned, and then on the frequency – you may need to play the recording twice. For the more able, challenge pupils to see how much they can understand on a first hearing.

1 – *Was machst du in deiner Freizeit?*
 – *Ich gehe schwimmen.*
 – *Schwimmen? Toll! Wie oft gehst du schwimmen?*
 – *Ich gehe zweimal pro Woche schwimmen.*

2 – *Was machst du in deiner Freizeit?*
 – *Ich fahre Rad.*
 – *Und wie oft fährst du Rad?*
 – *Ich fahre am Wochenende Rad.*

3 – *Was machst du in deiner Freizeit?*
 – *Ich sehe gern fern.*
 – *Fernsehen. Gut. Wie oft siehst du fern?*
 – *Ähm ... ich sehe jeden Tag fern. Meine Mutter findet das furchtbar!*

4 – *Was machst du in deiner Freizeit?*
 – *Ich gehe reiten.*
 – *Reiten? Das ist klasse! Wie oft gehst du reiten?*
 – *Ich gehe dreimal pro Woche reiten. Meine Schwester hat ein Pferd.*

5 – *Hallo. Gehst du auch in deiner Freizeit reiten?*
 – *Ähm, nein. Ich höre Musik.*
 – *Ist das Popmusik?*
 – *Ja.*
 – *Und wie oft hörst du Musik?*
 – *Jeden Tag. Das ist mein Lieblingshobby.*

6 – *Und du? Was machst du in deiner Freizeit?*
 – *Ich spiele gern Tennis und Federball.*
 – *Sehr gut. Du bist also sehr sportlich. Wie oft machst du das?*
 – *Ich spiele am Wochenende Tennis, und einmal pro Woche spiele ich Federball.*

Answers
1 schwimmen, × 2 pro Woche
2 Rad fahren, am Wochenende
3 fern sehen, jeden Tag
4 reiten × 3 pro Woche
5 Musik hören, jeden Tag
6 Tennis, am Wochenende; Federball, × 1 pro Woche

4 Partnerarbeit. (AT 2/3) `1.4b/Y7 4.2/Y8`

Speaking. Pairs ask and answer questions about frequency of leisure activities. Start by pointing out the examples of questions that could be asked in the Key Language box (which is revision from Units 1 and 2). Less confident learners could keep to sports and hobbies that use *spielen* and *gehen*.

More confident pupils could expand on the model dialogue by giving answers in full sentences. Firstly, explain that the time expression is usually inserted immediately after the verb (as in the example for exercise 5).

Suggestion
This task could be developed into a class survey, with pupils selecting a single question to ask, and recording results in their books.

5 Wie oft machst du das? Schreib Sätze. (AT 4/3) `4.4/Y7`

Writing. Pupils write sentences to say how often they do each of the given activities, selecting the correct phrase for each from the Key Language box and inserting a frequency expression. Elicit from pupils the difference in typical word order in these sentences from their English equivalents.

Those who finish quickly could write additional sentences of their own, perhaps including extra information (e.g. places, opinions). They could also check each other's work.

Starter 2 5.4

Aim
To use prior knowledge of context as preparation for reading a letter in German.

Write the following (mostly familiar) items from Viktor's letter (page 59) on the board or an OHT. Tell the class that these words come from something they will be looking at in this lesson, and ask what they think it is. Give pupils 20 seconds to put the words in the most logical order (before having seen the letter). Discuss why they know how to do this.

Viktor
D-35921 Rotesheim, den 23. März
dein Viktor
Wie geht's?
Lieber James
Schreib bald!

6 Hör zu und lies den Brief von Viktor. `2.3/Y7 2.3/Y8`

Listening/Reading. Before you play the recording, pupils take a first look at the letter and tell you what they can about its purpose, audience and content. Clarify that this is a postal letter rather than an email. Do any elements of the letter seem different from the way we set out a letter in English? Is it the first contact Viktor has had with James? If you have not already done so, you may wish to raise the use of *du / Sie*, and ask what this shows about James. They then listen to the recording and read through the letter.

Poststraße 72
D-35921 Rotesheim

 27

Rotesheim, den 23. März

Lieber James,
danke für deinen Brief. Wie geht's?

Naja, für mich ist die Schule immer so langweilig, aber am Wochenende gehen wir oft ins Stadion und sehen ein Fußballspiel. Das ist immer toll! Meine Lieblingsmannschaft ist Dynamo Dresden. Wir gewinnen am Samstag vier zu null ... ähm ... hoffentlich! Spielst du gern Fußball? Hast du eine Lieblingsmannschaft?

Meine Cousine spielt jeden Tag Basketball. Ich spiele keinen Basketball – das finde ich langweilig! Aber wir spielen manchmal am Wochenende Tischtennis. Das ist okay. Wir fahren auch Rad, aber nicht oft.

Ich besuche manchmal meine Freunde. Wir faulenzen und spielen am Computer (mein Lieblingsspiel ist Tombraider!). Wir sehen auch sehr oft fern. Meine Lieblingssendung heißt „Sportschau". Hast du eine Lieblingssendung?

Was machst du gern mit deinen Freunden?

Schreib bald!
Dein
Viktor

ECHO-Tipp: Writing letters

This panel reminds pupils of key phrases for letter-writing in German.

7 Schreib die Sätze zu Ende. (AT 3/4)

4.4/Y7

Reading. Pupils use the letter to finish each of the sentences about Viktor. You may wish to point out the plural verb ending used in two of the sentences, and with a more able class take the opportunity to demonstrate the use of *sie* (they).

Follow-up reading, translation and writing activities can be found in the Introduction on pages 9–10.

Answers
1 Dynamo Dresden
2 Basketball
3 (manchmal am Wochenende) Tischtennis
4 seine Freunde
5 faulenzen gern / spielen am Computer / sehen fern
6 Viktors Lieblingssendung heißt „Sportschau".

ECHO-Detektiv: Saying 'we' in German
5.1

Look at this panel with pupils, and at the English meanings for the German *wir* forms given. Ask pupils to pick out examples of *wir* sentences in Viktor's letter. For practice, they could write or say a sentence each about what they do with their friends.

8 Schreib einen Brief an Viktor. Beantworte seine Fragen. (AT 4/4)

2.5/Y7 5.7

Writing. Pupils write their own letter to Viktor, or to an imaginary penfriend, using Viktor's as a model. Firstly, discuss what types of information to include, and whether it is a first or later letter. For those in need of more support, a writing frame is available on **Arbeitsblatt 4.5**. This may be a suitable point to take up contact with real penfriends in a German-speaking country and send pupils' letters.

ICT Letters could be word-processed or desk top published, perhaps with illustrations, for display.

Plenary
5.8

Aim
To review language learned to date and identify areas for improvement.

Pupils work in pairs to check the language they have learned so far in this chapter, using the **Mini-Test** checklist. Ask pupils which points their partners found most difficult. Give them the task of improving these points by next lesson. Partners could then test them again.

Learning targets

- Arranging to go out and when to meet
- Using *möchtest du …?* (would you like …?) with an infinitive

Key framework objectives

4.4/Y8 Language – developing sentences

4.5/Y8 Language – (b) range of modal verbs

Grammar

- *Möchtest du?* + infinitive
- Introduction to *in* + accusative
- Verb as second idea

Key language

Hast du am … Zeit?
Donnerstag / Freitag / Samstag / Sonntag
Möchtest du …
Fußball / Tennis / Basketball / Cricket spielen?
in die Stadt / in die Disko / in den Jugendklub / ins Kino gehen?
Ja, gern.
Ja, das mag ich.
Nein, das mag ich nicht.
Nein, das ist langweilig.
Wann treffen wir uns?
Um … Uhr
Bis dann / Bis Samstag

High-frequency words

hast du?
möchtest du?
spielen
gehen
in

ins
ja
nein
gern
ich mag
nicht
Wann?
um
bis
dann
wir

Pronunciation

o / ö

Mathematics

Digital time

Resources

CD 2, tracks 28–30
Workbooks A and B, p.35
Echo Elektro 1 TPP, Express
Mod 4 4.1–4.6

Starter 1 4.2/Y8

Aim

To introduce vocabulary for making invitations.

Tell the class that in this unit they will learn how to arrange to go out. Using visual props if possible (e.g. magazine adverts for specific films, a football), make a suggestion to the class using *Möchtest du … ?* Pupils stand up if they wish to accept, or remain seated. Repeat, with further suggestions, until you have demonstrated the question formation several times. As soon as possible, select volunteers to make the invitations.

➕ If time allows, get confident learners to respond verbally to the invitations – write these phrases on the board, read them out with suitable facial expressions, and elicit meanings:

Ja gern.   Ja, das mag ich.
Nein danke, das ist langweilig.
Nein, das mag ich nicht.

1 Hör zu und lies. 1.3a/Y7 1.3a/Y8

Listening/Reading. Before playing the recording, tell the class that you will want to know afterwards what it is about. Pupils listen and follow the dialogue in their books.

– *Hallo Peter. Hast du am Samstag Zeit? Möchtest du Fußball spielen?*
– *Nein, das mag ich nicht.*
– *Hm … Möchtest du in die Disko gehen?*
– *Nein danke, das ist langweilig!*
– *Möchtest du ins Kino gehen?*
– *Ja, gern!*
– *Wann treffen wir uns?*
– *Hm … Um sieben Uhr?*
– *Ja, gut. Tschüs, bis Samstag!*

2 Finde Stefanies Frage für jede Antwort. (AT 3/4) 4.6a/Y7

Reading. Pupils scan through the dialogue in order to find the question that goes with each of four answers. Elicit the meanings of the questions and answers.

ECHO-Detektiv: Möchtest du ... ? = *Would you like ... ?*   4.5b/Y8

Pupils could practise this question form by pretending to ask you out – encourage more confident learners to demonstrate possible questions. You could start by revealing questions with the infinitives missing, and asking pupils to supply them.

Aussprache: o / ö (AT 1/)   4.1/Y7

Listening. Pupils note down which sound each of the words has. You could then display the words on the board/OHT, and chorus them with the class. You may wish initially to show pupils all the words, without any umlauts, and get them to add an umlaut where they have heard one.

1 *möchtest*
2 *hör zu*
3 *rot*
4 *zwölf*
5 *orange*

29

Suggestion
Use this, or a similar, tongue twister for further practice of the two sounds:

Oma möchte zwölf rote Hosen.

3 Schreib die Fragen auf. (AT 4/3)
4.6a/Y7 4.5b/Y8

Writing. Pupils form questions using *möchtest du?* with an infinitive, based on the four pictures. Remind weaker pupils to think carefully about which infinitive they need.

4 Partnerarbeit: Mach vier Dialoge. (AT 2/3)   1.3b/Y7 1.3b/Y8

Speaking. Pupils work in pairs. They practise just the first part of arranging to go out – when to meet will be introduced later. Encourage them to turn down their partner's first few suggestions, and to use the full range of language in the Key Language box. They could work with a number of different partners.

Starter 2   4.1/Y7

Aim
To practise key sounds from the language of this unit.

Write some or all of these tongue twisters on the board or an OHT. Start by practising them with the whole class, to clarify any pronunciation issues. Pairs can then work together to refine their accuracy and speed. Afterwards, ask for nominees/volunteers to demonstrate their skills to the class.

Am vierten November wird Vati vierundvierzig.
Monika möchte mit Michael Musik machen.
Hast du um zwanzig vor zwölf Zeit?
Susi spricht Spanisch und spielt in der Sporthalle.
Möchtest du Öl aus Österreich?

5 Hör zu und füll die Tabelle aus. (1–3) (AT 1/4)   1.1/Y7 1.1/Y8

Listening. Pupils listen to the recording and note brief answers in German to show the day, activity and time of each arrangement heard. Remind them to focus on picking out the details needed, and not to worry about extra words. Challenge more able pupils to see what they can understand on a first hearing. Answers can firstly be jotted down in abbreviated form. Less confident learners could listen for just one specific item each time the tape is repeated.

1 – Hallo, Viktor. Hast du am Samstag
    Zeit? Möchtest du Fußball spielen?
  – Ja, gern.
  – Wann treffen wir uns?
  – Um zehn Uhr?
  – Ja, gut. Tschüs, bis Samstag.
  – Tschüs.
2 – Hallo, Julia. Hast du am Freitag Zeit? Möchtest du
    in die Disko gehen?
  – Ja, das mag ich!
  – Wann treffen wir uns?
  – Um sechs Uhr dreißig?
  – Ja, prima. Bis dann.
  – Tschüs, bis dann.
3 – Hallo Nina, wie geht's?
  – Gut danke. Und dir?

 30

*– Auch gut, danke. Hast du am Sonntag Zeit?
  Möchtest du in die Stadt gehen?*
– Nein, das ist langweilig.
– Möchtest du Tennis spielen?
– Ja, gern!
– Wann treffen wir uns? Um elf Uhr?
– Ja, gut. Bis Sonntag um elf Uhr.
– Tschüs, bis dann.

Answers

	Tag?	Was?	Wann?
Viktor	Sa.	Fußball	10.00
Julia	Fr.	Disko	6.30
Nina	So.	Tennis	11.00

6 Richtig oder falsch? Sieh deine Notizen von Aufgabe 5 an. (AT 3/2) `2.1/Y7`

Reading. Pupils use their answers from the previous listening exercise to decide whether each statement is true or false. To help them, ensure that the correct answers from the previous exercise are jotted up on the board as a reference. After discussing the answers, ask pupils for comments about the word order in the statements. Confident learners could then re-write the false statements correctly, with the verb as second idea.

Answers
1 Richtig
2 Falsch (Freitag)
3 Falsch (Tennis)
4 Falsch (6.30)
5 Richtig

ECHO-Detektiv `4.4/Y8`

This panel explains the 'verb as second idea' rule. With a more able class, you may wish to spend time developing this issue, perhaps looking at some examples together or getting volunteers to stand at the front, each holding up a card with one word of a sentence, to be arranged in the correct order by the rest of the class. Pupils can then write or say sentences of their own.

7 Lies die SMS-Texte. Schreib sie in der richtigen Reihenfolge auf. (AT 3/3, AT4/2) `2.1/Y7`

Reading. Pupils work out the correct order of the text messages, and write them out. More able pupils could study the texts for one minute in pairs and then try to reconstruct the conversation with their books shut, before going back to check the answers.

Answers
e – Hi! Möchtest du am Samstag in die Stadt gehen?
c – Nein, das ist langweilig.
a – Hm, okay. Möchtest du schwimmen gehen?
g – Ja, gern!
b – Wann treffen wir uns?
f – Um elf Uhr?
d – Tschüs, bis dann!

8 Schreib Dialog 1 oder 2 und lern ihn auswendig. Du kannst ihn in der Klasse vortragen. (AT 4/4) `1.4b/Y8`

Writing. Pupils use the prompts given to write a dialogue for making arrangements to go out. Remind them to use the Key Language boxes and examples in this unit for support. Pairs could then rehearse and perform one of their dialogues on tape or to the class – encourage appropriate expression, and the use of extra words and opinions.

Plenary `4.5b/Y8`

Aim
To focus on the difference between *ich möchte* and *ich mag*.

Write the two sentences below on the board or an OHT. Ask for volunteers to translate them, and elicit the difference between the two forms of the same irregular verb, *mögen*. Have they heard of the conditional? Then give them pairs of sentences (e.g. I like playing tennis, I'd like to play tennis) to translate into (or from) German.

Ich mag Pommes Frites essen.
Ich möchte Pommes Frites essen.

Learning targets

- Understanding information about an adventure sports centre
- Using *man kann* to say what activities there are

Key framework objectives

4.5/Y7	Language – (b) modal verbs
2.1/Y8	Reading – authentic materials
3.2/Y8	Culture – (b) customs/ traditions
5.2	Strategies – memorising

Grammar

- Modal verbs
- *Man kann* + infinitive
- *Ich mag* + infinitive

Key language

Man kann …
Kann man … ?
Ich mag …
Basketball spielen
Kanu fahren
klettern
Mountainbike fahren
schwimmen
segeln
Tennis spielen
Tischtennis spielen
Volleyball spielen
Wildwasser fahren
windsurfen

High-frequency words

ich
mag
man
kann
fahren
spielen
auf
in
im

English

Letters of enquiry
Formal language

Citizenship

Getting information for a visit to another country

Resources

CD 2, tracks 31–32
Workbooks A and B, p.36
Arbeitsblatt 4.7, p. 64
Echo Elektro 1 TPP, Express
Mod 4 5.1–5.5

Starter 1
5.2

Aim

To encourage pupils to pay close attention to language and content when reading a text.

Memory test: give pupils 30 seconds to look at the *Abenteuerzentrum* webpage on page 62. Tell them you will be testing their memory of what they have seen and what they have managed to pick up from the text. When they have closed their books, ask them about the text. What kind of text was it? How do they know? What is it advertising? Who might it be aimed at? How does it try to encourage customers? What German words can they remember for activities available at the centre? Collate their answers on the board, and look at the text together.

1 Hör zu und lies. Finde die richtigen Wörter für die Fotos. (AT 3/2)
2.1/Y8 5.6

Reading. Pupils listen to the recording and read through the website text. They then find the correct highlighted word for each photo on the webpage. They should look up any they cannot guess.

Suggestion

Exploit the text further by asking pupils to read it aloud in pairs, concentrating on intonation and expression – they should swap readers each time they come to a punctuation mark. Alternatively, pairs could use it for a 'reading race' – one partner starts reading aloud; when he/she reaches the second exclamation mark, his/her partner also starts reading, and tries to catch up before the end of the text.

> *Was ist dein Lieblingssport?*
> *Kommt zum Abenteuerzentrum Spitzberg!*
> *Hier in den Bergen kann man Mountainbike fahren – toll, aber schwierig! Man kann auch auf dem Spitzberg gut klettern, und richtige Abenteurer können dort Wildwasser fahren! Auf dem See kann man Kanu*

31

fahren, segeln oder windsurfen. Natürlich kann man auch schwimmen gehen. Abends oder bei schlechtem Wetter kann man mit neuen Freunden in der Sporthalle Tennis oder Tischtennis spielen. Magst du Teamsport? Volleyball- und Basketballplätze sind auch da.

Answers

1 schwimmen
2 segeln
3 Wildwasser fahren
4 Kanu fahren
5 klettern
6 windsurfen
7 Mountainbike fahren

2 Wo kann man das machen? Finde die Antworten im Text. (AT 3/3) `2.2a/Y8`

Reading. Pupils identify the location where each person would be able to do the sport they like, using the website text. Elicit from the class the meaning of *ich mag*, and the fact that it is used here with an infinitive at the end of the sentence.

Follow-up reading, translation and writing activities can be found in the Introduction on pages 9–10.

Answers

1 auf dem See
2 auf dem Spitzberg
3 auf dem See
4 in der Sporthalle
5 auf dem See

3 Finde im Text die Wörter unten. `2.1/Y7`

Reading. Pupils look in the website text for the German equivalent of English expressions.

Answers

1 bei schlechtem Wetter
2 toll, aber schwierig
3 mit neuen Freunden
4 richtige Abenteurer
5 natürlich
6 in den Bergen

ECHO-Detektiv: Modal verbs – *mag* and *kann* `4.5b/Y7`

After looking at this grammar panel with pupils, you could give them further sentences using these structures to translate from German to English, or, with more confident learners, also from English into German.

4 Partnerarbeit: Stell Fragen über das Abenteuerzentrum Spitzberg. (AT 2/3) `4.5b/Y7`

Speaking. Pairs use the pictures as prompts for questions and answers about the sports available.

Starter 2 `4.5b/Y7 4.5b/Y8`

Aim

To reinforce *man kann* plus infinitive.

Write these three locations on the board:

Kantine
Sporthalle
Bergen

Read out the ten statements below, and perhaps other similar ones, with a pause between each. Pupils listen and, working with a partner, decide in which of the locations the activity takes place, writing the relevant word, or its first letter, on a mini-whiteboard or piece of paper, and holding it up for you to see. Get them to keep a tally of how many they get right. Afterwards, ask pupils what they can tell you about the word order of the statements (verb as second idea, infinitive at end of each).

Hier kann man Tennis spielen.
Hier kann man Volleyball lernen.
Hier kann man Orangensaft trinken.
Hier kann man Mountainbike fahren.
Hier kann man Volleyball spielen.
Hier kann man klettern.
Hier kann man Kekse essen.
Hier kann man Basketball spielen.
Hier kann man wandern.
Hier kann man Chips essen.

5 Was sagt Peter? Hör zu und füll die Lücken aus. (1–8) (AT 1/4) `1.1/Y7 1.1/Y8`

Listening. Pupils listen to Peter talking about his forthcoming trip to the *Abenteuerzentrum*, and find the correct word for each gap in the written statements. Challenge more able pupils to see what they can understand on the first hearing.

Ich fahre in den Osterferien zum Abenteurzentrum Spitzberg. Das ist wirklich super! Ich mag Wildwasserfahren und klettern. Man kann auch windsurfen – ich kann gut windsurfen, ich finde es toll! Tja, was mache ich noch? Ach ja, man kann Mountainbike fahren, und abends kann man in der Sporthalle Volleyball spielen. Ich mag Schwimmen nicht – ich finde es langweilig. 🔘 **32**

Answers
1 klettern
2 windsurfen
3 kann
4 fahren
5 man
6 spielen
7 mag
8 nicht

5 Lies den Brief. Was ist das auf Deutsch? (AT 3/3)   2.2a/Y7

Reading. Pupils look through Stefanie's letter and pick out the German phrases to match the English translations given. Before they do so, elicit first impressions of the type and content of this text.

Answers
1 Ich mag Mountainbike fahren.
2 Ich klettere sehr gern.
3 Sehr geehrte Damen und Herren!
4 Können Sie mir bitte helfen?
5 Kann man auch Kanu fahren?

Suggestion   3.2b/Y8

Write the words *du* and *Sie* on the board. Discuss with pupils the difference between them, if you have not previously done so. Elicit from the class which form is used in the letter, and why. Ask them for other evidence that this is a formal letter (*Sehr geehrte Damen und Herren, Ihre*), and what the English equivalents would be. Discuss with pupils different letter writing customs in England and Germany and also forms of address.

6 Schreib einen Brief ans Abenteuerzentrum Spitzberg. (AT 4/3–4)   2.5/Y7 2.5/Y8

Writing. Pupils write a similar letter of enquiry. Less confident learners can follow the writing frame given in the Pupil's Book, and take ideas from Stefanie's letter to fill the gaps. Others should be encouraged to add extra sentences of their own, including further opinions.

Plenary   4.2/Y7

Aim

To review the language for adventure activities.

Charades: ask a volunteer to mime one of the activities mentioned on the webpage in this unit. The rest of the class guess the activity (*Kann man Kanu fahren?* or just *Kanu fahren*, depending on ability). The pupil who guesses correctly does the next mime, or nominates someone else. This could be played as a timed team game. Points could be deducted for inaccurate pronunciation of cognates. You may wish to allow pupils to refer to their books.

Further mime activities can be found in the Introduction on page 10.

Lernzieltest 5.8

This is a checklist of language covered in Chapter 4. Pupils can work with the checklist in pairs to check what they have learned. Points which directly address grammar and structures are marked with a G. There is a **Lernzieltest** sheet in the Resource and Assessment File (page 67). Encourage pupils to look back at the chapter and to use the grammar section to revise what they are unclear about.

You can also use the **Lernzieltest** as an end-of-unit plenary.

Wiederholung

This is a revision page to prepare pupils for the **Kontrolle** at the end of the chapter.

Resources
CD 2, track 33

1 Hör zu. Was machen sie gern? (AT 1/3)
1.1/Y7 1.1/Y8

Listening. Pupils listen and match each speaker to the correct picture. Explain to weaker pupils that they will be hearing a continuous conversation, and must listen out for the names, which will be in the same order as they appear on the page.

– Also, Birgit, was machst du gern in
  deiner Freizeit?   33
– Ich spiele gern Federball. Das ist mein
  Lieblingssport.
– Und du, Thomas, was machst du gern?
– Ich gehe gern schwimmen, jeden Tag im Sommer.
– Gehst du gern schwimmen, Jakob?
– Nein, ich finde es zu doof. Ich gehe gern angeln.
  Das finde ich super. Es ist immer interessant.
– Was machst du gern, Elke?
– Also, Angeln finde ich schrecklich. Das ist sooo
  langweilig. Aber Fußball ist toll. Ich spiele dreimal
  pro Woche Fußball. Meine Lieblingsmannschaft ist
  Borussia Dortmund.
– Spielst du gern Fußball, Sabine?
– Nein, überhaupt nicht. Mein Lieblingssport ist
  Tennis. Möchtest du jetzt Tennis spielen?

Answers
a Thomas
b Sabine
c Birgit
d Jakob
e Elke

2 Partnerarbeit: Was machst du gern? (AT 2/2)
1.4b/Y7

Speaking. Pupils practise dialogues to revise leisure vocabulary with *gern* and identify the correct pictures.

3 Macht Lisa das gern (✓) oder nicht gern (✗)? (AT 3/3)
2.1/Y7

Reading. Pupils read the text to find out whether Lisa likes or dislikes each activity.

Answers
1 ✓ 2 ✗ 3 ✓ 4 ✓ 5 ✓ 6 ✗

4 Schreib die Sätze auf. (AT 4/2)
4.4/Y7

Writing. Pupils identify individual statements in the 'word snake', and copy them out correctly. Encourage pupils to check for capital letters.

Answers
Ich spiele gern Volleyball.
Er geht gern schwimmen.
Sie hört gern Musik.
Ich sehe gern fern.
Ich gehe gern reiten.

5 Beantworte die Fragen: Schreib einen Text über deine Freizeit. (AT 4/4)
2.4b/Y7 2.4b/Y8

Writing. Pupils use their answers to the questions to form a paragraph about their free time. Check that all the questions have been answered.

Learning targets
- Reading a letter about plans for next week
- Making plans to go out next week

Key framework objectives
1.4/Y8 Speaking – (a) classroom exchanges
2.2/Y8 Reading – (a) longer, more complex texts
5.8 Strategies – evaluating and improving

Grammar
- Present tense to talk about close future (receptive)

- Verb as second idea (revisited)
- *Möchtest du* (+ infinitive)? (revisited)

High-frequency words
am
bis
dann
gehen
gern
haben
möchtest du?
sein
spielen
wann?
was?
wie?

English
Letter-writing conventions

Resources
CD 2, tracks 34–35
Workbooks A and B, p. 37
Arbeitsblatt 4.6, p. 62

Starter 1   5.4

Aim
To practise a two-staged approach to reading a longer text – firstly scanning for gist, purpose and difficulty; then focusing on the meanings of individual words.

Vocabulary search: ask pupils to look at Julia's letter for 30 seconds. Ask them what type of text it is, who it is to and from, and for the gist of what the text is about. Then read out the following list of English words, some of which they may already know in German. After each one, pupils search through the letter to find its German equivalent, write it on a piece of paper or a mini-whiteboard, and hold it up – accept only correctly spelt versions, with capital letters for nouns. Award points to the first five (or more) correct answers each time (pupils could win points for a team or as individuals).

plans	*Pläne*
until	*bis*
the 30th of March	*den 30. März*
visit	*Besuch*
new	*neu(en)*
next	*nächste*

Hör zu und lies.   2.2a/Y8

Listening/Reading. Play the recording of Julia's letter, while pupils read along. They could then read the letter aloud in pairs – you may wish first to chorus the words with umlauts for practice.

> *Leipzig, den 30. März*
> *Liebe Nina,*
> *danke für deinen Brief. Ich habe große Pläne für deinen Besuch nächste Woche!*
>
> *Am Montag gehen wir ins Kino. Was ist dein Lieblingsfilm? Wir sehen den neuen Film von Benjamin Braun. Er ist super! Am Dienstag spielen wir mit meiner Cousine Tennis – sie spielt gut. Das ist mein Lieblingssport – hast du auch einen Lieblingssport? Am Mittwoch besuchen wir Stefanie, und am Donnerstag gehen wir in die Stadt.*
>
> *Gehst du gern in die Disko? Am Freitag haben wir eine Disko im Jugendklub. Viktor tanzt nicht sehr gut – das ist immer lustig! Man kann auch Tischfußball spielen, essen und trinken. Isst du gern Hamburger?*
>
> *Dann haben wir das Wochenende! Am Samstag gehen wir ins Konzert. Wir treffen Viktor und Peter um sieben Uhr.*
>
> *Möchtest du am Sonntag faulenzen? Ich mag fernsehen. Meine Lieblingssendung „Die Simpsons", kommt am Sonntag um achtzehn Uhr. Was ist deine Lieblingssendung?*
>
> *Bis Montag!*
> *Deine Julia*

2 Was sind die Pläne? (AT 3/4)   2.1/Y7

Reading. Pupils re-read Julia's plans, and match the correct activity to each day.

Answers
Montag – c
Dienstag – d
Mittwoch – a
Donnerstag – b
Freitag – g
Samstag – e
Sonntag – f

3 Beantworte die Fragen. (AT 3/4)   4.4/Y7

Reading. Pupils answer the comprehension questions about the letter in German. More able pupils could answer in full sentences – refer them to the **ECHO-Detektiv** panel on the use of the third person plural.

Answers
1 den neuen Film von Benjamin Braun
2 Tennis
3 Nein
4 Man kann tanzen, Tischfußball spielen und auch essen und trinken.
5 um sieben Uhr
6 faulenzen

ECHO-Detektiv: sie = *they*

This panel formalises the use of the pronoun *sie* and the third person plural verb ending.

4 Du bist Nina. Schreib einen Brief an Julia und beantworte ihre Fragen. (AT 4/4–5)   2.4b/Y7 2.4b/Y8

Writing. Pupils pick out the questions from Julia's letter (*Was ist dein Lieblingsfilm? Gehst du gern in die Disko? Isst du gern Hamburger? Möchtest du am Sonntag faulenzen? Was ist deine Lieblingssendung?*). Pretending to be Nina, they write a letter back to Julia, anticipating the planned visit and including answers to the five questions. Encourage pupils to

use Julia's letter as a model: start by looking at the structure and asking for examples of useful sentences. Note these on the board. Some pupils should be able to extend their letters by making up other details and opinions.

Starter 2   1.4a/Y8

Aim

To recap language for arranging to go out, in preparation for exercises 5 and 6.

Use a copy of **Arbeitsblatt 4.6**, a diary page, on an OHT. Cover it up. Divide the class into two teams. Explain that teams must find out on which night you are free next week, taking it in turns to ask *Möchtest du am (Montag) …?*. No team member may contribute more than once. Award one point for every correctly-phrased question (reply *Nein, ich …* if you are not free), two points for the team which discovers the free night (reply *Ja, gern* and reveal your 'diary'), and finally, a bonus point if they can then continue the conversation to make an arrangement to meet you (fill in the time and activity on your OHT). If time allows, play again, using the second 'diary page' on the OHT.

5 Was sind deine Pläne für nächste Woche? Du hast einen Tag frei. (AT 4/2)   2.4a/Y7

Writing. In preparation for exercise 6, pupils write their own imaginary diary for next week, filling each day except one with a leisure phrase from earlier in this chapter. Make sure they do not all copy the example and leave Wednesday free. They can refer back to Units 1 and 2 for ideas. Quick finishers could add extra activities, still keeping one day free, until everyone is ready. You could use an OHT copy of **Arbeitsblatt 4.6** (see Starter 2) to demonstrate.

6 Gruppenarbeit: Wer hat am (Mittwoch) auch frei? Stell Fragen in der Klasse. (AT2/4)   1.4a/Y7 1.4a/Y8

Speaking. Pupils use the example dialogues as models and aim to fill the 'free' day in their diary. Use your OHT copy of **Arbeitsblatt 4.6** to demonstrate the procedure with volunteers. It will be most realistic if pupils move around the class until they find a person who is free on the same day as them, and then arrange what to do and when to meet, writing the details into their diary page. More confident pupils should be able to use greetings, opinions and other extra language of their own.

7 Hör zu und sing mit. 5.4

Listening. After listening to and reading through the song for the first time, get pupils to work in small groups and give them two or three minutes to plan a series of relevant actions to perform whilst singing. Stronger pupils will be able to help weaker group members to understand the lines of the song. Then play the recording again, and ask all groups to perform their actions, whilst singing along.

Further ideas for exploiting the songs can be found in the Introduction on page 10.

Meine Lieblingszahl ist vierzehn.
Deine Lieblingszahl ist zwei.
Seine Lieblingszahl ist zwanzig.
Ihre Lieblingszahl ist drei.

 35

Farbe, Sport, Tier und Zahl,
Lieblingssachen überall.

Mein Lieblingssport ist Schwimmen.
Dein Lieblingssport ist Wandern.
Sein Lieblingssport ist Tennis.
Ihr Lieblingssport ist Angeln.

Farbe, Sport, Tier und Zahl.
Lieblingssachen überall.

Meine Lieblingsfarbe ist Orange.
Deine Lieblingsfarbe ist Blau.
Seine Lieblingsfarbe ist Lila.
Ihre Lieblingsfarbe ist Grau.

Farbe, Sport, Tier und Zahl.
Lieblingssachen überall.

Mein Lieblingshaustier ist eine Maus.
Dein Lieblingshaustier, eine Giraffe.
Sein Lieblingshaustier ist eine Schlange.
Ihr Lieblingshaustier ist ein Affe.

Farbe, Sport, Tier und Zahl.
Lieblingssachen überall.

Plenary 5.8

Aim

To encourage pupils to evaluate and improve the quality of written work.

Spot the mistake: write several sentences containing language from this chapter on the board or an OHT. Depending on the level of the group, the sentences should each contain one or more mistakes of a particular type (e.g. verb endings, word order, gender, use of umlaut and punctuation). Pupils work alone or in pairs for five minutes to identify the mistakes in each sentence, correct them, and identify the type of mistakes they are. Discuss answers (get volunteers to come up to the front and circle the mistakes) and award points for mistakes spotted and corrections.

SELF-ACCESS READING AND WRITING AT TWO LEVELS

A Reinforcement

1 Was macht Matthias gern oder nicht gern? Schreib sechs Sätze. (AT4/2)
4.4/Y7

Writing. Pupils use the information in the picture of Matthias to build sentences about his leisure likes and dislikes.

Answers
Er spielt gern Tennis.
Er geht gern angeln.
Er spielt gern Fußball.
Er geht gern reiten.
Er geht gern schwimmen.
Er spielt nicht gern Hockey.
Er spielt nicht gern Rugby.
Er geht nicht gern wandern.

2 Wie ist es richtig? Schreib die Sätze richtig aus. (AT3/2 AT4/2)
4.4/Y7

Writing. Pupils rearrange the mixed-up endings of sentences about favourite things, and copy each one out so that it makes sense.

Answers
1 Meine Lieblingsfarbe ist Grün.
2 Mein Lieblingsauto ist ein Mercedes.
3 Meine Lieblingszahl ist dreizehn.
4 Meine Lieblingsmannschaft ist Bayern München.
5 Mein Lieblingshaustier ist eine Katze.
6 Meine Lieblingsmusik ist Mozart.

3 Was passt zusammen? (AT3/2)
2.1/Y7

Reading. Pupils match each question to the correct answer.

Answers
1 b   2 d   3 e   4 c   5 a   6 f

4 Beantworte die Fragen. (AT4/2–3)
4.4/Y7

Writing. Pupils write their own answers to the six questions from the previous task.

B Extension

1 Wer mag was? Schreib die Tabelle ab und füll sie mit Häkchen (✓) aus. (AT3/3)
2.2a/Y8

Reading. Pupils read Anton's note and Karin's reply, then copy and complete the grid to show who likes what.

Answers

	Anton	Karin
Die Simpsons	✓	
Fußball	✓	
klassische Musik		✓
Windsurfen		✓
Jugendklub	✓	
Heavy Metal	✓	

2 Lies die Briefe aus Aufgabe 1 noch mal. Schreib die Sätze ab und füll die Lücken aus. (AT3/3)
4.4/Y7

Reading. Pupils re-read the letters in order to complete the sentences about Anton and Karin correctly. More able pupils should refer to the support box only to check their answers.

Answers
1 **Anton** spielt **Fußball** in der Schulmannschaft.
2 Karin **geht** gern am Wochenende windsurfen **und** Kanu fahren.
3 Anton ist sehr **schüchtern** in der **Schule**.
4 Karin ist zu **alt** für das Jugendklub.
5 Anton **hört** gern **Heavy Metal** Musik.
6 **Karin** findet **Fußball** furchtbar.
7 Anton findet Karin **toll** und **lustig**.

3 Schreib einen Brief und eine Antwort. (AT4/3–4)
2.5/Y7 2.5/Y8

Writing. Pupils invent their own scenario to write a note inviting somebody out, and either an enthusiastic acceptance, perhaps a more reluctant acceptance, or a rejection note in reply. Suggest using made up names, or their own name plus the name of a famous person. Remind them to keep to language they know, and to use the notes they have read as models.

Übungsheft A, Seite 32

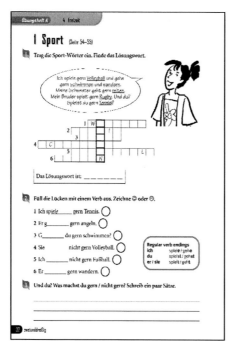

1 (AT3 Level 3, AT4 Level 1) 1 wandern **2** Tennis **3** Rugby **4** schwimmen **5** Volleyball **6** reiten

Das Lösungswort ist angeln.

2 (AT3 Level 2, AT4 Level 1) 1 Ich **spiele** gern Tennis. ☺ **2** Er **geht** gern angeln. ☺ **3 Gehst** du gern schwimmen? ☺ **4** Sie **spielt** nicht gern Volleyball. ☹ **5** Ich **spiele** nicht gern Fußball. ☹ **6** Er **geht** gern wandern. ☺

3 (AT3 Level 2–3)

Übungsheft B, Seite 32

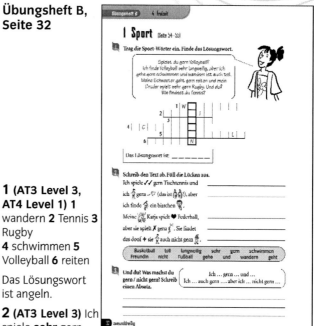

1 (AT3 Level 3, AT4 Level 1) 1 wandern **2** Tennis **3** Rugby **4** schwimmen **5** Volleyball **6** reiten

Das Lösungswort ist angeln.

2 (AT3 Level 3) Ich spiele **sehr** gern Tischtennis und ich **gehe** gern **schwimmen** (das ist **toll**!), aber ich finde **Fußball** ein bisschen **langweilig**. Meine **Freundin** Katja spielt **gern** Federball, aber sie spielt **nicht** gern **Basketball**. Sie findet das doof **und** sie **geht** auch nicht gern **wandern**.

3 (AT4 Level 3–4)

Übungsheft A, Seite 33

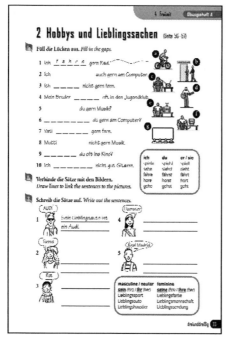

1 (AT3 Level 2, AT4 Level 1) 1 Ich **fahre** gern Rad. – a **2** Ich **spiele** auch gern am Computer. – f **3** Ich **sehe** nicht gern fern. – e **4** Mein Bruder **geht** oft in den Jugendklub. – b **5 Hörst** du gern Musik? – c **6 Spielst** du gern am Computer? – f **7** Vati **sieht** gern fern. – e **8** Mutti **hört** nicht gern Musik. – c **9 Gehst** du oft ins Kino? – g **10** Ich **spiele** nicht gut Gitarre. – d

2 (AT3 Level 2) 1 Sein Lieblingsauto ist ein Audi. **2** Ihr Lieblingssport ist Tennis. **3** Ihre Lieblingsfarbe ist Rot. **4** Ihr Lieblingshaustier ist ein Hamster. **5** Seine Lieblingsmannschaft ist Real Madrid.

3 (AT4 Level 3)

Übungsheft B, Seite 33

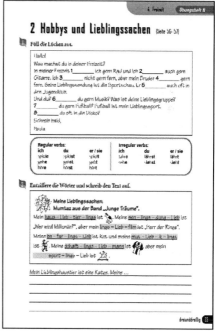

1 (AT4 Level 4) 1 fahre **2** spiele **3** sehe **4** sieht **5** geht **6** Hörst **7** Spielst **8** Gehst

2 (AT3 Level 3, AT4 Level 3) Mein **Lieblingshaustier** ist eine Katze. Meine **Lieblingssendung** ist „Wer wird Millionär?", aber mein **Lieblingsfilm** ist „Herr der Ringe". Meine **Lieblingsfarbe** ist Rot und meine **Lieblingsmusik** ist Rockmusik. Meine **Lieblingsmannschaft** ist Bayern München, aber mein **Lieblingssport** ist Tischtennis.

Übungsheft A, Seite 34

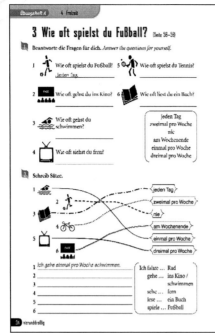

1 (AT3 Level 2, AT4 Level 1)

2 (AT4 Level 3) 1 Ich gehe einmal pro Woche schwimmen. **2** Ich spiele nie Fußball. **3** Ich lese jeden Tag ein Buch. **4** Ich fahre zweimal pro Woche Rad. **5** Ich sehe dreimal pro Woche fern. **6** Ich gehe am Wochenende ins Kino.

Übungsheft B, Seite 34

1 (AT4 Level 3) 1 Ich gehe einmal pro Woche schwimmen. **2** Wir spielen nie Fußball. **3** Ich lese jeden Tag ein Buch. **4** Ich sehe dreimal pro Woche fern. **5** Wir gehen am Wochenende ins Kino.

2 (AT3 Level 3, AT4 Level 1)
1 Lieber **2** danke
3 deinen **4** geht's
5 bin **6** spiele
7 dreimal **8** Woche
9 sportlich **10** Tag
11 schwimmen
12 Schreib **13** Deine

3 (AT3 Level 3) Dear Hakim, Thanks for your letter. How are you? I'm 14 years old and I like playing tennis. I play tennis three times a week. I'm very sporty. I go swimming every day. Write soon! Yours, Sandra

Übungsheft A, Seite 35

1 (AT4 Level 3) 1 Möchtest du am Montag ins Kino gehen? **2** Möchtest du am Dienstag Tennis spielen? **3** Möchtest du am Mittwoch in die Disko gehen? **4** Möchtest du am Donnerstag Basketball spielen? **5** Möchtest du am Freitag in die Stadt gehen?

2 (AT3 Level 2) 1 Bild 4 **2** Bild 1 **3** Bild 5 **4** Bild 4 **5** Bild 3 **6** Bild 5 **7** Bild 2

Übungsheft B, Seite 35

1 (AT4 Level 2–3)
1 Möchtest du am Freitag ins Kino gehen? – Ja, gern!
2 Möchtest du am Sonntag Tennis spielen? – Ja, wann treffen wir uns?
3 Möchtest du am Dienstag Basketball spielen? – Nein danke, das ist langweilig.
4 Möchtest du am Mittwoch in die Stadt gehen? – Ja, gern. Bis Mittwoch!
5 Möchtest du am Donnerstag Fußball spielen? – Nein, das mag ich nicht.

2 (AT4 Level 4)

● Möchtest du am Freitag in die Stadt gehen?
■ Nein danke, das ist langweilig.
● O.K., möchtest du am Samstag ins Kino gehen?
■ Nein danke, das mag ich nicht.
● Möchtest du am Mittwoch in die Disko gehen?
■ Ja, gern!
● Wann treffen wir uns?
■ Um acht Uhr.
● Bis dann! / Bis acht Uhr! / Bis Mittwoch!

**Übungsheft A,
Seite 36**

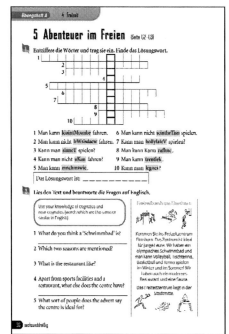

1 (AT3 Level 2, AT4 Level 2) 1 Mountainbike **2** Wildwasser **3** Tennis **4** Kanu **5** schwimmen **6** Tischtennis **7** Volleyball **8** fahren **9** klettern **10** segeln

Das Lösungswort ist Basketball.

2 (AT3 Level 4) 1 swimming pool **2** winter and summer **3** modern **4** a sauna **5** young people

**Übungsheft B,
Seite 36**

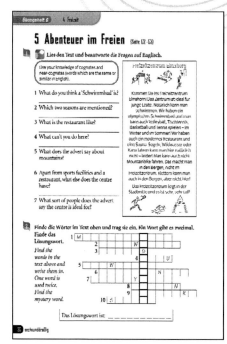

1 (AT3 Level 4) 1 swimming pool **2** winter and summer **3** modern **4** sailing, rafting, canoeing, mountain biking, climbing **5** you can go mountain biking and climbing in the mountains (but not in the leisure centre!) **6** a sauna **7** young people

2 (AT3 Level 3, AT4 Level 2) 1 Mountainbike **2** Wildwasser **3** Tennis **4** Kanu **5** schwimmen **6** Tischtennis **7** Volleyball **8** fahren **9** klettern **10** segeln

Das Lösungswort ist Basketball.

**Übungsheft A,
Seite 37**

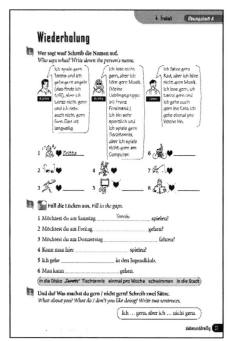

1 (AT3 Level 3) 1 Britta **2** Timo **3** Karim **4** Timo **5** Britta **6** Timo **7** Karim **8** Britta

2 (AT3 Level 2, AT4 Level 1) 1 Tennis / Tischtennis **2** in die Disko / schwimmen **3** in die Stadt **4** Tischtennis / Tennis **5** einmal pro Woche **6** schwimmen / in die Disko

3 (AT4 Level 3)

**Übungsheft B,
Seite 37**

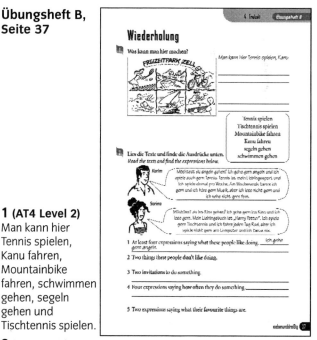

1 (AT4 Level 2)
Man kann hier Tennis spielen, Kanu fahren, Mountainbike fahren, schwimmen gehen, segeln gehen und Tischtennis spielen.

2 (AT3 Level 3)
1 *Any four of:* Ich gehe gern angeln. / Ich spiele gern Tennis. / Ich tanze gern. / Ich höre gern Musik. / Ich gehe gern ins Kino. / Ich lese gern. / Ich spiele gern Tischtennis. **2** *Any two of:* Ich lese nicht gern. / Ich sehe nicht gern fern. / Ich spiele nicht gern am Computer. / Ich tanze nie. **3** Möchtest du angeln gehen? / Möchtest du ins Kino gehen? **4** Ich spiele einmal pro Woche (Tennis). / Am Wochenende tanze ich gern. / Ich fahre jeden Tag Rad. / Ich tanze nie. **5** Tennis ist mein Lieblingssport. / Mein Lieblingsbuch ist „Harry Potter".

4 Workbooks

**Übungsheft A,
Seite 38**

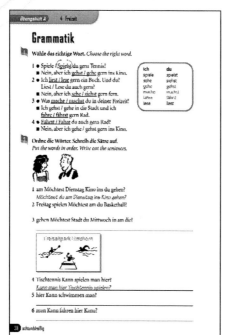

**Übungsheft B,
Seite 38**

1 (AT3 Level 3) 1 Spielst **2** gehe **3** lese, Liest **4** sehe **5** machst
6 gehe, fahre **7** Fährst **8** gehe

2 (AT4 Level 2) 1 Möchtest du am Dienstag ins Kino gehen?
2 Möchtest du am Freitag Basketball spielen? **3** Möchtest du am
Mittwoch in die Stadt gehen? **4** Kann man hier Tischtennis
spielen? **5** Kann man hier schwimmen? **6** Kann man hier Kanu
fahren?

1 (AT3 Level 3)

● **Spielst** du gern Tennis?
■ Nein, aber ich **gehe** gern ins Kino.
● Ich **lese** gern ein Buch. Und du? **Liest** du auch gern?
■ Nein, aber ich **sehe** gern fern.
● Was **machst** du in deiner Freizeit?
■ Ich **gehe** in die Stadt und ich **fahre** gern Rad.
● **Fährst** du auch gern Rad?
■ Nein, aber ich **gehe** gern ins Kino.

2 (AT4 Level 3) 1 Ihr Lieblings**auto** ist ein VW, aber **sein**
Lieblings**auto** ist ein Mercedes. **2 Ihre** Lieblings**farbe** ist Rot,
aber **seine** Lieblings**farbe** ist Grün. **3** Sein Lieblingshaustier ist
eine Katze, aber ihr Lieblingshaustier ist ein Hund. **4** Sein
Lieblingssport ist Tennis, aber ihr Lieblingssport ist Fußball.
5 Ihr Lieblingsbuch ist „Harry Potter", aber sein Lieblingsbuch
ist „Oliver Twist". **6** Seine Lieblingssendung ist „Big Brother",
aber ihre Lieblingssendung ist „Hollyoaks".

Arbeitsblatt 4.1

Das ist Tennis / Badminton

Arbeitsblatt 4.2

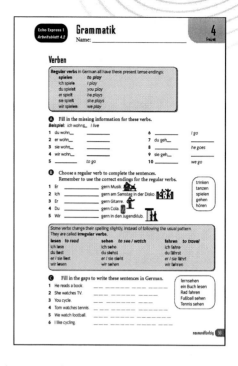

A

1 du wohnst / *you live* **2** er wohnt / *he lives* **3** sie wohnt / *she lives* **4** wir wohnen / *we live* **5** gehen **6** ich gehe **7** du gehst / *you go* **8** er geht **9** sie geht / *she goes* **10** wir gehen

B

1 hört **2** tanze **3** spielt **4** trinkst **5** gehen

C

1 Er liest ein Buch. **2** Sie sieht fern. **3** Du fährst Rad. **4** Tom sieht Tennis. **5** Wir sehen Fußball. **6** Ich fahre gern Rad.

Arbeitsblatt 4.3

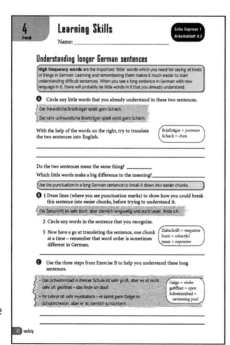

A

The friendly postman likes playing chess. The very unfriendly postman doesn't like playing chess.

B

3 The magazine is very colourful, but fairly boring and also expensive, I find.

C

The swimming pool in my school is very big, but it's not open very often – I find that stupid.

Her teacher is very musical – he likes playing the violin in the school orchestra, but he's fairly shy.

Arbeitsblatt 4.4

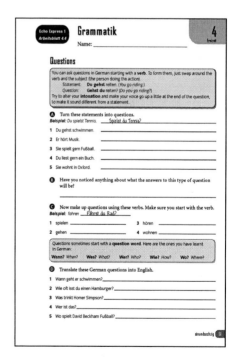

A

1 Gehst du schwimmen? **2** Hört er Musik? **3** Spielt sie gern Fußball? **4** Liest du gern ein Buch? **5** Wohnt sie in Oxford?

B

Yes or no.

D

1 When does he go swimming? **2** How often do you eat a hamburger? **3** What does Homer Simpson drink? **4** Who is that? **5** Where does David Beckham play football?

Resource and assessment file

Arbeitsblatt 4.5

Arbeitsblatt 4.6

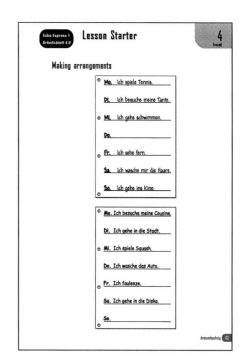

Arbeitsblatt 4.7

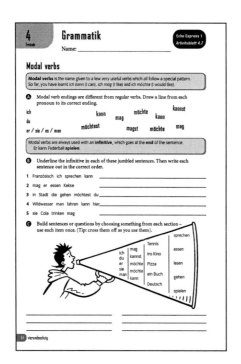

A
ich kann / mag / möchte
du kannst / magst / möchtest
er/sie/es/man kann / mag / möchte

B
1 sprechen / Ich kann Französisch sprechen.
2 essen / Er mag Kekse essen.
3 gehen / Du möchtest in die Stadt gehen.
4 fahren / Hier kann man Wildwasser fahren.
5 trinken / Sie mag Cola trinken.

C
Various possible answers

5 Mein Zuhause

Unit Learning targets	Key framework objectives	NC levels and PoS coverage	Grammar and key language	Skills
1 Wo wohnst du? (pp. 70–71) • Saying where you live • Learning to read long words	**1.1/Y7** Listening – gist and detail **1.3/Y8** Speaking – (b) using language for specific functions	NC levels 2–4 **2.2a** listen for gist **2.2d** pronunciation and intonation **2.2e** ask and answer questions **2.2f** initiate / sustain conversations **2.2k** deal with unfamiliar language **3b** sounds and writing **3c** apply grammar **3d** use a range of vocab / structures **4b** communicate in pairs etc.	*mein, dein, sein, ihr* *Wo wohnst du?* *Ich wohne in einem Dorf, in einer Stadt, in einer Großstadt, an der Küste, in den Bergen, auf dem Land.* *Ich wohne in einer Wohnung.* *Ich wohne in einem Einfamilienhaus, Doppelhaus, Reihenhaus, Bungalow.* *Wie ist deine Adresse?* *Meine Adresse ist …* *Wie ist deine Telefonnummer?* *Meine Telefonnummer ist …* *Er / Sie wohnt in …* *Seine / Ihre Adresse ist …* *Seine / Ihre Telefonnummer ist …* *Wie bitte? Langsamer, bitte.*	Reading compound words Asking for repetition
2 Mein Haus (pp. 72–73) • Saying what you do in different rooms • Using *es gibt* to say what there is	**1.5/Y8** Speaking – (a) unscripted talks **1.5/Y8** Speaking – (b) using simple idioms **4.6/Y8** Language – (b) range of negatives	NC levels 1–4 **2.2a** listen for gist **2.2b** skim and scan **2.2e** ask and answer questions **3b** sounds and writing **3c** apply grammar **3d** use a range of vocab / structures **4b** communicate in pairs etc.	*Es gibt* + accusative Indefinite article, accusative negative article, accusative Irregular verbs in 1st, 2nd, 3rd person singular: *essen, sehen, lesen, schlafen* *Mein Haus ist groß / mittelgroß / klein.* *der Garten / Balkon / Keller / Dachboden* *die Küche / Toilette* *das Wohnzimmer / Schlafzimmer / Badezimmer / Esszimmer* *Es gibt einen/keinen Garten / Balkon / Keller / Dachboden.* *Es gibt eine/keine Küche / Toilette.* *Es gibt ein/kein Wohnzimmer / Schlafzimmer / Badezimmer / Esszimmer.* *Ich höre / Er/Sie hört im Keller Musik.* *Ich spiele / Er/Sie spielt im Schlafzimmer am Computer.* *Ich koche / Er/Sie kocht in der Küche.* *Ich arbeite / Er/Sie arbeitet im Garten.* *Ich esse / Er/Sie isst im Esszimmer.* *Ich lese / Er/Sie liest im Badezimmer.* *Ich sehe / Er/Sie sieht im Wohnzimmer fern.* *Ich schlafe / Er/Sie schläft im Schlafzimmer.*	Improving pronunciation by recording and reviewing own speech Giving a presentation Looking up verbs

Unit Learning targets	Key framework objectives	NC levels and PoS coverage	Grammar and key language	Skills
3 In meinem Zimmer (pp. 74–75) • Describing your room • Understanding that the verb has to be the second idea	**4.2/Y8** Language – increasing vocabulary **4.4/Y7** Language – sentence formation	NC levels 2–4 **2.2a** listen for gist **2.2b** skim and scan **2.2g** write clearly and coherently **3b** sounds and writing **3c** apply grammar **3d** use a range of vocab / structures **4b** communicate in pairs etc.	Word order: verb as second idea Using *aber* and *und* to build complex sentences *der Schreibtisch / Kleiderschrank / Stuhl / Computer / Fernseher / Spiegel* *die Lampe / Kommode / Stereoanlage* *das Bett / Regal / Sofa* *In meinem Zimmer habe ich …* *einen Schreibtisch / Kleiderschrank / Stuhl / Computer / Fernseher / Spiegel* *eine Lampe / Kommode* *ein Bett / Regal / Sofa.* *Wie ist dein Zimmer?* *Mein Zimmer ist klein / groß / hell / dunkel / ordentlich / unordentlich.* *Sehr / ziemlich / nicht sehr*	Pronunciation Revising and improving written work
4 Wo ist es? (pp. 76–77) • Saying what is in your room • Using prepositions to describe where things are	**2.1/Y7** Reading – main points and detail **4.3/Y8** Language – gender	NC levels 2–4 **2.2a** listen for gist **2.2b** skim and scan **2.2c** respond appropriately **2.2e** ask and answer questions **3b** sounds and writing **3c** apply grammar **3d** use a range of vocab / structures **4b** communicate in pairs etc.	Prepositions with the dative Definite article, dative *Wo ist die Katze?* *Die Katze ist …* *auf dem Regal / unter dem Bett / in dem Kleiderschrank / neben dem Stuhl / zwischen dem Bett und dem Schreibtisch / hinter dem Computer.* *Wo ist der Bleistift?* *Der Bleistift ist auf / unter / in / neben / hinter dem Buch.*	Describing a picture
5 Liebes Traumhaus-Team (pp. 78–79) • Saying what you don't like about your room • Recognising sentences about the past	**2.3/Y8** Reading – text features: emotive **4.5/Y8** Language – (a) range of verb tenses (past)	NC levels 4–5 **2.1d** previous knowledge **2.2a** listen for gist **2.2b** skim and scan **2.2c** respond appropriately **2.2e** ask and answer questions **3b** sounds and writing **4b** communicate in pairs etc. **4g** language for a range of purposes	Recognising references to the past (*war, hatte, letzte Woche*, etc.) *Ich kann keine CDs spielen.* *Meine Freundinnen können (nicht) bei mir übernachten.* *Mein Zimmer war vorher dunkel / klein / unordentlich.* *Ich hatte vorher keinen Platz für meine Sachen.* *Der Kleiderschrank war sehr klein.* *Ich hatte keinen Fernseher und keinen Computer.* *Jetzt ist mein Zimmer hell / ordentlich.* *Jetzt habe ich viel Platz.* *Ich habe einen Computer / Fernseher / CD-Spieler / ein Sofabett.*	Listening for specific information Reading a longer text Unscripted speech
Lernzieltest und Wiederholung (pp. 80–81) • Pupils' checklist and practice test		NC levels 3–4 **2.2b** skim and scan **2.2c** respond appropriately **3c** apply grammar **3d** use a range of vocab / structures		

Unit Learning targets	Key framework objectives	NC levels and PoS coverage	Grammar and key language	Skills
Mehr (pp. 82–83) • Extension material	**2.2/Y8** Reading – (b) personal response to text **2.5/Y8** Writing – using researched language **5.5** Strategies – reference materials	**NC levels** 4–5 **2.1d** previous knowledge **2.1e** use reference materials **2.2a** listen for gist **2.2b** skim and scan **2.2c** respond appropriately **2.2e** ask and answer questions **2.2j** adapt previously-learnt language **3d** use a range of vocab / structures	Consolidation of language from Units 1–5	Reading a longer text for gist and detail Dictionary skills Unscripted speech
Extra (pp. 108–109) • Self-access reading and writing at two levels		**NC levels** 2–3 **2.2b** skim and scan **2.2c** respond appropriately **2.2e** ask and answer questions **3c** apply grammar **3d** use a range of vocab / structures		

Learning targets
- Saying where you live
- Learning to read long words

Key framework objectives
1.1/Y7 Listening – gist and detail
1.3/Y8 Speaking – (b) using language for specific functions

Grammar
- *mein, dein, sein, ihr*

Key language
Wo wohnst du?
Ich wohne …
in einem Dorf / in einer Stadt / in einer Großstadt / an der Küste / in den Bergen / auf dem Land.
in einem Bungalow / Einfamilienhaus / Doppelhaus / Reihenhaus
in einer Wohnung
Wie ist deine Adresse?
Meine Adresse ist …
Wie ist deine Telefonnummer?
Meine Telefonnummer ist …
Cardinal numbers 0–99
Wie bitte?
Langsamer, bitte.

High-frequency words
Cardinal numbers 0–99
an
auf
deine
du
in
meine
wie?
wie bitte?
wo?
wohnen

Pronunciation
Question intonation

Mathematics
Telephone numbers, addresses

Citizenship
The physical geography of German-speaking countries
The formats of postal addresses and phone numbers in German-speaking countries

Resources
CD 3, tracks 2–5
Workbooks A and B, p.42
Arbeitsblatt 5.1 Ex A, p. 80
Echo Elektro 1 TPP, Express
Mod 5 1.1–1.6

Starter 1   4.2/Y8

Aim
To build confidence in recognising and using compound nouns.

Present **Arbeitsblatt 5.1 Ex A** as an OHT or make individual photocopies for pupils. Pupils form as many compound nouns as they can from the fragments provided. Explain that each compound must be meaningful, i.e. pupils should be able to give an English translation if asked. Set a time limit, then gather compounds around the class and write them on the board.

To stretch more able pupils, you could then present some new compounds and elicit their meaning, e.g. *Lieblingsbruder, Computersendung, Lieblingssportsendung.*

1 Was passt zusammen? Hör zu und überprüfe es. (AT 3/2)   4.2/Y8

Reading/Listening. Pupils match the speech bubbles to the photos. They check their own answers by listening to the recording.

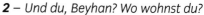

1 – *Wo wohnst du, Carsten?*
  – *Ich wohne in einer Großstadt.*
2 – *Und du, Beyhan? Wo wohnst du?*
  – *Ich wohne in einer Stadt.*
3 – *Olaf, wo wohnst du?*
  – *Ich wohne an der Küste.*
4 – *Und Carola? Wo wohnst du?*
  – *Ich wohne in Thalkirch in der Schweiz, in den Bergen.*
5 – *Und du, Heiko? Wo wohnst du?*
  – *Ich? Also, ich wohne in einem Dorf.*
6 – *Maren, wohnst du an der Küste?*
  – *Nein. Ich wohne auf dem Land.*

Answers
1 b **2** c **3** d **4** f **5** a **6** e

2 Partnerarbeit. (AT 2/3) `1.4b/Y7`

Speaking. Pupils work together in pairs to create dialogues based on the teenagers and locations shown in exercise 1.

3 Hör zu. Was passt zusammen? (1–5) (AT 1/2) `1.1/Y7`

Listening. Pupils listen to the recording and match the house pictures to the speakers. In preparation, look at the pictures with the class and elicit what the house types are called in English. You could go on to talk about which types of houses are most common where pupils live and point out that in Germany it is much more common to live in a flat than it is in Britain.

> 1 – *Wo wohnst du, Birgit?*
> – *Ich wohne in einem Doppelhaus.*
> 2 – *Wo wohnst du, Alex?*
> – *Ich wohne in einem Reihenhaus.*
> 3 – *Wo wohnst du, Bastian?*
> – *Ich wohne in einem Bungalow.*
> 4 – *Wo wohnst du, Maja?*
> – *Ich wohne in einer Wohnung.*
> 5 – *Wo wohnst du, Tim?*
> – *Ich wohne in einem Einfamilienhaus.*

 3

Answers
1 c   2 a   3 e   4 d   5 b

ECHO-Tipp: Long words `5.4`

This panel builds pupils' confidence in tackling long words. What do pupils think the individual elements of *Ein + familien + haus* mean? Can they guess what *Doppel-* means in *Doppelhaus*? See if pupils can think of any further compound nouns they have met in the course so far.

4 Wo wohnen sie? Schreib Sätze. (AT 4/3) `4.4/Y7`

Writing. Pupils write sentences in the third person singular in response to the picture cues. Draw pupils' attention to the sentence structure (type of house, then location).

➕ More able pupils can write and record short dialogues based on the picture cues, inventing names for the characters and expressing opinions, e.g.

A: *Wo wohnst du, Lisa?*
B: *Ich wohne in einem Reihenhaus, an der Küste. Das finde ich toll!*
etc.

Starter 2 `4.2/Y7`

Aim
To revise numbers 0 to 99.

Write six phone numbers on an OHT, each consisting of three two-digit numbers, e.g.

Max	24 10 39
Inge	92 23 48
Susi	23 63 55
Heiko	42 23 24
Hanna	94 23 11
Lexi	82 87 77

Pupils work together in pairs. Partner A sits facing the front of the class; partner B faces the back. When you call out a name, Partner A dictates the telephone number in German to partner B. Partner B writes it on paper or a mini-whiteboard and passes it to partner A to check (or holds it up for you to check). After three numbers, the partners swap seats.

5 Hör zu und lies. `1.1/Y7 1.3a/Y8`

Listening. Pupils listen to the recording and follow the dialogue in their books. Elicit from pupils the differences in address and phone number format in German (road name before number; telephone numbers read as two-digit numbers). In addition, elicit the phrases which are used in the conversation to get the speaker to repeat something.

> – *Wie ist deine Adresse, Julia?*
> – *Meine Adresse ist Gartenstraße 50.*
> – *Wie bitte?*
> – *Gartenstraße 50.*
> – *O.K. ... Und wie ist deine Telefonnummer?*
> – *Meine Telefonnummer ist 80 70 95.*
> – *Langsamer, bitte.*
> – *80 70 95.*
> – *Danke.*

 4

ECHO-Tipp `1.3b/Y8`

This panel introduces strategies for improving face-to-face communication. Practise this with the whole class by chorusing *Wie bitte?* and *Langsamer, bitte.*

6 Hör zu. Ergänze das Adressbuch. (AT 1/4) `1.1/Y7 1.1/Y8`

Listening. Pupils listen to the recording and note the missing numbers for the address book.

1 – Kati, wie ist deine Adresse?
  – Ahornweg 71.
  – Ahornweg 71 ... Und deine
    Telefonnummer?
  – Meine Telefonnummer ist 42 29 93.
  – Wie bitte?
  – 42 29 93.

2 – Wie ist deine Adresse, Alex?
  – Meine Adresse ist Lindenring 23.
  – 23?
  – Ja. Und meine Telefonnummer ist 45 03 42
  – Langsamer, bitte.
  – 45 03 42. O.K?
  – Ja, danke.

3 – Und du, Ulli? Wie ist deine Adresse?
  – Hafenstraße 90.
  – Hafenstraße ... 90.
  – Ja.
  – Und deine Telefonnummer?
  – Meine Telefonnummer ist 41 92 78.
  – Wie bitte?
  – 41 92 78.
  – O.K, danke.
  – Bitte.

4 – Hi, Jana!
  – Hi!
  – Du, wie ist deine Adresse?
  – Meine Adresse? Adlerweg 89!
  – Ach, ja, natürlich! ... Adlerweg 89.
  – Ja. Und meine Telefonnummer ist ...
  – 35 23 65!
  – Richtig! 35 23 65.

Answers

a 71   b 29   c 23   d 45   e 90   f 78   g 89
h 65

7 Partnerarbeit. (AT 2/3–4) 1.4b/Y7 1.3b/Y8

Speaking. Pupils work in pairs, asking each other where they live, their address and phone number. In order to add a feeling of authenticity, pupils could make up a mock German address before starting, using, for example, *Straße* with a noun or adjective from elsewhere in the book (*Braunstraße 45*, etc). Pupils could write down the information they hear and then confirm it with their partner. Remind pupils to use *Wie bitte?* and *Langsamer, bitte* if they have difficulty understanding what their partner says. Encourage them to start using these expressions spontaneously in class. If time permits, pupils could exchange this information with several classmates.

A further variation on pairwork can be found in the Introduction on page 10.

8 Schreib einen Text über deinen Partner / deine Partnerin. (AT 4/3–4)
4.4/Y8

Writing. Pupils write a short text in the third person singular about their partner, saying what their name is, where they live and giving their address and phone number. Encourage them to use *und* at least once to join statements together. Draw their attention to the change in verb forms from exercise 7 to exercise 8 and the use of *seine* and *ihre*.

More able pupils can include any other relevant language they have learned, e.g. favourite things, age, etc. They can build more complex sentences using *und* and *aber*.

Plenary
4.4/Y8

Aims

To improve pupils' ability to adapt and extend sentences.

To improve pupils' fluency and confidence in unscripted speech.

Divide the class into groups of 4–6 pupils. Give each group the same simple sentence, e.g. *Ich wohne in einer Wohnung.* Each group member in turn says the sentence, changing one part of it:

A: *Ich wohne in einer Wohnung.*
B: *Ich wohne in einem Haus.*
C: *Sie wohnt in einem Haus.*
etc.

Demonstrate with the whole class first how the activity works. Pupils then practise in groups. After one to two minutes, stop the groups and ask each one for its latest version of the sentence. If time permits, you could then give the groups another sentence to work with.

Learning targets
- Saying what you do in different rooms
- Using *es gibt* to say what there is

Key framework objectives
1.5/Y8 Speaking – (a) unscripted talks
1.5/Y8 Speaking – (b) using simple idioms
4.6/Y8 Language – (b) range of negatives

Grammar
- *Es gibt* + accusative
- *einen / eine / ein* (accusative)
- *keinen / keine / kein* (accusative)
- Irregular verbs: *essen, sehen, lesen, schlafen*

Key language
der Garten / Balkon / Keller / Dachboden
die Küche / Toilette / Garage
das Wohnzimmer / Esszimmer / Badezimmer / Schlafzimmer
Es gibt einen/keinen Garten / Balkon / Keller / Dachboden.
Es gibt eine/keine Küche / Toilette / Eingangshalle.
Es gibt ein/kein Wohnzimmer / Schlafzimmer / Badezimmer / Esszimmer.
Mein Haus ist groß / mittelgroß / klein.

High-frequency words
es gibt	*da*
ein	*manchmal*
kein	*dort*
wo?	*leider*

ziemlich	*aber*
sehr	*mein, dein*
auch	*in, im*
er, sie	

Pronunciation
Improving pronunciation by recording and reviewing own speech

Resources
CD 3, tracks 6–8
Workbooks A and B, p.43
Arbeitsblatt 5.1 Ex B, p. 80
Arbeitsblatt 5.2, p. 81
Flashcards 70–80
Echo Elektro 1 TPP, Express Mod 5 2.1–2.8

Starter 1
5.4

Aims
To introduce the new vocabulary needed for this lesson.
To build confidence in inferring the meanings of unknown words.

Prepare an OHT with the names of the rooms shown on **Arbeitsblatt 5.1, Ex B**:

die Garage	*das Badezimmer*
der Garten	*das Esszimmer*
die Toilette	*das Schlafzimmer*
der Balkon	*das Wohnzimmer*
der Keller	*der Dachboden*
die Küche	

Distribute photocopies, one copy per pair of pupils. Reveal the rooms on the OHT one word at time, reading the word aloud. Pupils speculate which room it is, and hold up the letter of the room on paper or a mini-whiteboard.

---

1 Hör zu. Welches Zimmer ist das? (1–11) (AT 2/1)
1.1/Y7

Listening. Pupils listen to the recording and find the matching rooms in their books.

Draw attention particularly to the *z* in *Zimmer*.

1 *das Esszimmer*
2 *das Wohnzimmer*
3 *das Badezimmer*
4 *der Dachboden*
5 *der Garten*
6 *der Keller*
7 *die Garage*
8 *die Küche*
9 *der Balkon*
10 *das Schlafzimmer*
11 *die Toilette*

6

Answers
1 h   2 f   3 g   4 a   5 k   6 j   7 i   8 e
9 c   10 b   11 d

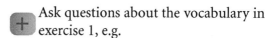

Ask questions about the vocabulary in exercise 1, e.g.

- How many cognates are there?
- Find three masculine/two feminine/four neuter nouns.
- Find a noun with four syllables.

2 **Lies die E-Mails und sieh dir das Bild in Aufgabe 1 an. Ist das Viktors oder Stefanies Haus? (AT 3/4)** `2.2a/Y8 2.3/Y8`

Reading. Pupils read the two emails and decide who the house in exercise 1 belongs to. Draw pupils' attention to the **ECHO-Detektiv** panel on page 72, where *es gibt* and the negative article *kein* are explained. Follow-up reading, translation and writing activities can be found in the Introduction on pages 9–10.

> **Answer**
> Viktor

R Read out some true/false sentences to check pupils' comprehension, e.g. *Richtig oder falsch? Viktors Haus ist klein.*

+ Discuss features of the texts which pupils can use to bring authenticity to their own writing, e.g. *Das ist schade; natürlich; leider; Was sonst?*

3 **Was gibt es? Was gibt es nicht? Füll die Tabelle aus. (AT 1/4)** `1.2/Y8`

Listening. Pupils listen to the interviews and note which rooms there are and aren't in each speaker's house. Before doing the exercise, look back at the emails in question 2 and elicit which word is used to say that there **isn't** something in a house.

1 – *Welche Zimmer gibt es in deinem Haus, Peter?* 🔘 **7**
 – *Also … es gibt ein Esszimmer … Es gibt ein Wohnzimmer. Es gibt eine Küche, ein Badezimmer und drei Schlafzimmer.*
 – *Und was hast du nicht in deinem Haus?*
 – *Wir haben keinen Keller, und keinen Dachboden, aber das ist nicht schlimm!*
2 – *Hallo, Julia. Welche Zimmer gibt es in deinem Haus?*
 – *Hallo. Es gibt eine Küche, es gibt ein Esszimmer … es gibt vier Schlafzimmer … es gibt einen Keller – und es gibt drei Badezimmer.*
 – *Drei Badezimmer!*
 – *Ja. Mein Haus ist groß.*
 – *Und was gibt es nicht?*
 – *Es gibt keine Garage und keinen Balkon, aber sonst gibt es alles.*

> **Answers**
> Peter: ✓ h, f, e, g, b; ✗ j
> Julia: ✓ e, h, b, j, g; ✗ c

> **ECHO-Detektiv: es gibt – *there is / there are*** `4.6b/Y8`
> This panel explains how to say that there is/isn't something in German, using *es gibt*. If you wish, refer pupils to the **Grammatik** on page 124 for more information and practice.

4 **Halte einen Vortrag. (AT 2/4)** `1.5a+b/Y8 4.6b/Y8`

Speaking. Pupils prepare and give a presentation about their own home. Give them the option of describing their 'dream home' instead. Pupils' presentations could be recorded (audio or video) and played back to review and improve their pronunciation. They could also be encouraged to use phrases from the emails in exercise 2 in order to make the speech sound more natural.

Suggestion

ICT Pupils use a graphics or DTP application to produce a plan of their ideal home, labelling the rooms in German.

> ## Starter 2 `4.5a/Y7`
>
> **Aims**
> To revise verbs for leisure activities from Chapter 4.
> To introduce new verbs for leisure activities.
> To promote fluency and confidence in speech.
>
> Present these sentences on an OHT. The sentences marked * are new:
>
> *Ich höre Musik.*
> *Ich koche.* *
> *Ich arbeite im Garten.* *
> *Ich esse.*
> *Ich lese.*
> *Ich schlafe.* *
>
> Elicit the meanings from the class, using mime or visuals to show the meanings of the new verbs. Ask pupils *Was machst du?*, prompting them as necessary to respond *Ich lese, Ich höre Musik*, etc. After a few responses, play 'throw-and-catch' with a soft toy or ball. Throw it to a pupil and ask him/her: *Was machst du?*. He/She must respond quickly, then throw the toy/ball to another pupil, who also responds, and so on round the class. (In a boisterous class, you may prefer pupils simply to name another pupil.) Alternatively, divide the class into two or three large groups and give each group a toy/ball.

5 Was passt zusammen? Hör zu und überprüfe es. (AT 1/2)   4.5a/Y7

Listening. Pupils listen and match the sentences to the cartoon characters. You could then elicit the meanings of the verbs. *Ich lese, ich sehe fern, ich höre Musik, ich esse* and *ich spiele am Computer* are known from earlier chapters; *ich koche, ich arbeite* and *ich schlafe* are unknown. Can pupils infer the meanings of the new verbs from context and the illustrations?

1 – *Was machst du, Wolfi?*
   – *Ich spiele im Schlafzimmer am Computer.*

2 – *Was machst du, Mutti?*
   – *Ich schlafe im Schlafzimmer.*

3 – *Oma! Was machst du, Oma?*
   – *Ich koche in der Küche.*

4 – *Und was machst du, Opa?*
   – *Ich arbeite im Garten.*

5 – *Was machst du, Vati?*
   – *Ich esse im Esszimmer.*

6 – *Ulrike! ... Ulrike! ... Was machst du, Ulrike?*
   – *Ich lese ... im Badezimmer.*

7 – *Und was machst du, Onkel Fritz?*
   – *Ich sehe im Wohnzimmer fern.*

8 – *Tante Frieda! Was machst du?*
   – *Ich höre im Keller Musik.*

Answers

1 b	2 h	3 c	4 d	5 f	6 f	7 g	8 a

6 Was machst du in jedem Zimmer? Mach Notizen. (AT 4/2)   4.2/Y7

Writing. Pupils make notes on what they do in each of the rooms from exercise 5, in preparation for the pairwork speaking exercise 7. You could brainstorm ideas with the class, making sure that there are at least two ideas for each room.

7 Partnerarbeit. (AT 2/4)   4.5a/Y7

Speaking. Pupils ask each other what they do in each of the rooms, using the notes they have made from exercise 6. Make sure that they know how to transform the infinitive in their notes into sentences in the first person about themselves, doing a few examples on the board if necessary. Pupils should note down their partner's responses (for use in exercise 8).

+ More able pupils could be encouraged to mention more than one activity that they do in each room.

ECHO-Detektiv: Irregular verbs
4.5a/Y8

This panel reviews irregular verbs in the first, second and third person singular. Recap on the concept of irregular verbs and check that pupils can identify what makes each verb irregular. If you wish, refer pupils to the **Grammatik** on page 119 for more information and practice.

8 Was macht dein Partner / deine Partnerin? (AT 4/3)   4.5a/Y8

Writing. Pupils write down their partners' responses to exercise 7 in the third person. Draw pupils' attention to the use of *er* to refer to a boy and *sie* to refer to a girl, rather than continually repeating the person's name. Encourage pupils to refer back to the **ECHO-Detektiv** box to check that they have used the verbs correctly in their sentences.

+ More able pupils write more complex sentences (including connectives and qualifiers).

Plenary   4.5a/Y7 4.5a/Y8 5.8

Aim

To review knowledge of verbs.

Pupils work in groups to prepare a presentation on verbs. Each group creates an OHT. You could give them these questions to start them off:

- What do I need to think of when I use a verb?
- Regular or irregular – how do I know?
- Verb forms – where can I check them?
- What irregular verbs have we learned?

Set a time limit. After the time limit has expired, ask for a volunteer group to give its presentation. Depending on time, other groups could then give their presentations, or simply add any extra points they think are important.

Learning targets
- Describing your room
- Understanding that the verb has to be the second idea

Key framework objectives
4.2/Y8 Language – increasing vocabulary
4.4/Y7 Language – sentence formation

Grammar
- Word order: verb as second idea
- Using *und* and *aber*

Key language
der Schreibtisch / Kleiderschrank / Stuhl / Computer / Fernseher / Spiegel
die Lampe / Kommode / Stereoanlage
das Bett / Regal / Sofa
In meinem Zimmer habe ich …
einen Schreibtisch / Kleiderschrank / Stuhl / Computer / Fernseher / Spiegel
eine Lampe / Kommode
ein Bett / Regal / Sofa
Wie ist dein Zimmer?
Mein Zimmer ist klein / groß / hell / dunkel / ordentlich / unordentlich.
sehr / ziemlich / nicht sehr

High-frequency words
ich habe, du hast
in
meinem
klein
groß
aber
sehr
nicht sehr
ziemlich

Resources
CD 3, tracks 9–11
Workbooks A and B, p.44
Arbeitsblatt 5.3, p.82
Arbeitsblatt 5.5, p.84
Echo Elektro 1 TPP, Express
Mod 5 3.1–3.7

Starter 1   4.1/Y7

Aim

To improve pupils' recognition of sound patterns.

Use OHT 25 to present the furniture vocabulary. Ask pupils to predict to a partner how the words are pronounced. Then ask individual pupils to attempt to pronounce the words. Do not correct errors directly – elicit further suggestions from other pupils or guide the class to the right answer by looking at the pronunciation of other words they know with the same sound patterns. You could point out that the emphasis is usually on the first syllable – *Computer* and *Regal* being among the rare exceptions.

1 Hör zu und lies.   4.2/Y7

Listening/Reading. Pupils listen to the recording and follow the text in their books.

a *der Fernseher*
b *der Kleiderschrank*
c *die Kommode*
d *das Bett*
e *die Stereoanlage*
f *der Stuhl*
g *die Lampe*
h *der Spiegel*
i *das Regal*
j *das Sofa*
k *der Computer*
l *der Schreibtisch*

9

2 Hör zu. Welche Sachen werden genannt? (1–6) (AT 1/3)   1.1/Y7

Listening. Pupils listen to the recording and note down the letters (from exercise 1) of the items of furniture mentioned.

1 – *Was hast du in deinem Zimmer, Carsten?*
  – *In meinem Zimmer habe ich ein Bett … ein Sofa und … einen Schreibtisch.*
2 – *Und du, Beyhan? Was hast du in deinem Zimmer?*
  – *O.K. … also … in meinem Zimmer habe ich ein Bett und ein Regal – und einen Computer.*

10

3 – *Und Olaf, was hast du in deinem Zimmer?*
   – *Tja, in meinem Zimmer habe ich einen Kleiderschrank, eine Stereoanlage und ein Bett.*
4 – *Maren, was hast du in deinem Zimmer?*
   – *Uff! ... In meinem Zimmer? ... In meinem Zimmer habe ich einen Spiegel, eine Kommode ... und einen Stuhl.*
5 – *Was hast du in deinem Zimmer, Heiko?*
   – *In meinem Zimmer habe ich einen Fernseher, ein Bett und einen Kleiderschrank.*
6 – *Und Carola. Was hast du in deinem Zimmer, Carola?*
   – *In meinem Zimmer habe ich einen Schreibtisch, einen Stuhl und ... und ein Regal.*

Answers
1 d, j, l
2 d, i, k
3 b, e, d
4 h, c, f
5 a, d, b
6 l, f, i

▌3 Gedächtnisspiel. (AT 2/3–4)   `4.2/Y7`

Speaking. Pupils work in groups to play a 'chain game' with items of furniture. The first pupil says *In meinem Zimmer habe ich …* and names an item of furniture; subsequent pupils repeat the sentence, each adding another item of furniture to the end, and so on until a pupil forgets the order, hesitates or makes a mistake. He/She restarts the game with a new sentence. Whilst less able pupils may use this exercise purely to improve their fluency and reinforce furniture vocabulary, encourage more able pupils to focus on the accurate use of *einen / eine / ein* as well. This exercise prompts pupils to use inverted word order – more able pupils could be encouraged to notice this.

ECHO-Detektiv   `4.4/Y7` `4.4/Y8`

This panel looks at inverted word order and the 'verb second' rule. If pupils have difficulty understanding that *in meinem Zimmer* is one 'idea', you could explain that this is because it gives one piece of information (i.e. it answers the question 'where?'). With a higher-ability class, you could use this example to introduce the concept of adverbs (words or phrases in a sentence which tell you when, where or how). Pupils can be referred to the **Grammatik** on page 123 for more information and practice.

▌4 Schreib einen langen Satz über dein Zimmer. (AT 4/3)   `4.4/Y7` `4.4/Y8`

Writing. Pupils use connectives to write long sentences about their rooms. Remind the class about the use of *und* and *auch* in order to add extra information to the sentence.

+ Encourage more able pupils to make their sentences as long and complex as possible, using *aber ich habe keinen / keine / kein* and giving opinions. Pupils could then work in pairs to extend, improve and correct each other's sentences.

Starter 2   `4.4/Y7` `4.4/Y8`

Aim
To improve pupils' understanding of the 'verb second' idea.

Make four large cards which will be visible from the back of the class and label them:

front	back
ich	subject
habe	verb
eine Lampe	object
in meinem Zimmer	adverb (or 'details' for a lower-ability class)

Ask four pupils to come to the front of the room. Give each of them a card and ask them to stand in a line. Ask them to hold the cards in front of them, with the German words towards the class. Ask the class whether the sentence is correct: *Ist das richtig?* If not, pupils direct the card holders to move *nach links* or *nach rechts* until a correctly ordered sentence is formed. The card holders then turn the cards around so that the grammatical functions are revealed. Then ask the class to find another correct order for the cards.

▌5 Hör zu. Wie sind ihre Zimmer? (1–6) (AT 1/2)   `1.1/Y7`

Listening. Pupils listen to the recording and note the characteristics of each speaker's room.

1 – *Wie ist dein Zimmer, Micha?*
   – *Mein Zimmer? Also, mein Zimmer ist klein.*
2 – *Und du, Britta? Wie ist dein Zimmer?*
   – *Mein Zimmer ist ... unordentlich.*
3 – *Wie ist dein Zimmer, Fabian?*
   – *Mein Zimmer ist hell.*
4 – *Und Silke. Wie ist dein Zimmer, Silke?*
   – *Ach ... mein Zimmer ist dunkel.*

5 – Wie ist dein Zimmer, Matthias?
– Mein Zimmer ist groß.
6 – Wie ist dein Zimmer, Heike?
– Ähmm ... mein Zimmer ist ordentlich.

Answers
1 klein
2 unordentlich
3 hell
4 dunkel
5 groß
6 ordentlich

➕ Pupils conduct a survey amongst their classmates, asking *Wie ist dein Zimmer?* and writing sentences about their findings. Encourage more confident pupils also to use other adjectives they know.

6 Wessen Zimmer ist das? (AT 3/4)
2.1/Y7 5.5

Reading. Pupils read the descriptions and decide whose bedroom is illustrated.

Answer
Viktor

➕ Give the class five minutes to read the texts again thoroughly. They use the **Wortschatz** to look up any words they do not recognise. After five minutes, ask individual pupils to translate sentences into English. If they get stuck, they could nominate another pupil to help them – *(Jim), kannst du mir helfen?* For further reading activities, see pages 9–10 of this book.

7 Korrigiere die Sätze. (AT 3/4)
4.2/Y8

Reading. Pupils correct the false sentences about the boys' rooms.

Answers
(Accept any alternatives that make sense.)
1 Peters Zimmer ist sehr unordentlich.
2 Peter hat einen Schreibtisch, einen Computer und einen Fernseher.
3 Viktors Zimmer ist klein und unordentlich.
4 Viktor findet sein Zimmer toll.
5 Heikos Zimmer ist nicht sehr groß / ziemlich klein und ziemlich dunkel.
6 Heiko hat einen Computer (aber keinen Fernseher).

ECHO-Tipp
4.2/Y8 4.4/Y8

Look at the **ECHO-Tipp** panel with the class prior to doing exercise 8. It suggests ways of making a sentence more interesting. Write a simple sentence on the board or an OHT, e.g. *Mein Zimmer ist klein.* Pupils work in pairs to make the sentence more interesting and complex. Examples might include:

Mein Zimmer ist klein, aber ordentlich.
Mein Zimmer ist sehr klein und ich finde es doof.
Mein Zimmer ist klein und schwarz – das ist furchtbar!

Set a time limit of about two minutes. After the time limit has expired, collect suggestions around the class, writing them below the original sentence. The class could then have a vote on which they think was the most interesting sentence.

8 Wie ist dein Zimmer? Schreib einen Text. (AT 4/3–4)
4.2/Y8 4.4/Y8

Writing. Pupils write a short text describing their own room. Encourage more able pupils to write sentences with connectives, give opinions and use inverted word order with *In meinem Zimmer habe ich / gibt es …* In preparation, collect expressions they have learned in order to give opinions. Point out that this is an important skill, so they should build and use these phrases as often as possible.

Plenary
5.8

Pupils work in pairs to check the language they have learned so far in this chapter, using the **Mini-Test** checklist. Ask pupils which points their partners found most difficult. Give pupils the task of improving those points by next lesson. Partners could then test them again.

Learning targets
- Saying what is in your room
- Using prepositions to describe where things are

Key framework objectives
2.1/Y7 Reading – main points and detail
4.3/Y8 Language – gender

Grammar
- Prepositions with the dative
- Definite article: dative

Key language
Wo ist die Katze?
Die Katze ist …
auf dem Regal / unter dem Bett / in dem Kleiderschrank / neben dem Stuhl / zwischen dem Bett und dem Schreibtisch / hinter dem Computer.
Wo ist der Bleistift?
Der Bleistift ist auf / unter / in / neben / hinter dem Buch.

High-frequency words
wo?
ist
auf
hinter
in
neben
unter
zwischen
darin
nicht?
was?
also

English
Prepositions

Resources
CD 3, track 12
Workbooks A and B, p.45
Arbeitsblatt 5.4, p. 83
Echo Elektro 1 TPP, Express Mod 5 4.1–4.5

Starter 1
4.2/Y7

Aim
To revise furniture vocabulary.

Option 1: Pupils mime an item of furniture and their classmates ask closed questions such as *Bist du ein Kleiderschrank?*, etc. For further mime activities, see the Introduction on page 10.

Option 2: Play hangman using items of furniture and items in a schoolbag. Set a time limit and elicit answers. Ask for a class consensus before confirming the correct answers. You could then write additional similar sentences, and give pupils further time to confer. Ask the class to guess what today's lesson will be about, before they open their books.

Suggestion
4.2/Y8

Present the six prepositions *auf, hinter, in, neben, unter* and *zwischen* on an OHT or on the board. Demonstrate their meaning using simple diagrams on the board, or objects in the classroom, while chorusing the preposition with the class. Continue to demonstrate the prepositions without saying them – pupils have to call out the correct preposition.

1 Hör zu und lies. Wo ist die Katze? (AT 3/2)
4.4/Y8

Listening. Pupils listen to the recording, following the conversation and focusing on the key phrases under each picture in their book. Emphasise that they should concentrate on hearing and understanding the key phrases as the conversation progresses.

> – *Wo ist die Katze?*
> – *Die Katze ist auf dem Regal. Nein …*
>   *die Katze ist unter dem Bett. Ach,*
>   *die Katze ist in dem Kleiderschrank!*
> – *Und jetzt? Wo ist die Katze jetzt?*
> – *Die Katze ist neben dem Stuhl. Nein … die Katze*
>   *ist zwischen dem Bett und dem Schreibtisch. Ach,*
>   *nein! Die Katze ist hinter dem Computer!*

12

2 Wie heißt das auf Englisch? (AT 3/4)
4.2/Y8

Reading. Pupils translate the prepositions into English, using the illustrations from exercise 1 to infer the meanings.

145

Answers
1 on (top of)
2 under
3 in
4 next to
5 behind
6 between

3 Partnerarbeit. (AT 2/3) `4.2/Y8`

Speaking. Pupils work in pairs to practise prepositions, using the Key Language panel for support. Partner A positions a pencil relative to a schoolbook and partner B says where it is. Then the roles are reversed. Pupils could practise further with other pairs of objects.

Suggestion

For further practice, partner A says a sentence describing the position of the object, and partner B moves the object accordingly.

4 Sieh dir Zogs Zimmer an und lies die Sätze auf Seite 77. Was ist richtig? (AT 3/2) `2.1/Y7`

Reading. Pupils compare the sentences with the picture and choose the correct preposition to complete each sentence.

Answers
1 neben
2 auf
3 auf
4 unter
5 hinter
6 zwischen

Starter 2 `4.2/Y8`

Aim

To reinforce the meanings of prepositions.
Draw two simple identical sketches of items of furniture (e.g. two wardrobes) on the board, side by side. Divide the class into two teams. Each team elects a representative who goes to the board. The teams take turns to call out a German preposition – the representative who draws a cross in the correct place first wins a point for his/her team. Change the representatives a few times.

Alternatively, the representatives could demonstrate the prepositions using two objects, e.g. a pencil and a schoolbag. Encourage stronger pupils to say a whole phrase e.g. *auf dem Kleiderschrank* rather than just one preposition.

ECHO-Detektiv: Prepositions in the dative `4.3/Y8`

This panel shows the change in the definite article after a preposition which takes the dative case. Check comprehension of the term 'preposition' by asking for examples in English, or by calling out words in English including some prepositions – pupils put up their hands whenever you say a preposition. If you wish, refer pupils to the **Grammatik** on page 114 for more information and practice.

5 Sieh dir das Bild noch mal an. Beantworte die Fragen. (AT 4/3) `4.3/Y8`

Writing. Pupils answer the questions about the picture from exercise 4 in full sentences. In preparation, go through the **ECHO-Detektiv** panel with the class. With less able pupils, you may wish to concentrate further on the meaning of the prepositions; with more able pupils, focus also on accuracy in the form of the definite article.

Answers
1 Die Gitarre ist unter dem Bett.
2 Der Taschenrechner ist auf dem Bett.
3 Die Jacke ist in dem Kleiderschrank.
4 Die Diskette ist neben dem Computer.

6 Lies den Text und zeichne das Zimmer. (AT 3/4)   2.1/Y7

Reading. Pupils read the description, then draw the bedroom. They use the **Wortschatz** (less able pupils) or their dictionaries (more able pupils) to look up the meanings of any unknown words.

R Draw the outline of the room and one or two items in it on the board to help less able pupils to get started.

+ Draw pupils' attention to the use of *er*, *sie* and *es* to refer back to items that have already been mentioned, rather than repeating the name of the item every time. Can they identify which noun each pronoun refers back to?

7 Zeichne dein Zimmer. Beschreib es. (AT 4/3 or 4)   4.3/Y8

Writing. Pupils draw a picture of their bedroom, then write a description based on the one in exercise 6. A partner could then check the description against the picture, making sure the prepositions and articles are correct as they read. Emphasise that it is good to concentrate on specific areas when checking work in order to spot specific types of mistake better.

Plenary   4.2/Y8 4.3/Y8

Aims

To consolidate furniture vocabulary and prepositions.
To improve pupils' fluency and confidence in unscripted speech.

Photocopy **Arbeitsblatt 5.4** and cut it in half at the dotted line. Pupils work in pairs. Partner A receives the top half of the worksheet and partner B the bottom half. Each partner must ask questions in German to locate and draw in missing items on their sheet. Their partner answers and they draw in the missing item. Finally, pairs can check their partner's picture against their own.

Alternative: pairs revise changes to articles when they are used with the prepositions in this unit. An able pupil can then be elected to report the rule back to the whole class.

Learning targets
- Saying what you don't like about your room
- Recognising sentences about the past

Key framework objectives

2.3/Y8 Reading – text features: emotive

4.5/Y8 Language – (a) range of verb tenses (past)

Grammar
- *sein: ich war* (receptive only)
- *haben: ich hatte* (receptive only)
- *können: ich kann, sie können*
- *keinen / keine / kein*
- Time expressions which signal past reference (receptive only)

Key language
General consolidation of language from Units 1–4

High-frequency words
bitte
helfen
Sie
mir
alt

aber
mein / meine
keinen / keine / kein
ich kann, sie können
sehr
nur
jetzt
vorher
es war
ich hatte
Sachen
bei

Resources
CD 3, tracks 13–14
Workbooks A and B, p.46
Arbeitsblatt 5.6, p. 85
Arbeitsblatt 5.7, p. 86
Echo Elektro 1 TPP, Express
Mod 5 5.1–5.5

Starter 1
1.4b/Y8

Aim

To improve pupils' fluency and confidence in unscripted speech.

Write on the board the question *Wie ist dein Zimmer?*. Brainstorm vocabulary which would be useful in answering this question.

Pupils work in pairs. Partner A attempts to talk for one minute about his/her bedroom, while partner B takes notes. Then the roles are reversed. Ask for volunteers to report back to the class about their partners' rooms, in German (higher ability) or English (lower ability).

▌ Hör zu und lies. (AT 1/4)   2.2a/Y8   2.3/Y7

Listening/Reading. Pupils listen to the recording and read the letter in their books. After a first listening, ask pupils to close their books. Ask for volunteers to (a) say what the text is about and (b) relate any details they remember. Play the recording a second time. Stop after each sentence and ask the class to repeat the text in unison, trying to match not just the pronunciation, but also the tone of voice and the intonation of the sentence. See pages 9–10 of this guide for further activities to practise reading skills. You may wish to draw pupils' attention to *Sie*, as a polite way of saying 'you' to adults. (The usage of *du / Sie* is discussed in Chapter 6.)

> *Liebes Traumhaus-Team,*
> *bitte helfen Sie mir! Ich bin dreizehn Jahre alt, aber mein Zimmer ist ein Baby-Zimmer:*
> *Es ist dunkel und klein, und die Wände sind rosa und blau – furchtbar!*
> *Mein Zimmer ist unordentlich – ich habe keinen Platz für meine Sachen. Der Kleiderschrank ist sehr klein und meine Klamotten liegen auf dem Schreibtisch.*
> *In meinem Zimmer habe ich keinen Fernseher und keinen Computer. Ich kann auch keine CDs spielen – meine Stereoanlage ist sehr alt! Ich brauche eine neue Stereoanlage!*
> *Was noch? Ach ja, meine Freundinnen können nicht bei mir übernachten – ich habe nur ein Bett!*
> *Hilfe!*
> *Ihre*
> *Beate Ohlers*

🔘 **13**

2 Lies Beates Brief und beantworte die Fragen auf Englisch. (AT 3/4)

2.3/Y8 5.4

Reading. Pupils read the letter again, then answer the questions in English. You could ask pupils to look for colloquial phrases which make Beate's letter feel more natural (*Was noch? Ach ja …*). How would they say these if writing a letter in English?

> **Answers**
> 1 Thirteen
> 2 It's dark, small, pink and blue.
> 3 Because she doesn't have enough room for her things.
> 4 It's very small.
> 5 Her stereo is very old.
> 6 She only has one bed.

R Give pupils a list of English words and phrases to find the German equivalents of in the letter, e.g.:

1 but (*aber*)
2 dark (*dunkel*)
3 pink (*rosa*)
4 awful (*furchtbar*)
5 untidy (*unordentlich*)
6 my things (*meine Sachen*)
7 on the desk (*auf dem Schreibtisch*)
8 no TV (*keinen Fernseher*)
9 my stereo (*meine Stereoanlage*)
10 my friends (female) (*meine Freundinnen*)

+ Ask the class what they remember about using the verb *kann* in a sentence. Ask for volunteers to spot and read out two sentences containing forms of this verb (*Ich kann auch keine CDs spielen; Meine Freundinnen können nicht bei mir übernachten.*). Warn them that it may be in a slightly different form to the way in which they have already seen it. Write up the sentences on the board and ask for other volunteers to come to the board and underline the verb and the infinitive in each sentence.

ECHO-Tipp: new words   **5.4/Y8**

This panel encourages pupils to infer the meanings of new words from the context. Ask for volunteers to guess the meanings of the two words *Klamotten* and *übernachten*, asking for evidence to support their guesses. With a less able class, you may prefer to provide three alternative meanings for each word (different parts of speech as well as widely different meanings), for pupils to choose from. Finally, ask the class to check the meanings of the two words in the **Wortschatz** or in their dictionaries.

3 Gedächtnisspiel: Mein Zimmer ist furchtbar! (AT 2/4)   **5.2**

Speaking. Pupils work in pairs or small groups. The first speaker says the core sentence, *Mein Zimmer ist furchtbar*, and adds one more detail. The next speaker repeats what the first speaker said, and adds another detail, and so on. When a speaker can't remember the sequence, can't think of anything new to add, or hesitates, the game starts again from the core sentence.

Starter 2   **1.3b/Y8**

Aim

To improve fluency and confidence in unscripted speech.

Provide the following expressions on the board and demonstrate their pronunciation:

Ach, weißt du …
Also …
OK …
Tja …
Na ja.

Explain that these are 'fillers' like 'umm' and 'well' in English, and that they are useful to provide thinking time when speaking spontaneously. Chorus the expressions with the class.

Divide the class into groups of three or four. One group member starts to talk about his/her bedroom. As soon as he/she hesitates or runs out of things to say, another group member can start to talk. The aim is to be the person talking when you call out *Stopp!* (after an interval of 30 seconds to two minutes). The winner in each group could get a small prize.

4 Füll die Lücken aus. Hör zu und überprüfe es. (AT 3/5)   **4.5a/Y8**

Reading/Listening. Pupils read the letter and attempt to predict which word goes in each gap, selecting from the words provided. They listen to the recording to check their answers. Use this letter, the **ECHO-Tipp** and the **ECHO-Detektiv** to introduce how to spot references to the past.

> *Liebes Traumhaus-Team,*
> *Hallo! Mein Zimmer ist jetzt toll!*
> *Es war vorher dunkel, aber jetzt ist es hell.*
> *Es war rosa und blau, jetzt ist es grün. Grün ist meine Lieblingsfarbe!*

14

Ich hatte keinen Platz für meine Sachen, aber jetzt habe ich viel Platz. Ich habe einen großen Kleiderschrank und ein Regal für meine CDs und DVDs. Ich habe endlich einen Computer und einen Fernseher – spitze! Meine Stereoanlage war sehr alt, aber jetzt habe ich einen neuen CD-Spieler.
Ich hatte vorher nur ein Bett. Jetzt habe ich ein Bett und ein Sofabett. Toll! Meine Freundinnen können jetzt bei mir übernachten!
Ihre
Beate Ohlers

Answers
1 danke
2 aber
3 ist
4 Lieblingsfarbe
5 meine
6 habe
7 Kleiderschrank
8 Regal
9 Stereoanlage
10 Bett
11 übernachten

ECHO-Tipp   4.2/Y8
This draws pupils' attention to adverbs of time as signals for the past and present tenses. Ask the class to find and read out sentences containing examples of *jetzt* and *vorher* from the letter.

ECHO-Detektiv: war / hatte   4.5a/Y8
This panel introduces the imperfect tense forms of *sein* and *haben*. Check comprehension by asking pupils to spot further examples in the letter in exercise 4. If you wish, refer pupils to the **Grammatik** for further information and practice.

5 Wie war Beates Zimmer vorher und wie ist es jetzt? Mach zwei Listen. (AT 3/5)   4.5a/Y8

Reading. Pupils re-read Beate's letter (exercise 4) and list what her room was like before the makeover and what it is like now. In preparation, work through the sample answers and make sure that pupils understand that they have to (a) scan the text for information about Beate's room and (b) decide (using clues like *jetzt / vorher*, *ist / war* and *habe / hatte*) whether the information applies to the present or the past. Follow-up reading, translation and writing activities can be found in the Introduction on pages 9–10.

Suggested answers

vorher	jetzt
dunkel	hell
rosa und blau	grün
keinen Platz	viel Platz
Kleiderschrank klein	Kleiderschrank groß
keinen Fernseher	Computer
keinen Computer	Fernseher
Stereoanlage	CD-Spieler
Bett	Bett und Sofabett

+ Particularly able pupils can write up their notes as full sentences, using *war / hatte* as necessary.

6 Schreib einen Brief an das Traumhaus-Team. (AT 4/4 or 4/5)   2.4a/Y8

Writing. Pupils write a letter to the *Traumhaus-Team* saying what they don't like about their bedrooms, using Beate's first letter (exercise 1) as a model. More able pupils should be encouraged to write as independently as possible, recycling language from Beate's letter but using their own ideas and expressing their own opinions. Less able pupils could be provided with a writing frame, or encouraged to stick closely to the structure of Beate's letter, just changing specified details.

+ Particularly able pupils could also write a 'thank you' letter, using *war* and *hatte* as well as the present tense.

Plenary   4.5a/Y8

Aim
To reinforce recognition of references to the past.

Pupils share a pair of mini-whiteboards. They write 'past' on one and 'present' on the other and place them on their desk. Read out ten or more sentences. Some of them should be statements about the present, some about the past and some contain reference to both, e.g.

Mein Zimmer war dunkel.
Meine Oma ist laut.
Susi war unpünktlich, aber jetzt ist sie immer pünktlich.
etc.

Pupils try to take and hold up the correct whiteboard(s) before their partners can.

Lernzieltest

5.8

This is a checklist of language covered in Chapter 5. Pupils can work with the checklist in pairs to check what they have learned. Points which directly address grammar and structures are marked with a G. There is a **Lernzieltest** sheet in the Resource and Assessment File (page 89). Encourage pupils to look back at the chapter and to use the grammar section to revise what they are unclear about.

You can also use the **Lernzieltest** as an end-of-unit plenary.

Wiederholung

This is a revision page to prepare pupils for the **Kontrolle** at the end of the chapter.

Resources
CD 3, tracks 15–16

Hör zu. Füll die Tabelle aus. (AT 1/4)
1.1/Y7 1.1/Y8 1.3a/Y7

Listening. Pupils copy the grid. They then listen to the recording and fill it in. Encourage them to listen to the tone of voice as well as to the language to identify the positive and negative points.

1 – Wo ist das erste Haus?
– Gartenstraße 74.

15

– Gartenstraße 74 ...Und wie ist das Haus?
– Ziemlich gut. Es gibt drei Schlafzimmer.
– Ja, das ist gut. Und wie viele Badezimmer?
– Zwei Badezimmer.
– Auch gut.
– Ja, aber es gibt keine Garage. Das finde ich nicht so gut.
– Keine Garage? Nein, das ist schlecht.
– Und der Garten ist klein.
– Hmm, das ist auch nicht so toll.

2 – OK, und das zweite Haus?
– Auch in der Gartenstraße, Hausnummer 32.
– 32 ...Und? Wie ist es?
– Auch nicht schlecht. Es gibt eine Garage ...
– He! Toll!
– ... und das Wohnzimmer ist groß.
– Gut.
– Ja, aber es gibt auch ein Problem: Das Haus hat nur zwei Schlafzimmer.
– Nur zwei? Also, das ist sehr schlecht.
– Ja, und ich finde die Küche nicht gut. Sie ist ziemlich dunkel.
– Hmm, nein. Das geht nicht.
– Ja, das denke ich auch.

3 – OK, und das dritte Haus?
– Auch in der Gartenstraße, Hausnummer 45.
– Auch dort? 45 ...Und wie ist das?
– Ziemlich gut. Also, es gibt einen Balkon ...
– Sehr gut!
– ... und drei große Schlafzimmer.
– Das ist toll! Gibt es auch einen Garten?
– Ja, der Garten ist sehr schön! Das Problem ist nur: das Wohnzimmer ist klein.
– Ein kleines Wohnzimmer? Also, das ist nicht so gut.
– Ja, ich finde es auch nicht gut.
– Und, was machen wir jetzt?!

Answers

Adresse	☺	☹
Gartenstraße 74	3 Schlafzimmer 2 Badezimmer	keine Garage Garten – klein
Gartenstraße 32	Garage Wohnzimmer – groß	2 Schlafzimmer Küche – dunkel
Gartenstraße 45	Balkon Garten – schön 3 Schlafzimmer	Wohnzimmer – klein

Hör zu. Schreib die Zahlen auf. (1–8) (AT 1/3)
1.1/Y7 1.1/Y8

Listening. Pupils listen to the recording and write down the numbers they hear.

1 – Wie ist deine Adresse?
– Meine Adresse? Bachmannstraße 82.

16

2 – Ist deine Adresse Joachimstraße 19?
– Ja, richtig. Joachimstraße 19.

3 – Wie ist deine Adresse?
– Meine Adresse ist Märzweg 123.
– 123?
– Ja, genau.

4 – Du, Uwe, wie ist deine Adresse?
– Ingolfsweg 36.

5 – Meine Adresse ist Märchenallee 47.
– Wie bitte?
– Märchenallee 47.

6 – Und wie ist deine Adresse?
– Meine Adresse ist Seestraße 53.

7 – Wie ist Katis Adresse?
– Katis Adresse ... Adlerstraße 43.
– Danke.

8 – Meine Adresse ist Josephstraße 56.
– Langsamer, bitte.
– Josephstraße 56.

Answers
1 82 **2** 19 **3** 123 **4** 36 **5** 47 **6** 53 **7** 43 **8** 56

3 Partnerarbeit: Mach Interviews. (AT 2/3) 1.4b/Y7

Speaking. Pupils work in pairs. They interview each other using the questions provided.

4 Lies den Brief. Beantworte die Fragen auf Englisch. (AT 3/3) 2.2a/Y8

Reading. Pupils read the letter and answer the questions in English.

Answers
1 a flat
2 small and dark
3 two bedrooms, a bathroom, a kitchen, a living room
4 an extra bedroom and bathroom, a toilet, a dining room, a balcony
5 untidy

5 Wie ist dein Zimmer? Was gibt es in deinem Zimmer? (AT 4/3 or 4)
2.4b/Y7 2.4b/Y8

Writing. Pupils write a short text about their bedrooms.

Learning targets
- Reading and discussing events in a story
- Writing an imaginary interview with a celebrity

Key framework objectives
2.2/Y8 Reading – (b) personal response to text
2.5/Y8 Writing – using researched language
5.5 Strategies – reference materials

Key language
Consolidation of language from Units 1–5

High-frequency words
komm!
spielen
gleich
was?
hier
los
auf
er
wer?

er/sie/es war, wir waren
weg
mein/meine
dein
wo?

Resources
CD 3, track 17
Workbooks A and B, p.47

Starter 1   2.2a/Y8 5.2

Aims
To practise scanning and summarising texts.
To improve recall of written language.

Ask the class to read the story in exercise 1. Set a time limit of about two minutes. At the end of the time limit, pupils close their books. Ask pupils what they remember from the text, including individual words/phrases, details of illustrations and gist (characters, subject matter, plot). Write this on the board or an OHT for review after exercise 1.

1 Hör zu und lies. (AT 1/5, 3/5)   2.2b/Y8 5.6
Listening/Reading. Pupils listen to the dialogue and follow the story in their books. Check comprehension by asking pupils to modify/extend the summary they created for Starter 1. Ask them to spot and translate examples of reference to the past. Ask pupils for their opinion of the text. Did it help reading it in this format? Why/why not?

Suggestion
Pupils could then read the story aloud in pairs, trying to copy the tone of voice and intonation of the speakers, as well as focusing on basic accuracy of pronunciation.

– Uwe! Komm, wir spielen Frisbee!
– O.K, O.K. Ich komme gleich ...
– Was ist hier los? Mein Skateboard ist auf dem Boden ... wo ist mein Musik-Player? Er

🔘 17

war im Schreibtisch. Er war ein Geburtstagsgeschenk. Wer war in meinem Zimmer?
– Kati, Hilfe! Ein Dieb war im Haus. Mein Musik-Player ist weg!
– O.K. Wir waren im Garten ...
– Ja, und mein Musik-Player war hier, im Schreibtisch ...
– Aber dein Computer ist noch da, und dein Geld auch ... Hmm. Ich habe eine Idee ...
– Aha! Hier ist der Dieb!
– Tobi!! Böser Hund!

2 Wie heißt das auf Englisch? Rate mal, dann schlag es nach. (AT 3/5)   5.4 5.5
Reading. Pupils attempt to work out the meanings of the new words from the context, then look up the words in the **Wortschatz** (lower ability) or in their dictionaries (higher ability) to check.

Answers
1 floor
2 birthday present
3 gone
4 thief
5 money
6 also

➕ More able pupils could go on to look up other vocabulary from the story in their dictionaries. In particular, they could look up the components of the phrases in the vocabulary box on page 82, to see the range of meanings offered by the dictionary. Stress the importance of selecting the most appropriate meaning from the dictionary, e.g. in this context, *gleich* means 'straight away', not 'equal' or 'equally'. Can pupils see that *Ich komme gleich* is not rendered adequately by a literal translation 'I come straight away'?

3 Gedächtnisspiel. (AT 2/4) | 5.2

Speaking. Pupils work in pairs. Partner A looks at picture 1 from the story (page 82) and attempts to memorise the details, then closes his/her book, while partner B asks him/her the questions and confirms whether his/her answers are correct. Then the roles are reversed with picture 3. More able pupils should be encouraged to respond using full sentences with *war*.

4 Lies das Star-Interview. Welches Haus gehört Benjamin Braun? | 2.2a/Y8

Reading. Pupils read the interview and work out which picture show Benjamin Braun's house.

> **Answer**
> b

5 Schreib ein Star-Interview mit einem Fußball-Profi oder einem Popstar. | 2.5/Y8

Writing. Pupils write an interview with another celebrity. To get them going you could brainstorm the sort of things that celebrities might have in their houses and give them the vocabulary they need. You could also get them to scan the text for useful phrases that they would like to re-use.

Plenary | 1.4a+b/Y8

Aim

To improve pupils' fluency and confidence in unscripted speech.

Brainstorm language which would be useful in showing someone around a house, e.g. names of rooms, colours, other adjectives to describe rooms. Also remind pupils of the 'stalling' expressions: *Ach, weißt du … Also … OK … Tja … Na ja.*

Pupils work together in pairs to create role plays. One partner plays the part of an estate agent showing a potential buyer around a house. The other partner plays the role of the buyer. The estate agent explains what each room is, and the buyer asks questions and makes comments, e.g.:

A: *Hier ist die Küche.*
B: *Super! Wo ist der Keller?*
A: *Hier. Man kann dort Musik hören.*
B: *Hmm, also … es ist ziemlich dunkel.*
etc.

Give pupils three to five minutes to prepare and practise their role plays, then ask for volunteers to perform their role play to the class.

SELF-ACCESS READING AND WRITING AT TWO LEVELS

A Reinforcement

Was passt zusammen? (AT3/2)
`4.2/Y7`

Reading. Pupils read the 'small ads' for accommodation, and match them to the correct illustrations.

> **Answers**
> **1** d **2** c **3** a **4** b

Schreib Untertitel für die Bilder. (AT4/2)
`4.4/Y7`

Writing. Pupils use the pictures and Key Language panel to construct sentences about activities and rooms.

> **Answers**
> **1** Ich spiele im Wohnzimmer am Computer.
> **2** Ich lese in der Toilette.
> **3** Ich höre im Badezimmer Musik.
> **4** Ich sehe in der Küche fern.
> **5** Ich schlafe im Garten.
> **6** Ich arbeite in der Garage.

Schreib die Sätze aus. (AT4/2)
`4.4/Y7`

Writing. Pupils copy out the sentences, inserting gaps to separate the words. More confident learners should be expected to use correct capital letters.

> **Answers**
> **1** Ich wohne in einem Einfamilienhaus auf dem Land.
> **2** Wir haben sieben Schlafzimmer und sechs Badezimmer.
> **3** Mein Zimmer ist sehr klein und unordentlich.
> **4** Meine Adresse ist Teichstraße fünfundneunzig.
> **5** Mein Computer ist zwischen dem Bett und dem Schreibtisch.

> ### ECHO-Tipp
> Pupils are reminded to start a noun with a capital letter in German.

B Extension

Welches Zimmer ist das? Was macht man in dem Zimmer? (AT3/2)
`4.2/Y7`

Reading. Pupils unjumble the words for rooms and write them out correctly. They then match the most logical activity to each room.

> **Answers**
> **1** Die Küche – b
> **2** Das Schlafzimmer – e
> **3** Das Wohnzimmer – d
> **4** Das Esszimmer – a
> **5** Der Garten – c

Wo ist das im Zimmer? Was passt zusammen? (AT3/3)
`2.1/Y7`

Reading. Pupils read the description of the bedroom, and work out which item each number in the picture represents.

> **Answers**
> **1** der Stuhl   **4** eine Diskette
> **2** der Fernseher   **5** die Stereoanlage
> **3** das Regal   **6** meine Bücher

Wie ist die richtige Reihenfolge? Schreib den Text ab und füll die Lücken aus. (AT3/3 AT4/2)
`4.4/Y7`

Reading/Writing. Pupils firstly scan through the text and work out how to re-order the lines so that it makes sense. They then copy the text out in the correct order, replacing each picture with the correct word (checking spellings as necessary by looking words up).

> **Answers**
> 5, 1, 3, 2, 4, 6
> Hallo! Ich bin Zorka. Mein **Hund** heißt Zluk. Ich wohne in Bloork, das ist ein Dorf auf dem Planeten Blik. Wir haben einen großen **Garten**. Ich wohne in einem Einfamilienhaus. Wir haben ein **Wohnzimmer**, eine Küche, ein **Badezimmer** und zwei Schlafzimmer. Wir haben keinen **Keller**. Mein Schlafzimmer ist sehr unordentlich, aber es ist groß und hell. Es gibt ein **Bett** und einen Stuhl. Auf dem **Schreibtisch** habe ich einen **Fernseher**. Ich sehe gern fern. Mein Zimmer ist toll!

Übungsheft A,
Seite 42

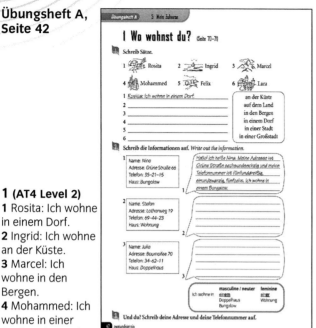

1 (AT4 Level 2)
1 Rosita: Ich wohne in einem Dorf. **2** Ingrid: Ich wohne an der Küste. **3** Marcel: Ich wohne in den Bergen. **4** Mohammed: Ich wohne in einer Großstadt. **5** Felix: Ich wohne auf dem Land. **6** Lara:Ich wohne in einer Stadt.

2 (AT3 Level 2, AT4 Level 3) 1 Hallo! Ich heiße Nina. Meine Adresse ist Grüne Straße sechsundsechzig und meine Telefonnummer ist fünfunddreißig, einundzwanzig, fünfzehn. Ich wohne in einem Bungalow. **2** Hallo! Ich heiße Stefan. Meine Adresse ist Lotharweg neunzehn und meine Telefonnummer ist neunundsechzig, vierundvierzig, dreiundzwanzig. Ich wohne in einer Wohnung. **3** Hallo! Ich heiße Julia. Meine Adresse ist Baumallee siebzig und meine Telefonnummer ist vierunddreißig, zweiundsechzig, elf. Ich wohne in einem Doppelhaus.

3 (AT4 Level 2–3)

Übungsheft B,
Seite 42

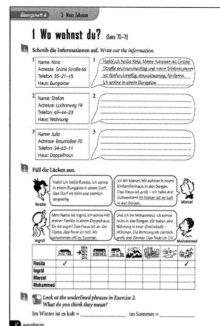

1 (AT3 Level 2,
AT4 Level 3) 1
Hallo! Ich heiße Nina. Meine Adresse ist Grüne Straße sechsundsechzig und meine Telefonnummer ist fünfunddreißig, einundzwanzig, fünfzehn. Ich wohne in einem Bungalow. **2** Hallo! Ich heiße Stefan. Meine Adresse ist Lotharweg neunzehn und meine Telefonnummer ist neunundsechzig, vierundvierzig, dreiundzwanzig. Ich wohne in einer Wohnung. **3** Hallo! Ich heiße Julia. Meine Adresse ist Baumallee siebzig und meine Telefonnummer ist vierunddreißig, zweiundsechzig, elf. Ich wohne in einem Doppelhaus.

2 (AT3 Level 3) Rosita: tick bungalow and village. **Ingrid:** tick semi-detached and coast. **Marcel:** tick detached and mountains. **Mohammed:** tick flat and city

3 (AT3 Level 3) Im Winter ist es kalt = *it's cold in the winter*; im Sommer = *in the summer*

Übungsheft A,
Seite 43

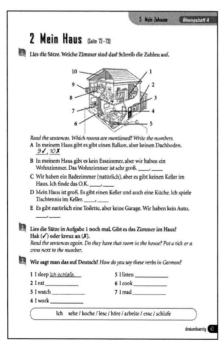

1/2 (AT3 Level 3) A 9 ✓, 10 ✗ **B** 3 ✗, 4 ✓ **C** 1 ✓, 5 ✗ **D** 5 ✓, 7 ✓ **E** 6 ✓, 2 ✗

3 (AT4 Level 1–2) 1 Ich schlafe. **2** Ich esse. **3** Ich sehe. **4** Ich arbeite. **5** Ich höre. **6** Ich koche. **7** Ich lese.

Übungsheft B,
Seite 43

1 (AT3 Level 4) *Circle:* ein Esszimmer, einen Garten, keinen Balkon, zwei Badezimmer, zwei Schlafzimmer

2 (AT3 Level 4, AT4 Level 2) Opa: Ich schlafe im Schlafzimmer. **Olli:** Ich lese im Badezimmer. **Anja:** Ich höre in der Küche Musik. **Mutti:** Ich arbeite im Garten. **Vati:** Ich sehe im Schlafzimmer fern.

**Übungsheft A,
Seite 44**

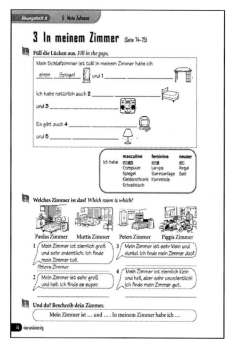

1 (AT3 Level 3, AT4 Level 1) Mein Schlafzimmer ist toll! In meinem Zimmer habe ich **einen Spiegel** und **1 einen Schreibtisch**. Ich habe natürlich auch **2 ein Bett** und **3 eine Stereoanlage**. Es gibt auch **4 einen Computer** und **5 eine Lampe**.

2 (AT3 Level 3) 1 Peters Zimmer **2** Muttis Zimmer **3** Paulas Zimmer **4** Piggis Zimmer

3 (AT4 Level 3–4)

**Übungsheft B,
Seite 44**

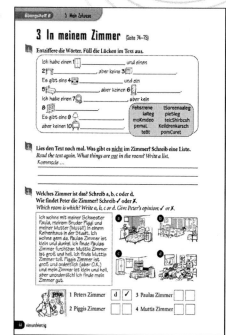

**1 (AT3 Level 3,
AT4 Level 2)**
Ich habe einen
1 Kleiderschrank und einen **2 Schreibtisch**, aber keine **3 Kommode**. Es gibt eine **4 Stereoanlage** und ein **5 Bett**, aber keinen **6 Spiegel**. Ich habe einen **7 Computer**, aber kein **8 Regal**. Es gibt eine **9 Lampe**, aber keinen **10 Fernseher**.

2 (AT3 Level 3, AT4 Level 1) Es gibt keine Kommode, keinen Spiegel, kein Regal und keinen Fernseher.

3 (AT3 Level 4) 1 Peters Zimmer:d, ✓ **2** Piggis Zimmer:c, ✓ **3** Paulas Zimmer:a, ✗ **4** Muttis Zimmer:b, ✓

**Übungsheft A,
Seite 45**

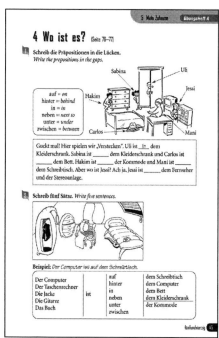

1 (AT3 Level 3) Guckt mal! Hier spielen wir „Verstecken". Uli ist **in** dem Kleiderschrank. Sabina ist **hinter** dem Kleiderschrank und Carlos ist **unter** dem Bett. Hakim ist **neben** der Kommode und Mani ist **auf** dem Schreibtisch. Aber wo ist Jessi? Ach ja, Jessi ist **zwischen** dem Fernseher und der Stereoanlage.

2 (AT4 Level 4) Der Computer ist auf dem Schreibtisch. Der Taschenrechner ist auf dem Bett. Die Jacke ist in dem Kleiderschrank. Die Gitarre ist unter dem Bett. Das Buch ist auf dem Computer.

**Übungsheft B,
Seite 45**

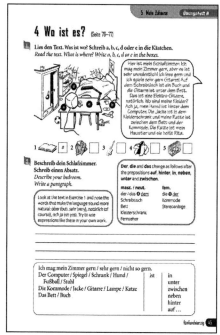

1 (AT3 Level 4) 1e 2a 3b 4c 5d

2 (AT4 Level 4)

**Übungsheft A,
Seite 46**

**Übungsheft B,
Seite 46**

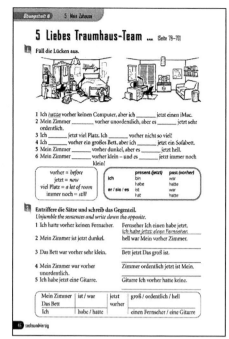

1 (AT3 Level 2) 1B 2B 3A 4A 5A 6B 7A 8B

2 (AT3 Level 4) 1 present 2 present 3 past 4 past 5 past
6 present 7 past 8 present

3 (AT4 Level 4) 1 Ich **hatte** vorher keinen Computer. 2 Jetzt
habe ich viel Platz. 3 Jetzt **habe** ich ein Sofabett. 4 Vorher **war**
mein Zimmer dunkel. 5 Jetzt **ist** mein Zimmer hell. 6 Mein
Zimmer **war** vorher klein.

1 (AT3 Level 5) 1 Ich **hatte** vorher keinen Computer, aber ich
habe jetzt einen iMac. 2 Mein Zimmer **war** vorher
unordentlich, aber es **ist** jetzt sehr ordentlich. 3 Ich **habe** jetzt
viel Platz. Ich **hatte** vorher nicht so viel! 4 Ich **hatte** vorher ein
großes Bett, aber ich **habe** jetzt ein Sofabett. 5 Mein Zimmer
war vorher dunkel, aber es **ist** jetzt hell. 6 Mein Zimmer **war**
vorher klein – und es **ist** jetzt immer noch klein!

2 (AT4 Level 5) 1 Ich habe jetzt einen Fernseher. 2 Mein
Zimmer war vorher hell. 3 Das Bett ist jetzt groß. 4 Mein
Zimmer ist jetzt ordentlich. 5 Ich hatte vorher keine Gitarre.

**Übungsheft A,
Seite 47**

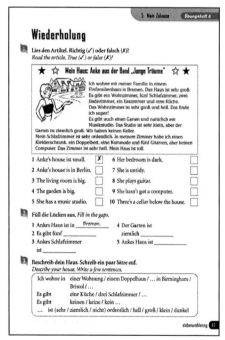

**Übungsheft B,
Seite 47**

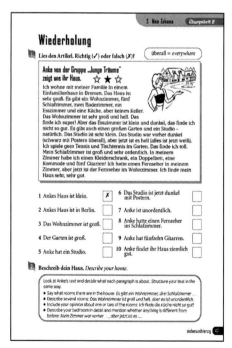

1 (AT3 Level 4) 1 ✗ 2 ✗ 3 ✓ 4 ✓ 5 ✓ 6 ✗ 7 ✗ 8 ✓ 9 ✓ 10 ✗

2 (AT3 Level 4) 1 Ankes Haus ist in **Bremen**. 2 Es gibt fünf
Schlafzimmer / Gitarren. 3 Ankes Schlafzimmer ist **ordentlich
/ hell**. 4 Der Garten ist ziemlich **groß**. 5 Ankes Haus ist **toll /
groß**.

3 (AT4 Level 4)

1 (AT3 Level 5) 1 ✗ 2 ✗ 3 ✓ 4 ✓ 5 ✓ 6 ✗ 7 ✗ 8 ✓ 9 ✗ 10 ✗

2 (AT4 Level 4–5)

**Übungsheft A,
Seite 48**

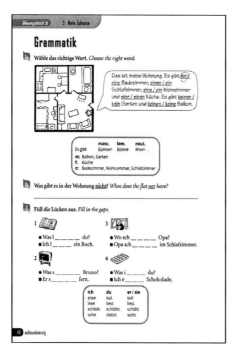

**Übungsheft B,
Seite 48**

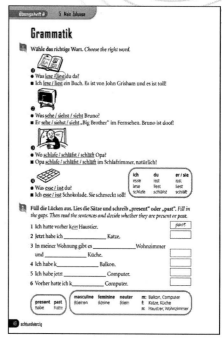

1a (AT3 Level 3) Das ist meine Wohnung. Es gibt **ein** Badezimmer, **ein** Schlafzimmer, **ein** Wohnzimmer und **eine** Küche. Es gibt **keinen** Garten und **keinen** Balkon.

1b (AT3 Level 3) Es gibt keinen Garten und keinen Balkon.

2 (AT4 Level 2) 1 Was **liest** du? – Ich **lese** ein Buch. **2** Was **sieht** Bruno? – Er **sieht** fern. **3** Wo **schläft** Opa? – Opa **schläft** im Schlafzimmer. **4** Was **isst** du? – Ich **esse** Schokolade.

1 (AT3 Level 3) 1 Was **liest** du da? – Ich **lese** ein Buch. Es ist von John Grisham und es ist toll! **2** Was **sieht** Bruno? – Er **sieht** „Big Brother" im Fernsehen. Bruno ist doof! **3** Wo **schläft** Opa? – Opa **schläft** im Schlafzimmer, natürlich! **4** Was **isst** du? – Ich **esse** Schokolade. Sie schmeckt toll!

2 (AT3 Level 5)

1 Ich hatte vorher **kein** Haustier. *(past)*
2 Jetzt habe ich **eine** Katze. *(present)*
3 In meiner Wohnung gibt es **ein** Wohnzimmer und **eine** Küche. *(present)*
4 Ich habe **keinen** Balkon. *(present)*
5 Ich habe jetzt **einen** Computer. *(present)*
6 Vorher hatte ich **keinen** Computer. *(past)*

Arbeitsblatt 5.1

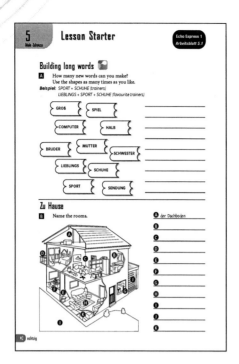

A
Halbschwester, Halbbruder, Großmutter, Computerspiel, Lieblingssendung

B
A der Dachboden **B** das Badezimmer **C** das Schlafzimmer **D** der Balkon **E** die Toilette **F** die Küche **G** das Esszimmer **H** das Wohnzimmer **I** der Garten **J** die Garage **K** der Keller

Arbeitsblatt 5.2

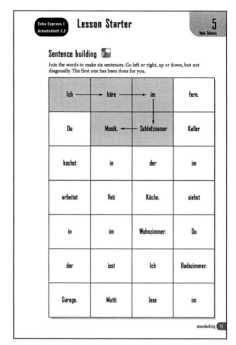

Ich höre im Schlafzimmer Musik. Du kochst in der Küche. Vati arbeitet in der Garage. Mutti isst im Wohnzimmer. Ich lese im Badezimmer. Du siehst im Keller fern.

Arbeitsblatt 5.3

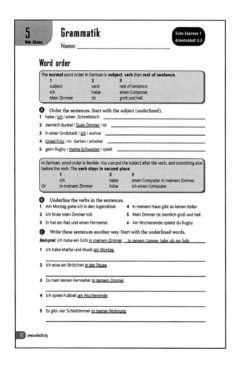

A
1 Ich habe einen Schreibtisch. **2** Susis Zimmer ist ziemlich dunkel. **3** Ich wohne in einer Großstadt. **4** Onkel Fritz arbeitet im Garten. **5** Meine Schwester spielt gern Rugby.

B
1 gehe **2** finde **3** hat **4** gibt **5** ist **6** spielst

C
1 Am Montag habe ich Mathe und Musik. **2** In der Pause esse ich ein Brötchen. **3** In deinem Zimmer hast du keinen Fernseher. **4** Am Wochenende spiele ich Fußball. **5** In meiner Wohnung gibt es vier Schlafzimmer.

Arbeitsblatt 5.4

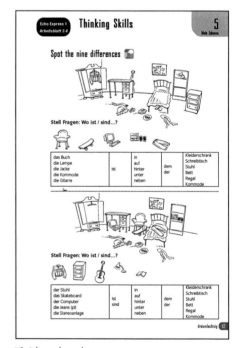

Die Jacke ist in dem Kleiderschrank.
Die Kommode ist neben dem Regal.
Die Gitarre ist hinter dem Schreibtisch.
Die Lampe ist auf dem Regal.
Das Buch ist unter dem Bett.

Der Stuhl ist neben dem Bett / dem Schreibtisch.
Das Skateboard ist unter dem Stuhl.
Der Computer ist unter dem Schreibtisch.
Die Jeans sind auf dem Bett.
Die Stereoanlage ist auf dem Regal.

Arbeitsblatt 5.5

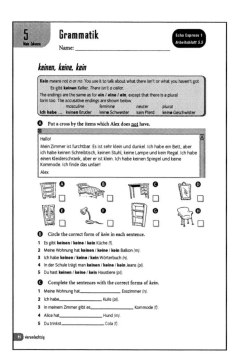

A
A, C, D, F, G, H

B
1 keine 2 keinen 3 kein 4 keinen 5 keine

C
1 kein 2 keine 3 keine 4 keinen 5 keine

Arbeitsblatt 5.7

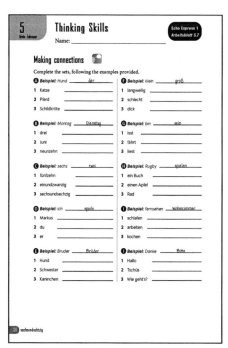

A 1 die 2 das 3 die
B 1 vier 2 Juli 3 zwanzig
C 1 fünf 2 sieben 3 zweiundzwanzig
D 1 spielt 2 spielst 3 spielt
E 1 Hunde 2 Schwestern 3 Kaninchen
F 1 interessant 2 gut 3 schlank
G 1 essen 2 fahren 3 lesen
H 1 lesen 2 essen 3 fahren
I 1 Schlafzimmer 2 Garage / Garten 3 Küche
J 1 Hallo 2 Tschüs 3 Gut, danke (or similar)

Arbeitsblatt 5.6

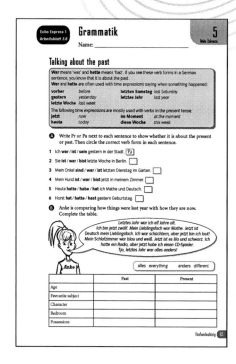

A
1 Pa / war 2 Pa / war 3 Pa / war 4 Pr / ist 5 Pr / habe 6 Pa / hatte

B

	Past	Present
Age	11	12
Favourite subject	maths	German
Character	shy	noisy
Bedroom	blue and white	purple and black
Possessions	radio	CD player

6 Stadt und Land

Unit Learning targets	Key framework objectives	NC levels and PoS coverage	Grammar and key language	Skills
1 Wo liegt das? (pp. 86–87) • Learning about some towns and cities in Germany, Austria and Switzerland • Talking about the weather	**1.1/Y8** Listening – understanding on first hearing **2.4/Y8** Writing – (b) organising paragraphs	NC levels 2–4 **2.2d** pronunciation and intonation **2.2e** ask and answer questions **3b** sounds and writing **3c** apply grammar **3d** use a range of vocab / structures **3e** different countries' cultures **3f** compare experiences **4b** communicate in pairs etc.	Revision of *man kann* + infinitive Revision of verb as second idea (*hier kann man*) *Leipzig, Berlin, Kiel, München, Wien, Salzburg, Bern, Klosters* *Wo liegt das?* *Das liegt in Deutschland / Österreich / der Schweiz* *im Norden / Süden / Osten / Westen von …* *die Stadt / die Großstadt / das Dorf* *Das ist die Hauptstadt von …* *bekannt für* (receptive only) *Man kann / Hier kann man … ins Kino / ins Sportzentrum gehen* *Wie ist das Wetter?* *Es ist schön / sonnig / windig / wolkig / nebelig / frostig / heiß / warm / kalt.* *Es regnet.* *Es schneit.* *Es donnert und blitzt.*	Learning some basic geographical facts about the main German-speaking countries Pronunciation: names of cities Formulating basic questions Understanding a weather forecast
2 In der Stadt (pp. 88–89) • Saying what there is in a town, and talking about types of transport • Recognising plural forms	**4.5/Y7** Language – (b) modal verbs **4.3/Y8** Language – plurals **5.4** Strategies – working out meaning	NC levels 1–4 **2.1c** knowledge of language **2.1e** use reference materials **2.2a** listen for gist **2.2e** ask and answer questions **2.2g** write clearly and coherently **3b** sounds and writing **3c** apply grammar **3d** use a range of vocab / structures **4b** communicate in pairs etc.	Revision of *es gibt* + accusative Further revision of *man kann* + infinitive *der Bahnhof(∺ e)* *der Markt(∺ e)* *der Park(s)* *der Supermarkt(∺ e)* *die Kirche(n)* *die Post(en)* *das Rathaus(∺ er)* *das Schloss(∺ er)* *das Schwimmbad(∺ er)* *das Verkehrsamt(∺ er)* *Es gibt …* *einen / eine / ein / plural* *keinen / keine / kein* *Im Frühling / Sommer / Herbst / Winter* *mit dem Auto / Bus / Zug / Taxi / Flugzeug* *mit der Straßenbahn / U-Bahn* *zu Fuß* *Man kann … fahren / gehen*	Checking/ looking up plurals of nouns Using a dictionary/ other resources appropriately
3 Wo ist der Markt? (pp. 90–91) • Asking for and giving directions • Understanding the difference between *du* and *Sie*	**5.6** Strategies – reading aloud	NC levels 1–3 **2.2e** ask and answer questions **2.2j** adapt previously-learnt language **3b** sounds and writing **3c** apply grammar **3d** use a range of vocab / structures **4b** communicate in pairs etc. **4g** language for a range of purposes	Use of *du* and *Sie* Introduction to the imperative *Wo ist …?* *der Markt / Park* *die Kirche / Post /* *das Rathaus / Schwimmbad / Verkehrsamt* *Geh / Gehen Sie …* *links / rechts / geradeaus* *Nimm / Nehmen Sie …* *die erste / zweite / dritte Straße* *auf der linken / rechten Seite bitte* *danke*	Social conventions Polite little words

Unit Learning targets	Key framework objectives	NC levels and PoS coverage	Grammar and key language	Skills
4 An der Imbissbude (pp. 92–93) ● Buying food and drink at a snack stand using euros ● Using *ich möchte* to say what you would like	3.1/Y8 Culture – changes in everyday life 2.4/Y8 Writing – (a) using text as stimulus	NC levels 1–4 2.1c knowledge of language 2.2j adapt previously-learnt language 3b sounds and writing 3c apply grammar 3d use a range of vocab / structures 3e different countries' cultures 3f compare experiences 4b communicate in pairs etc. 4d make links with English	*ich möchte* + direct object *sie sind* (receptive) Identifying nouns, verbs, adjectives Nouns written with capital letter (revision) *Ich möchte …* *einmal / zweimal* *Bratwurst / Hamburger / Pizza / Pommes frites / Schaschlik / Ketchup / Mayonnaise / Senf / Kaffee / Tee* *mit Milch / Zitrone* *Cola* *Limonade* *Das macht …* *Euro / Cent*	Speaking skills Cultural information about currency, snacks and snack stands Identifying words already known from other languages Revision of numbers for prices Polite little words
5 In den Sommerferien (pp. 94–95) ● Talking about your plans for the summer holidays ● Talking about the future (using the present tense)	1.2/Y8 Listening – new contexts 1.3/Y8 Listening – (a) understanding language for specific functions 3.2/Y8 Culture – (a) young people: aspirations 4.5/Y8 Language – (a) range of verb tenses (future)	NC levels 1–5 2.1a identify patterns 2.1c knowledge of language 2.2e ask and answer questions 2.2g write clearly and coherently 2.2h redraft to improve writing 2.2j adapt previously-learnt language 3b sounds and writing 3c apply grammar 3d use a range of vocab / structures 4b communicate in pairs etc. 4c use more complex language	Using the present tense to talk about the future Verb as second idea (revisited) *Was machst du in den Sommerferien?* *Für wie lange?* *Wie fährst du dahin?* *Ich fahre / Er/Sie fährt / Wir fahren …* *nach … Schottland / Wales / Devon / Spanien / Österreich* *für … Tage / Wochen* *Ich bleibe zu Hause.* *mit dem Auto / Bus / Flugzeug / Zug* *In den Sommerferien* *Morgen* *nächste Woche* *am Montag / Dienstag / Mittwoch*	
Lernzieltest und Wiederholung (pp. 96–97) ● Pupils' checklist and practice test		NC levels 3–5 2.1b memorising		
Extra (pp. 110–111) ● Self-access reading and writing at two levels		NC levels 1–5 2.2b skim and scan 2.2e ask and answer questions 3c apply grammar 3d use a range of vocab / structures		

Learning targets
- Learning about some towns and cities in Germany, Austria and Switzerland
- Talking about the weather

Key framework objectives
1.1/Y8 Listening – understanding on first hearing

2.4/Y8 Writing – (b) organising paragraphs

Grammar
- Revision of *man kann* + infinitive
- Revision of verb as second idea (*hier kann man …*)

Key language
Wo liegt (Leipzig)?
Das liegt in Deutschland / Österreich / der Schweiz
im Norden / Süden / Osten /
Westen von …
die Stadt / die Großstadt / das Dorf
Das ist die Hauptstadt von …
Berlin, Bern, Kiel, Klosters, Leipzig, München, Salzburg, Wien
bekannt für Bier, Fußball, Wintersport, Wassersport, Mozart
Man kann / Hier kann man …
ins Kino / Sportzentrum gehen
toll / super / langweilig / interessant
Wie ist das Wetter?
Es ist schön.
Es ist sonnig.
Es ist windig.
Es ist wolkig.
Es ist nebelig.
Es ist frostig.
Es ist heiß.
Es ist warm.
Es ist kalt.
Es regnet.
Es schneit.
Es donnert und blitzt.

High-frequency words
für
gehen
hier
im
in
ins
ist
ich finde es
von
man kann
wo?

Pronunciation
Names of cities

Citizenship
Learning about towns and cities in other countries

Resources
CD 3, tracks 18–21
Workbooks A and B, p.52
Arbeitsblatt 6.1, p. 106
Echo Elektro 1 TPP, Express
Mod 6 1.1–1.8

Starter 1
3.1/Y7

Aim
To recap what pupils already know about the German-speaking countries, and to introduce them to more geographical facts in preparation for this unit.

Give the class one minute to look at the map on page 86 of the Pupil's Book – tell them they will be tested on how many country and city names they can remember. They then close their books. Give a copy of **Arbeitsblatt 6.1** to each pupil, and ask them to fill in as many names as they can in the correct places on the map. Now, or later, they can also colour in the three flags correctly. Answers could be quickly checked by referring back to the Pupil's Book. Alternatively, a volunteer pupil completes an OHT copy of the **Arbeitsblatt** as you speak. Give information about the cities to introduce new vocabulary as the class mark their answers:

Berlin ist die Hauptstadt von Deutschland.
Kiel liegt im Norden von Deutschland.

Welche Stadt ist das? (1–8) (AT 1/2)
1.1/Y7

Listening. Pupils listen to the recording and look at the map in their book. They identify the towns being described, and write down the names. Weaker pupils may prefer to write on **Arbeitsblatt 6.1** instead, and number the towns. They can listen to the recording for exercise 2 to check their answers.

1 *Das liegt im Osten von der Schweiz.*
2 *Das liegt im Norden von Deutschland.*
3 *Das liegt im Süden von Deutschland.*
4 *Das liegt im Osten von Deutschland.*
5 *Das liegt im Westen von Österreich.*
6 *Das ist die Hauptstadt von der Schweiz.*
7 *Das ist die Hauptstadt von Deutschland.*
8 *Das liegt im Osten von Österreich und ist die Hauptstadt von Österreich.*

18

2 Hör zu und überprüfe es. (AT 1/2)

1.1/Y7

Listening. Pupils check their answers to exercise 1. Then refer pupils to the Key Language box and ask questions about where the towns are, to reinforce the new language.

1 *Also, das liegt im Osten von der Schweiz. Ach ja, das ist Klosters.* 19
2 *Und das liegt im Norden von Deutschland, im Norden von Deutschland – das ist Kiel.*
3 *Das liegt im Süden von Deutschland. Das ist München.*
4 *Und das ist in Deutschland, im Osten. Das ist Leipzig.*
5 *Das ist im Westen von Österreich also, im Westen … das ist Salzburg.*
6 *Das ist die Hauptstadt von der Schweiz. Das ist Bern.*
7 *Das ist die Hauptstadt von Deutschland. Das ist Berlin.*
8 *Und das ist die Hauptstadt von Österreich, und liegt im Osten. Ähm, das ist Wien.*

Answers
1 Klosters
2 Kiel
3 München
4 Leipzig
5 Salzburg
6 Bern
7 Berlin
8 Wien

Aussprache (AT 1/)

4.1/Y7

Listening. Pupils listen to and repeat the German pronunciation of European city names that are commonly pronounced differently in English. They could then chorus them for practice.

Berlin
Salzburg
Bern
London
Paris
20

3 Partnerarbeit: Erdkundequiz. (AT 2/3)

1.4b/Y7

Speaking. In pairs, pupils quiz each other on the location of the towns and cities on the map, collecting points for immediately correct answers.

+ More confident learners could extend this activity to other cities and countries.

Starter 2

1.1/Y7 1.1/Y8

Aim

To encourage pupils to pay close attention when listening.

Pupils look at the map on page 86 for one minute to refresh their memories about where places are. They then take turns to come to the front and read aloud the following statements about towns in the German-speaking countries. After each one, the rest of the class must stand up if they think it is false. Ask a volunteer to correct it (to make this easier for weaker pupils, you could at this stage reveal the false sentence on an OHT). Less confident learners could be allowed to refer to the map in the Pupil's Book. More able pupils could themselves prepare some true/false statements to be used. Encourage pupils to listen carefully and try to understand sentences on a first hearing.

München ist die Hauptstadt von Deutschland. (Berlin)
Bern liegt in Österreich. (in der Schweiz)
Kiel liegt im Norden von Deutschland. (richtig)
Wien ist die Hauptstadt von der Schweiz. (Österreich)
Salzburg ist bekannt für Mozart. (richtig)
Leipzig liegt im Westen von Deutschland. (im Osten)

4 Hör zu. Wie ist das Wetter? (1–10) (AT 1/3)

1.1/Y8

Listening. Pupils listen to the statements about weather, and match each one to the relevant symbol. Before pupils open their books to start the task, you could play the first one or two statements and ask them what they think they are listening to, and how they could tell.

Und jetzt der Wetterbericht für heute.
Wie ist das Wetter?

 21

1 *Zuerst, Norddeutschland. Es ist kalt in Hamburg.*
2 *Es ist windig in Kiel.*
3 *In der Hauptstadt, Berlin, ist es nebelig.*
4 *In Leipzig ist es sonnig, aber frostig.*
5 *Jetzt Süddeutschland, und es regnet in München. Temperaturen, zwölf Grad.*
6 *In Stuttgart ist es heiß. Das Wetter ist schön.*
7 *Und jetzt, die Schweiz. In Bern ist es stürmisch. Es donnert und blitzt.*
8 *Es schneit in Klosters. Die Temperatur liegt bei minus zwei Grad.*
9 *Und in Österreich, wie ist das Wetter? Es ist warm in Wien.*
10 *In Salzburg ist es kalt und wolkig.*

Answers

1 i	2 c	3 e	4 b ,f	5 j	6 g, a
7 l	8 k	9 h	10 i, d		

Suggestion

Practise the new weather vocabulary using weather symbols on pieces of card or cut-up OHT (see the suggestions for games in the Introduction).

5 Partnerarbeit. Wie ist das Wetter? (AT 2/2)

1.4b/Y7

Speaking. Pupils ask and answer questions about the weather in various European cities, using the information given. Encourage accurate pronunciation of the city names by drilling them first.

+ Quick finishers could go on to ask questions about other cities, and to make up answers. Encourage them to include several weather phrases for each, and to add exclamations and opinions.

6 Lies die Texte. Schreib die Tabelle ab und füll sie auf Englisch aus. (AT 3/4)

2.2a/Y8

Reading. Pupils read the texts in order to find the information needed to complete a copy of the grid in English. After completing the exercise, you could ask pupils to look for examples of a verb (*kann*) used with an infinitive at the end of the sentence in these texts. Pupils could read through the texts once and locate sentences they find hard to understand. After reading in more detail, ask pupils whether they managed to work out what the sentences meant and what helped them to work them out.

Answers

	1	2
Country	Switzerland	Germany
N/S/E/W	East	South
City/Village	village	city
Famous for	winter sports	football, beer
Activities	snowboarding	cinema
	skiing	sports centre
Opinion	super	never boring
Weather	snow in winter	often sunny, sometimes rainy
Place name	Klosters	München

7 Schreib über eine Phantasiestadt. (AT 4/4)

2.4b/Y8

Writing. Pupils write a text about an imaginary town, based on answers to the five questions. Encourage more able pupils to extend their sentences and to give as much detail as possible. Remind them that they will find useful language in the texts from the previous exercise, including modals with an infinitive.

Plenary

4.1/Y7 5.1

Aim

To practise sound–spelling links encountered in this unit, and extend pupils' knowledge of places in Germany.

Read out to pupils some, or all, of the following list of towns and cities in Germany, slowly and clearly. They listen carefully to each one and write it down, aiming to spell it correctly. Tell them to focus on each syllable, and to think whether they already know how to spell that syllable from other words or place names. Reveal each one after reading it out and discuss the pronunciation – what word did it sound like? Offer a reward to any pupil who can show you on a map where the places are, by next lesson.

Bernau	*(Bern, 'au' blau)*
Düsseldorf	*('ü' München, Dorf)*
Freiburg	*('ei' Leipzig, 'burg' Salzburg)*
Schwerin	*(Berlin)*
Trier	*(Kiel)*
Weimar	*('ei' Leipzig)*

Learning targets
- Saying what there is in a town, and talking about types of transport
- Recognising plural forms

Key framework objectives

4.5/Y7 Language – (b) modal verbs
4.3/Y8 Language – plurals
5.4 Strategies – working out meaning

Grammar
- *es gibt* + accusative (revision)
- *man kann* + infinitive (revision)

Key language

der Bahnhof (∴ e)
der Markt (∴ e)
der Park(s)
der Supermarkt (∴ e)
die Kirche(n)
die Post(en)
das Rathaus (∴ er)
das Schloss (∴ er)
das Schwimmbad (∴ er)
das Verkehrsamt (∴ er)
Es gibt einen / eine / ein / zwei / drei …
Es gibt keinen / keine / kein …
Man kann … fahren
mit dem Auto / Bus / Zug / Taxi / Flugzeug
mit der Straßenbahn / U-Bahn
Man kann zu Fuß gehen
im Frühling / Sommer / Herbst / Winter

High-frequency words

was?	*kann*
wie?	*mit*
es gibt	*gehen*
ein	*fahren*
kein	*im*
man	

Resources

CD 3, tracks 22–24
Workbooks A and B, p.53
Arbeitsblatt 6.2, p. 107
Arbeitsblatt 6.5, p. 110
Flashcards 81–88
Echo Elektro 1 TPP, Express
Mod 6 2.1–2.7

Starter 1
4.1/Y7

Aim
To encourage pupils to predict the pronunciation of 'difficult' new words.

Write these six new words on the board, or use pieces of an OHT copy of **Arbeitsblatt 6.2** on a projector:

Kirche
Rathaus
Schloss
Schwimmbad
Supermarkt
Verkehrsamt

In pairs or groups, pupils attempt to pronounce each word. They then consolidate and build their confidence through whole-class chorusing (you can use louder/quieter, etc. to make this fun). Before starting, look at potential problem areas, such as *sch, w, v, s*.

At this stage, pupils may not understand the words. Ask if anyone knows what type of words they are (e.g. nouns, places in a town), and whether they can guess the meanings of any of the words. If you are using OHT pieces on a projector, volunteers could come to the front of the class and try to match words to pictures.

① Wie heißt das auf Deutsch? (AT3/1 AT4/1)
4.2/Y7

 Writing. Pupils match each word to the correct picture, and copy the word correctly. They will need to look up the meanings of some of the words. After checking answers, you could chorus the words with the class, perhaps firstly asking them to predict the correct pronunciation of each one.

Answers
a der Supermarkt
b die Kirche
c der Park
d das Schloss
e der Bahnhof
f das Schwimmbad
g die Post
h der Markt
i das Verkehrsamt
j das Rathaus

Suggestion

Photocopy **Arbeitsblatt 6.2** (two for each pair of pupils), and cut up the copies to make playing cards. Pupils shuffle their set of cards and spread them face down on the table. They then play Pelmanism to collect matching pairs of cards, turning two cards face up each time, and saying the word on each card aloud. The cards could be used again later in the unit, with pupils forming *es gibt* sentences as they turn them over.

2 Was gibt es in der Stadt? (1–3) (AT1/3)

1.1/Y7 1.1/Y8

Listening. Pupils listen to the interviews about people's towns, and identify the pictures for the features each town has by writing down the letters each time. Before starting, elicit from the class the meaning of *es gibt*, and remind them about the difference between *ein* and *kein*. Ask pupils if they find *es gibt* easy or difficult to remember. What do they think the words mean literally? Explain that they will come across other phrases like this in German which have to be translated as a 'chunk' rather than word for word and that it would be useful to start a list of them in their exercise books.

> **1** – *Andreas, was gibt es in deiner Stadt?*
> – *Ähm …Es gibt ein Schwimmbad. …Es gibt auch einen Supermarkt und einen Park.* **22**
> **2** – *Und Herr Detmold, was gibt es in Ihrer Stadt?*
> – *Also, es gibt ein Verkehrsamt. Ja, und es gibt auch ein Schloss, eine alte Kirche und ein Rathaus. Das ist sehr interessant.*
> **3** – *Frau Schmidt, was gibt es in Ihrer Stadt?*
> – *Es gibt eine Post. Es gibt auch zwei Supermärkte, aber wir haben keinen Markt.*

> **Answers**
> **1** f, a, c   **2** i, d, b, j   **3** g, a (x2)

3 Gedächtnisspiel: Was gibt es in der Stadt? (AT 2/3–4)

5.2

Speaking. Small groups play a memory game, building up a chain of places in a town – this information could be made up, or be based on a place they all know. Draw attention to the Key Language panel for support. Weaker pupils can focus on simply using the correct items of vocabulary, while more able learners should aim for accuracy in their use of the indefinite article, and could also include *kein* and plural forms of nouns.

Starter 2

4.2/Y7

Aim

To consolidate the vocabulary for places in a town.

Use an OHT copy of **Arbeitsblatt 6.2.** Cut up the individual cards (with or without the words), and scatter them on the projector. Start by running through the vocabulary, using *es gibt*. You could initially cover, or half conceal, the words, revealing each one as you elicit it from the class.

Then turn the projector off, remove one card, and turn it on again. Pairs of pupils write a sentence on mini-whiteboards or paper to say what is missing, using *es gibt + keinen / keine / kein*, and hold up their answers. With a less able group, you may want to colour-code the cards (or write the endings on them), to help with the correct ending for *kein.*

4 Wie viele gibt es? (AT 3/4)

4.3/Y8 5.4

Reading. Pupils read the tourist information leaflet and record how many of each of the features a–j pictured in exercise 1 there are in Parkstadt. Before starting, draw their attention to the **ECHO-Tipp** panel about the plural forms of nouns.

Follow-up reading, translation and writing activities can be found in the Introduction on pages 9–10.

> **Answers**
> **a** 4   **b** 3   **c** 1   **d** 0   **e** 0   **f** 2   **g** 1   **h** 1
> **i** 1   **j** 1

ECHO-Tipp

4.3/Y8

This panel reminds pupils about the range of plural noun forms in German. Discuss with pupils where and how to find the plural forms of nouns. They could then note the plural forms of places in a town – by picking out those used in the text for exercise 4, and looking up others themselves.

ECHO-Tipp: Words in context 5.4

After reading this tip box, pupils look at the text about Parkstadt again, and find the words for the four seasons. Ask pupils how they managed to work out the meanings. This could be developed into a list of strategies on the board.

5 Hör zu. Finde den richtigen Untertitel für jedes Foto. (1–8) (AT 1/2) 4.5b/Y7

Listening. Pupils listen to the statements about transport, and identify the correct transport noun for each photo from those given on the right. You may then wish to chorus the new vocabulary to practise pronunciation. Ask more able pupils why some are *mit dem* and others are *mit der*. Also focus on the difference in verb for modes of transport and for going by foot. You could point out that these are also expressions which can't be translated word for word from German into English: we don't say 'with the bus'! Looking at the rest of the phrase or text will help them to work out the most suitable translation of a word.

1 – Wie kann man in die Stadt fahren?
 – Man kann mit dem Auto fahren. *23*
2 – Wie kann man in die Stadt fahren?
 – Man kann mit dem Bus fahren.
3 – Wie kann man in die Stadt fahren?
 – Man kann mit dem Zug fahren.
4 – Wie kann man in die Stadt fahren?
 – Man kann mit dem Taxi fahren.
5 – Wie kann man in die Stadt fahren?
 – Man kann mit dem Flugzeug fliegen.
6 – Wie kann man in die Stadt fahren?
 – Man kann mit der Straßenbahn fahren.
7 – Wie kann man in die Stadt fahren?
 – Man kann mit der U-Bahn fahren.
8 – Wie kann man in die Stadt fahren?
 – Man kann zu Fuß gehen.

Answers
1 Auto
2 Bus
3 Zug
4 Taxi
5 Flugzeug
6 Straßenbahn
7 U-Bahn (short for Untergrund-Bahn)
8 zu Fuß

6 Partnerarbeit. (AT 2/2) 4.5b/Y7

Speaking. Using the Key Language panel for support, pupils ask and answer questions about transport, using the pictures from exercise 5. Before starting, ask pupils what question they heard each time during the listening exercise. Remind weaker pupils about *man kann*, and that the verb (*fahren, gehen* or *fliegen*) goes to the end of the sentence.

7 Hör zu und füll die Tabelle aus. (1–3) (AT 1/4) 1.2/Y8

Listening. Pupils listen to three young people talking about the town where they live, and note as many details as possible in English in the grid. Warn them that they must spell the place names correctly, and offer bonus marks if they can also note extra details (e.g. opinions, weather).

1 Hallo, ich wohne in Zürich. Das schreibt man Z Ü R I C H. Das liegt in der Schweiz, im Norden. Die Stadt ist sehr groß und ich wohne gern hier. Es gibt einen schönen Park und ein großes Schwimmbad – das ist toll im Sommer. Man kann mit dem Flugzeug nach Zürich fliegen, oder natürlich mit Bus oder dem Auto fahren. *24*
2 Hallo, ich komme aus Deutschland. Ich wohne in Stuttgart, im Süden. Das schreibt man S T U T T G A R T. Wir haben Kinos, zwei Schwimmbäder und eine große Kirche. Der Park ist schön im Herbst und im Frühling. Man kann mit dem Zug, mit dem Bus oder mit der Straßenbahn fahren. Es ist toll hier!
3 Ich wohne in Zell, im Westen von Österreich. Das schreibt man Z E L L. Zell ist ein Dorf, und ist nicht sehr groß. Im Winter schneit es sehr oft hier und man kann gut Ski fahren. Es gibt auch alte Häuser und eine Kirche. Es ist manchmal langweilig, aber ich wohne gern hier. Mann kann mit dem Zug oder mit dem Bus nach Zell fahren.

Answers
	Town	Location	What there is	Transport
1	Zürich	Switzerland North	Nice park / Big swimming pool	Plane / Bus / Car
2	Stuttgart	Germany South	Cinemas / 2 swimming pools / Big church / Park	Train / Bus / Tram
3	Zell	Austria West	Old houses / Church	Train / Bus

8 Schreib über deine Stadt / dein Dorf. (AT 4/4)

2.4a+b/Y8

Writing. Pupils write about their town or village. They should include as much detail as possible. You could use **Arbeitsblatt 6.5** to assist pupils in doing this task. They must focus on accuracy by checking genders and plurals, the correct use of *es gibt* and *man kann*, and other verb forms.

Plenary

4.2/Y7

Aims

To recap vocabulary from the unit.
To focus thinking on why one word in a group of three is the odd-one-out.

Write the following groups of three words from this unit on the board or an OHT. In pairs, pupils work out which word is the odd-one-out, and why. There may be more than one possible answer – accept any valid reasons when you discuss them. Then give pairs two minutes to come up with their own set of three, referring to their book if necessary, for the class to try.

Rathaus
Verkehrsamt
Parks
(*Park* – not a place you go to for advice; not a *das* word; cognate; plural)
Straßenbahn
Bus
U-Bahn
(*Bus* – does not travel on rails; *der* word; cognate)

Learning targets

- Asking for and giving directions
- Understanding the difference between *du* and *Sie*

Key framework objectives

5.6   Strategies – reading aloud

Grammar

- Use of *du* and *Sie*
- Introduction to the imperative

Key language

Wo ist …?
der Markt / Park
die Kirche / Post
das Rathaus / Schwimmbad / Verkehrsamt
Geh / Gehen Sie …
links
rechts
geradeaus
Nimm / Nehmen Sie …
die erste / zweite / dritte Straße
bitte
danke

High-frequency words

wo?
geh / gehen Sie
nimm / nehmen Sie
Sie
erste / zweite / dritte
bitte
danke

Resources

CD 3, tracks 25–28
Workbooks A and B, p.54
Arbeitsblatt 6.3, p. 108
Echo Elektro 1 TPP, Express
Mod 6 3.1–3.8

Starter 1
4.2/Y7

Aim

To introduce and practise basic vocabulary for giving directions, using the imperative.

Blindfold directions game: tell the class that they are going to learn how to give and understand directions in German. Write the key words *geh links, geh rechts, geh geradeaus*, with arrows, on the board, and briefly introduce them by means of pointing and repetition. Ask for a volunteer who does not mind being blindfolded, and get another pupil to tie a scarf around his/her eyes. Choose reliable members of the class to direct the volunteer safely around furniture to the opposite corner of the room, by calling out the relevant direction word whenever a change of direction is needed. Involve as many pupils as possible by frequently changing the 'caller', so that everybody stays alert in case they are chosen.

1 Hör zu. Was passt zusammen? (1–8) (AT 1/1)
1.1/Y7

Listening. Pupils listen to the recording and match the words they hear to the correct directions icon. Check answers and elicit the meaning of *Straße*.

---

1 *links*
2 *die erste Straße links*
3 *geradeaus*
4 *auf der linken Seite*
5 *die zweite Straße links*
6 *rechts*
7 *auf der rechten Seite*
8 *die dritte Straße rechts*

25

> **Answers**
> **1** b   **2** d   **3** a   **4** h   **5** e   **6** c   **7** g   **8** f

2 Hör zu. Sieh dir den Plan von Echostadt an. Wo geht man hin? (1–6) (AT 1/3)
1.1/Y7

Listening. Pupils listen to the directions given, follow them on the map and work out which place they are being directed to. Afterwards, elicit the meaning of *auf der linken / rechten Seite*. Confident learners may also notice the difference between *geh* and *gehen Sie, nimm* and *nehmen Sie*. This is looked at in exercises 4 and 5.

1 – *Wo ist [beep], bitte?*
   – *Geh geradeaus und nimm die erste Straße links. Das ist auf der rechten Seite.*
   – *Danke.*
   – *Bitte.*

26

2 – Guten Tag. Wo ist hier [beep], bitte?
  – Also, gehen Sie geradeaus und nehmen Sie die dritte Straße links. Das ist auf der rechten Seite.
  – Danke schön.
  – Bitte sehr.

3 – Entschuldigen Sie, bitte. Wo ist [beep], bitte?
  – Gehen Sie geradeaus und nehmen Sie die zweite Straße rechts. Das ist auf der linken Seite.
  – Danke.
  – Bitte.

4 – Hallo. Wo ist [beep], bitte?
  – Geh geradeaus und nimm die zweite Straße links. Das ist auf der rechten Seite.
  – Danke schön.
  – Bitte sehr.

5 – Wo ist [beep], bitte?
  – Geh geradeaus und nimm die dritte Straße rechts. Das ist auf der linken Seite.
  – Danke.
  – Bitte.

6 – Wo ist [beep], bitte?
  – Geh geradeaus und nimm die erste Straße rechts. Das ist auf der linken Seite.
  – Danke.
  – Bitte.

Answers

1 a   2 c   3 e   4 b   5 f   6 d

---

3 Partnerarbeit. Wo ist das in Echostadt? (AT 2/3)   1.4b/Y7

Speaking. Pupils follow the model dialogue given in order to ask for and give directions to four different places on the map, as indicated by the picture cues.

A variation on pairwork can be found in the Introduction on page 10.

Suggestion
Quick finishers could create further dialogues for the remaining places on the map. They could then write out complete dialogues, perhaps including greetings or other extra language.

Starter 2   1.4b/Y7

Aim
To reinforce the language learnt in the previous lesson for asking for and giving simple directions.

Information-gap speaking task: give out copies of **Arbeitsblatt 6.3**. Pupils each fold their sheet (or a single copy could be cut in two) so that one partner is looking at role A and the other at role B. Before starting, elicit the key language of asking for and giving directions, writing this on the board as necessary for support. Pairs work through the necessary dialogues, and label the 'missing' places on their maps.

4 Hör die Dialoge von Aufgabe 2 noch mal an. „Du" oder „Sie"? (1–6) (AT 1/2)   1.3a/Y8

Listening. Pupils listen to the recording, which is the same as from exercise 2, but with beeps replaced by locations, and identify whether *geh / nimm* – for somebody being addressed as *du* – or *gehen Sie / nehmen Sie* is used. Before playing the recording, look at the **ECHO-Tipp** panel with the class. After checking answers, draw pupils' attention to the imperative forms in the **ECHO-Detektiv** before starting exercise 5.

1 – Wo ist der Markt bitte?
  – Geh geradeaus und nimm die erste Straße links. Das ist auf der rechten Seite.
  – Danke.
  – Bitte.

2 – Guten Tag. Wo ist hier das Rathaus bitte?
  – Also, gehen Sie geradeaus und nehmen Sie die dritte Straße links. Das ist auf der rechten Seite.
  – Danke schön.
  – Bitte sehr.

3 – Entschuldigen Sie, bitte. Wo ist die Kirche bitte?
  – Gehen Sie geradeaus und nehmen Sie die zweite Straße rechts. Das ist auf der linken Seite.
  – Danke.
  – Bitte.

4 – Hallo. Wo ist die Post bitte?
  – Geh geradeaus und nimm die zweite Straße links. Das ist auf der rechten Seite.
  – Danke schön.
  – Bitte sehr.

5 – Wo ist das Verkehrsamt, bitte?
  – Geh geradeaus und nimm die dritte Straße rechts. Das ist auf der linken Seite.
  – Danke.
  – Bitte.

27

6 – Wo ist der Park, bitte?
  – Geh geradeaus und nimm die erste Straße rechts.
    Das ist auf der linken Seite.
  – Danke.
  – Bitte.

Answers
1 du 2 Sie 3 Sie 4 du 5 du 6 du

ECHO-Detektiv: Giving instructions
This formalises for pupils the imperative of *gehen* and *nehmen*, in the *du* and *Sie* forms.

5 Wo ist das in Echostadt? Schreib Dialoge. „Du" oder „Sie"? (AT 4/3)
2.4a/Y7

Writing. Pupils write directions for each of the unknown people shown (using the map on the facing page), taking into account their evident age in order to decide whether to use the *du* or *Sie* form.

Answers
1 Geh geradeaus und nimm die zweite Straße rechts. Die Kirche ist auf der linken Seite.
2 Gehen Sie geradeaus und nehmen Sie die dritte Straße rechts. Das Verkehrsamt ist auf der linken Seite.
3 Geh geradeaus und nimm die erste Straße links. Der Markt ist auf der rechten Seite.

Pupils who finish quickly could write directions to other places on the map, without including the word for the destination, using the *du* or *Sie* form. Partners could then work out the destinations.

6 Hör zu und sing mit. 5.6
Listening. Pupils listen, then have a go at singing. For authenticity, divide them into two groups to sing the questions and directions. With more able pupils, write the words *Schloss, Marktplatz, Schwimmbad* on the board. The class could firstly listen to the song with their books shut, and tell you where these places are. Pupils could work in pairs and read the song out loud to practise accurate pronunciation. Further ideas for exploitation of songs can be found in the Introduction on page 10.

Wo ist bitte der Marktplatz?
Geh hier geradeaus.
Nimm die erste Straße links.
Das ist fünf Minuten vom Haus!

 28

Danke, danke, danke.
Bitte, bitte, bitte.
Ich fahre in die Stadt
Gibt es hier ein Schloss?
Ja, geh geradeaus.
Das Schloss ist neben der Post!
Danke, danke, danke.
Bitte, bitte, bitte.
Ich gehe heute schwimmen.
Gibt es hier ein Schwimmbad?
Ja, nimm die dritte Straße links.
Das geht schnell mit dem Rad!
Danke, danke, danke.
Bitte, bitte, bitte.

Plenary 5.8
Aim
To encourage pupils to reflect on what they have learnt in this unit.

Discuss with pupils the usefulness for tourists of knowing how to ask for and understand directions. Tell them to imagine they have to teach these useful phrases to a friend or relative who is going to a German-speaking country for work or on holiday. What would they need to explain, and which would be the most important words (a) to be able to use (question form, useful place names, polite words) and (b) to understand (direction words, imperative forms)? Get pairs of pupils to produce two lists, and collate answers on the board. Ask them to try teaching this to someone at home or a friend who is not learning German, and to report back next lesson on how they got on.

Alternatively, you may wish to use the **Mini-Test** as your plenary.

Mini-Test 5.8
Aim
To review language learned to date and identify areas for improvement.

Pupils work in pairs to check the language they have learned so far in this chapter, using the **Mini-Test** checklist. Ask pupils which points their partners found most difficult. Give them the task of improving these points by next lesson. Partners could then test them again.

Learning targets
- Buying food and drink at a snack stand using euros
- Using *ich möchte* to say what you would like

Key framework objectives
3.1/Y8 Culture – changes in everyday life
2.4/Y8 Writing – (a) using text as stimulus

Grammar
- *ich möchte* + direct object
- Identifying nouns, verbs, adjectives
- Nouns written with capital letter (revision)

Key language
ich möchte
einmal / zweimal / dreimal
Bratwurst
Hamburger
Pizza
Pommes
Schaschlik
Ketchup
Mayonnaise
Senf
Kaffee
Tee
mit Milch / Zitrone
Cola
Limonade
Das macht …
Euro
Cent

High-frequency words
ich möchte
einmal / zweimal / dreimal
mit
sie sind
das macht

Mathematics
Calculating prices

Citizenship
Cultural origins of food words and different types of food

Resources
CD 3, tracks 29–30
Workbooks A and B, p.55
Arbeitsblatt 6.4, p. 109
Flashcards 89–96
Echo Elektro 1 TPP, Express Mod 6 4.1–4.6

Starter 1 · 3.1/Y8

Aim
To look at words for food and drink which are used in more than one language.

Give pupils 30 seconds to look for any food and drink words that they recognise from other languages, using the snack list on page 92 of their books. Discuss their findings (they do not need to write them down at this stage), and which language they think each comes from (see answers for exercise 1). You could then ask them why this might be, e.g. international food trends, adopting popular foods from other countries. Discuss how this may have changed over time. When their parents and grandparents were young, it was not so common to eat food from other countries. Point out that although the words look the same, they may be pronounced differently.

1 Essen ist international! Welche Wörter erkennst du schon? (AT 3/1) 3.1/Y8
Reading. Pupils read through the list of snack items, and write down any they recognise from other languages. They should then make a note of any remaining words with their meanings. The origins of the words are shown below – pupils may know some of these. Introduce the others as you work through the list.

Answers
Cola = used in English
Hamburger = used in English ('Hamburger steak', i.e. steak in Hamburg style)
Ketchup = used in English (Chinese origin)
Limonade = French
Mayonnaise = used in English (French)
Pizza = used in English (Italian)
Pommes (frites) = French
Shaschlik = Turkish, via Russian

ECHO-Tipp 3.1/Y7
Ask if any pupils have seen such a snack stand in other countries, and whether they themselves drink tea with lemon or eat chips with mayonnaise. You could point out that Germans think it strange to put salt and vinegar on chips.

2 Hör zu. Was möchten sie? (1–6) (AT 1/3)

`1.1/Y7 1.1/Y8`

Listening. Pupils listen to the dialogues at a snack stand, and work out which items, and how many of them, each customer wants. Play each dialogue twice, and suggest to pupils that they firstly listen for the items, and secondly for the quantity. Weaker pupils could listen solely for the items.

1 – Bitte schön?
  – Ich möchte einmal Bratwurst und einmal Kaffee, bitte.

`29`

2 – Bitte schön?
  – Ich möchte einmal Schaschlik, einmal Pommes und einmal Senf, bitte.

3 – Guten Tag. Bitte schön?
  – Ich möchte einmal Pizza und zweimal Limonade, bitte.

4 – Guten Tag. Bitte schön?
  – Guten Tag. Ich möchte dreimal Pommes, zweimal Ketchup und eine Portion Mayonnaise, bitte.
  – Sonst noch etwas?
  – Ja, dreimal Cola, bitte.

5 – Guten Tag.
  – Ich möchte zweimal Hamburger und eine Tasse Tee mit Zitrone, bitte.

6 – Guten Tag, kann ich dir helfen?
  – Ja, bitte. Ich möchte viermal Bratwurst, viermal Pommes, und achtmal Mayonnaise.

Answers

1 b × 1, i × 1
2 d × 1, e × 1, m × 1
3 c × 1, f × 2
4 e × 3, k × 2, l × 1, g × 3
5 a × 2, j × 1
6 b × 4, e × 4, l × 8

Refer pupils to the Key Language panel, and practise the pronunciation of *ich möchte*. Then practise the use of *einmal*, etc. with food words: hold up one of the flashcards for snack items, and write the number '1' on the board (or indicate with one finger). Get a confident volunteer to ask for that item, using *ich möchte einmal …, bitte*. Repeat, getting the whole class to chorus the answers, and using different numbers and items, perhaps progressing on to pairs of items.

3 Was isst und trinkt Friedrich jeden Tag? Schreib eine Liste. (AT 4/3)

`2.4a/Y7`

Writing. Pupils use the information in the picture to write a long sentence about what Friedrich eats every day.

Answers
(Accept any order and suitable wording.)
Friedrich isst fünfmal Bratwurst, dreimal Pommes, dreimal Mayonnaise, viermal Hamburger, zweimal Pizza und trinkt achtmal Cola.

Starter 2

`4.2/Y7`

Aims
To revise numbers 1–100.
To practise saying prices of snacks in euros and cents.

If you have not already done so, discuss euros and cents with the class, referring pupils to the panel in their books. Explain that they are going to be learning more about buying snacks, so will need to practise saying and understanding prices. Write an example price in figures on the board and elicit how it would be said in German.

Mental arithmetic: read out a short list of single food and drink items and their prices from the price list in the Pupil's Book. Pupils listen, with books closed, and work out the total cost – writing it in figures on paper or a mini-whiteboard and holding it up as soon as they have finished. Confirm the correct answer by writing it on the board.

ECHO-TIPP
Draw pupils' attention to this panel on the euro before they tackle exercise 4.

4 Hör zu. Was möchten Sie? Was kostet das? (1–6) (AT 1/4)

`1.2/Y8`

Listening. Pupils listen to longer dialogues at a snack stand. For each one, they note the items bought (in German or English, depending on your group), and the total price paid. Remind them that they can make use of the price list in exercise 1 for support.

Elicit the meanings of the extra questions heard in the recording: *Sonst noch etwas? Und zu trinken? Ist der Tee mit Milch oder Zitrone?* Encourage pupils to include such questions to extend their speaking in the next task.

1 – *Guten Tag. Ich möchte zweimal Pommes und zweimal Cola, bitte.*
  – *Zweimal Pommes und zweimal Cola. … Bitte schön. Das macht acht Euro, bitte.*
  – *Acht Euro, bitte schön.*
  – *Danke schön, auf Wiedersehen.*
2 – *Guten Tag. Was darf's sein?*
  – *Ich möchte einmal Pizza, bitte.*
  – *Sonst noch etwas?*
  – *Nein danke, das ist alles.*
  – *Das macht zwei Euro fünfzig, bitte.*
  – *Zwei Euro fünfzig, bitte schön.*
  – *Danke schön, auf Wiedersehen.*
3 – *Guten Tag. Ich möchte einmal Bratwurst, bitte.*
  – *Einmal Bratwurst. Mit Senf?*
  – *Nein, mit Ketchup bitte.*
  – *Also, einmal Bratwurst und einmal Ketchup, das macht zwei Euro siebzig, bitte.*
  – *Zwei Euro siebzig, bitte schön.*
  – *Danke schön, auf Wiedersehen.*
4 – *Guten Tag. bitte schön?*
  – *Ich möchte dreimal Hamburger, bitte.*
  – *Und zu trinken?*
  – *Zweimal Cola und einmal Limonade bitte.*
  – *Dreimal Hamburger, zweimal Cola, und eine Limonade … Das macht zwölf Euro sechzig, bitte.*
  – *Zwölf Euro sechzig, bitte schön.*
  – *Danke schön, auf Wiedersehen.*
5 – *Guten Tag. Ich möchte einmal Schaschlik und zweimal Bratwurst, bitte.*
  – *Einmal Schaschlik und zweimal Bratwurst. Sonst noch etwas?*
  – *Ja, dreimal Mineralwasser bitte.*
  – *Also … Das macht vierzehn Euro, bitte.*
  – *Vierzehn Euro, bitte schön.*
  – *Danke schön, auf Wiedersehen.*
6 – *Guten Tag. Ich möchte viermal Kaffee und einmal Tee, bitte.*
  – *Ist der Tee mit Milch oder Zitrone?*
  – *Tee mit Zitrone, bitte.*
  – *Sonst noch etwas?*
  – *Nein, danke.*
  – *Also … Das macht zehn Euro, bitte.*
  – *Zehn Euro, bitte schön.*
  – *Danke schön, auf Wiedersehen.*

Answers
1 2 × Pommes, 2 × Cola, 8,00 Euro
2 1 × Pizza, 2,50 Euro
3 1 × Bratwurst, 1 × Ketchup, 2,70 Euro
4 3 × Hamburger, 2 × Cola, 1 × Limonade, 12,60 Euro
5 1 × Schaschlik, 2 × Bratwurst, 3 × Mineralwasser, 14,00 Euro
6 4 × Kaffee, 1 × Tee mit Zitrone, 10,00 Euro

---

5 Partnerarbeit: Mach Dialoge an der Imbissbude. (AT 2/4)   `1.4b/Y7`

Speaking. Pupils work with a partner, taking it in turns to be the customer at a snack stand and to ask for the items pictured. A sample dialogue is given, which can be extended by more confident learners. The vendor will need to refer to the price list at the start of the unit. Quick finishers could go on to make up their own extended dialogues, or write out a dialogue. A variation on pairwork can be found in the Introduction on page 10.

6 Was essen und trinken sie gern oder nicht gern? (AT 3/3)   `2.1/Y7`

Reading. Pupils read the three texts and complete a simple grid in English for each person, to show what they do and do not like eating and drinking. You may wish to elicit the meaning of *sie sind*, and to direct pupils to page 120 for further practice of conjugating the verb *sein*.

Answers

	✓	✗
Nina	hamburger chips lemonade	cola
Viktor	chips mayonnaise cola	tea coffee
Stefanie	kebab ketchup coffee	chips cola lemonade

+ Quick finishers could translate one or more of the texts into English. Additional follow-up activities can be found in the Introduction on pages 9–10.

7 Lies die Texte noch mal. Finde zehn Substantive, fünf Verben und fünf Adjektive. (AT 3/3)   `2.1/Y7`

Reading/Writing. Pupils re-read the three texts from exercise 6 in order to identify nouns, verbs and adjectives. Support weaker pupils by writing a few examples for each category on the board and emphasising how to recognise them (e.g. nouns begin with capital letter, common verb endings). You could also remind them that verbs are always the second idea in the sentence.

ECHO-Tipp
This is a reminder to pupils that all nouns in German are written with capital letters.

8 Schreib die Sätze zu Ende. (AT 4/4)

2.4a/Y8

Writing. Pupils construct a paragraph about their own taste in food and drink, to include each of the given sentence beginnings at least once. You could start by looking at the sentence beginnings and putting them into the order in which they think they would come in a paragraph. They can make use of the texts from exercise 6 as models for their own writing – encourage them to read through the texts and pick out useful phrases that they would like to re-use, drawing particular attention to adding details about opinions and using *gern* and *nicht gern* correctly.

Plenary

5.2

Aim

To focus on selecting useful language items from a source text.

Top Five Phrase Learning: tell the class they must decide on the Top Five phrases they could use again, from the three texts in exercise 6. Elicit ideas and collate a list of five on the board, voting on any about which there is disagreement. All pupils copy the list down. Give them a fixed time to work in small groups, testing each other or helping each other to learn the five phrases. Finally, as each pupil passes you at the door on their way out of the lesson, they must say a sentence of their own including one of the phrases.

Suggestions:

Das ist lecker!
Das schmeckt gut.
zu Hause
Das finde ich (langweilig).
Ich finde … furchtbar.
mein Lieblingsessen
… ist (nicht) sehr gut für mich.
nicht so gern

Learning targets

- Talking about your plans for the summer holidays
- Talking about the future (using the present tense)

Key framework objectives

1.2/Y8 Listening – new contexts
1.3/Y8 Listening – (a) understanding language for specific functions
3.2/Y8 Culture – (a) young people: aspirations
4.5/Y8 Language – (a) range of verb tenses (future)

Grammar

- Using the present tense to talk about the future
- Verb as second idea (revisited)

Key language

Was machst du in den Sommerferien?
Für wie lange?
Wie fährst du dahin?
Ich fahre / Er/Sie fährt / Wir fahren …
nach Schottland / Wales / Devon / Spanien / Österreich
für …Tage / Wochen
Ich bleibe zu Hause.
mit dem Auto / Bus / Flugzeug / Zug
in den Sommerferien
morgen
nächste Woche
am Montag / Dienstag / Mittwoch, etc.

High-frequency words

was?	*nach*
wie?	*in*
bleiben	*zu*
fahren	*am*
machen	*nächste*
für	*morgen*
mit	

ICT

Word-processing

Resources

CD 3, tracks 31–32
Workbooks A and B, p.56
Arbeitsblatt, 6.6, p. 111
Arbeitsblatt 6.7, p. 112
Echo Elektro 1 TPP, Express
Mod 6 5.1–5.7

Starter 1
4.2/Y7

Aim

To introduce the idea of holiday plans, revise country names, and give pupils the names of other countries they may need for holiday destinations.

Write the following 'word halves' of German names for countries on the board or an OHT, scattered randomly – beginnings on the left-hand side, endings on the right. Some are already known to the class; others will be new. Working in pairs, pupils write down what they think are the correct words, and their English meanings. When most have finished, link up the correct pairings and elicit meanings.

Schott	*land*	*Ita*	*lien*
Spa	*nien*	*Frank*	*reich*
Griechen	*land*	*Amer*	*ika*
Öst	*erreich*	*Austra*	*lien*
Eng	*land*	*Bel*	*gien*

---

1 Was passt zusammen? (AT 3/1)
4.5a/Y7

Reading. Pupils read the statements about plans for the summer holidays, and match each one to the correct picture postcard.

> **Answers**
> **1** c   **2** d   **3** b   **4** a

Suggestion

At this point, you could ask pupils where they are going in the summer holidays. Start by giving your own answer, then choose confident members of the class to demonstrate. Elicit the meanings of *ich fahre nach …* and *ich bleibe.*

+ After five people have said their plans, ask a sixth person to re-cap as many as they can remember, using *er / sie* verb forms. Then continue with another five.

2 Hör zu. Was sagen sie noch? (1–3) (AT 1/4)
1.1/Y7 1.1/8

Listening. Pupils listen to the interviews and pick out the extra information given. Before playing the recording, elicit what type of details pupils think will be heard (length of stay and mode of travel). With a less confident class, play the recording twice: encourage pupils to make brief notes on the first hearing and then write out the answers in full on the second hearing. Confident pupils could report the details in a full sentence using third person verb forms.

1 – *Peter, was machst du in den*
   Sommerferien?
   – *Ich fahre nach Österreich.*
   – *Für wie lange?*
   – *Für zehn Tage.*
   – *Wie fährst du dahin?*
   – *Wir fahren mit dem Auto.*
2 – *Nina, was machst du in den Sommerferien?*
   – *Ich fahre nach Schottland.*
   – *Für wie lange?*
   – *Für zwei Wochen.*
   – *Wie fährst du dahin?*
   – *Ich fliege mit dem Flugzeug, und fahre mit dem Auto.*
3 – *Julia, was machst du in den Sommerferien?*
   – *Stefanie und ich fahren im August nach Spanien.*
   – *Für wie lange?*
   – *Für eine Woche.*
   – *Wie fährt ihr dahin?*
   – *Wir fahren mit dem Bus.*

31

Answers
Peter: 10 Tage, Auto
Nina: zwei Wochen, Flugzeug + Auto
Julia und Stefanie: eine Woche, Bus

ECHO-Detektiv: Talking about the future
4.5a/Y8

Reinforce the fact that the present tense can be used to talk about the future by asking pupils to tell you one thing they are going to do this weekend or in the summer holidays. This could simply be a sentence with *ich fahre nach ...*, or could include other verbs (*ich esse, ich spiele, ich besuche, ich sehe*, etc.). More able pupils could use the *wir* form or make compound sentences. You could also use **Arbeitsblatt 6.6**.

3 Interviews über die Sommerferien. Mach Notizen. (AT 2/4–5) **1.4b/Y7 1.4b/Y8**

Speaking. Pairs interview each other about plans for the next summer holidays, and make notes. Encourage more able pupils to add opinions to their replies. Before starting, make sure the words needed for different countries are known. Explain that *nach* is used with named places.

Suggestion
The speaking task could be extended to become a class survey, or to become questions and answers about an imaginary ideal holiday.

4 Schreib einen Bericht. (AT 4/4)
2.4b/Y8

Writing. Pupils use the information gathered in exercise 3 to write a report about what their interviewees are planning to do in the summer holidays, using third person verb forms. The example given structures ideas in the time, manner, place order. With stronger classes you could emphasise this order and go on to do **Arbeitsblatt 6.7**, which practises the point in more detail.

Starter 2   **5.1**

Aim
To practise using familiar verbs in the *wir* form, and revise vocabulary for leisure activities, in preparation for the next tasks.

Huddle miming: ask the class to stand up. Tell them to mime any 'holiday' activity you say, to show that they understand its meaning. If the verb is with *ich*, pupils must stand individually and mime. If it is with *wir*, they must move to stand in a huddle with others and mime together. Any lack of clarity about whether they're standing alone or with others will result in them being out (although some sensitivity towards class 'loners' will of course be needed). Call out these verbs repeatedly, making a sentence with each one (initially miming as well yourself, to give pupils ideas). If any pupil mimes incorrectly or too slowly, they must sit down, until only a few winners are left – depending on the time available. Pupils who are out could do some of the calling for you. To make it more challenging, you could play the game as *Simon sagt*.

wir fahren / ich fahre
wir bleiben / ich bleibe
wir spielen / ich spiele
wir gehen / ich gehe
wir sehen / ich sehe
wir lesen / ich lese
wir besuchen / ich besuche
wir hören / ich höre

5 Füll die Lücken (1–6) mit dem richtigen Verb aus. (AT 3/5) `5.1`

Reading. Pupils focus on the first two paragraphs of the text, paying attention to details in order to select the correct verb and its form from the panel, for insertion into each gap. More able pupils should try this task without looking at the panel, using it only to check their answers.

Suggestion

Before starting the task, give pupils one minute to skim the whole text. Ask them to tell you how difficult they find it, what it is about, and to outline the content of each of the three paragraphs.

> **Answers**
> 1 fahre
> 2 fahren
> 3 haben
> 4 ist
> 5 gibt
> 6 kann

6 Was machen sie am Montag, Dienstag, usw.? (AT 3/5) `2.2a/Y8`

Reading. Pupils now read the final paragraph of the text and work out what Julia's plans are for each day of the holiday, matching pictures to days. They will need to pay extra attention to the activities Julia mentions once, but will be doing more than once (i.e. swimming every day). Follow-up reading, writing and translation activities can be found in the Introduction on pages 9–10.

> **Answers**
> Mo.   a, d
> Di.   a, h
> Mi.   a, f
> Do.   a, b, g
> Fr.   a, e
> Sa.   a, c

ECHO-Detektiv `4.5a/Y8`

This panel highlights a number of time phrases for talking about the future with the present tense. Here, you could ask pupils what phrases they use in English and show that there are equivalent phrases that they will both see and use in German. Highlight the point that these are the main clue that someone is talking about the future when they use the present tense, so pupils should learn them carefully.

7 Hör zu und füll die Tabelle aus. (AT 1/5) `1.2/Y8 1.3a/Y8 3.2a/Y8`

Listening. Pupils listen to three people talking in detail about their holiday plans, and note the relevant information in English in the grid. After completing the exercise, pupils could listen again to pick out the colloquial expressions in the listening that make the speech feel authentic. These are highlighted in the transcript below. Ask pupils also to listen for the tone and intonation the speakers use. Discuss with pupils how the holiday plans of the speakers compare to their own holiday plans.

1   Hallo. **Also,** meine Pläne für die Sommerferien. **Naja,** wir fahren nach Toulouse. Das liegt im Süden von Frankreich. Ich war auch letztes Jahr dort. Wir fahren mit dem Auto und wir bleiben zwei Wochen im August. Das Wetter ist immer toll – sonnig und heiß. **Was wir dort machen… ? Also,** wir besuchen Freunde und … **ah ja** … wir gehen wandern. Das ist alles **ein bisschen** langweilig. Ich mag das Essen in Frankreich, aber mein Französisch ist nicht sehr gut! `32`

2   **Was ich in den Sommerferien mache?** Nicht sehr viel, aber ich fahre nach Süddeutschland nach München zu meiner Großmutter. Ich fahre mit dem Zug dorthin und ich bleibe drei Tage. Das Wetter ist **meistens** schön und warm im Sommer. Meine Großmutter ist sehr lustig! Wir gehen in die Stadt, wir sehen fern und wir faulenzen auf dem Balkon. Es ist immer super in München und nie langweilig!

3   In den Sommerferien fahre ich mit meinem Vater nach London. Das ist die Hauptstadt von Großbritannien und liegt im Süden von England. Wir fliegen mit dem Flugzeug und haben eine Woche dort. Es regnet oft in London und es ist manchmal kalt. Wir gehen in die Stadt und ins Kino. Man kann auch im Hotel schwimmen gehen oder Squash spielen. **Und was noch? Ach ja** … Ich möchte den Buckingham Palast sehen. Das ist **wirklich** toll!

> **Answers**
>
> | | Where | How travelling? | How long for? | Weather | Plans? | Opinion |
> |---|---|---|---|---|---|---|
> | 1 | South of France | car | 2 weeks | sunny and hot | visit friends, good food hiking | boring, bad French super, |
> | 2 | Munich (Grandmother) | train | 3 days | | go into town, watch TV, laze on balcony | never boring, Grandmother is funny |
> | 3 | London | plane | 1 week | | go into town cinema swim/squash Buckingham Palace | great |

This panel reminds pupils that the verb must be the second idea in a German sentence. Refer pupils to it before they tackle exercise 8. Elicit some examples of this in Julia's text.

With a class of confident learners, you may wish at this point to introduce the concept of 'time, manner, place' word order, using **Arbeitsblatt 6.7** for practice of this.

8 Schreib über deine Phantasieferien mit einem Freund / einer Freundin. (AT 4/5)   **2.4b/Y8 2.5/Y8**

Writing. Pupils write an extended text about an imaginary plan for a holiday with a friend. They should model their writing on the text about Julia in exercise 5. Encourage more confident pupils to include opinions and as much detail as possible. The finished texts will be of interest to others in the class, and can be used for the plenary below.

Suggestion

ICT Pupils could word-process their texts and add visuals to enhance their work.

Plenary   5.6

Aims

To consolidate the language of this unit.
To practise authentic pronunciation and intonation.

Select pupils who have completed exercise 8 to read aloud their text about an imaginary holiday. The rest of the class listen and try to remember three facts from what they have heard – elicit these afterwards (in English, or in German using the third person singular, depending on the abilities of the group). Finally, pupils vote on their favourite text from those heard.

Lernzieltest
5.8

This is a checklist of language covered in Chapter 6. Pupils can work with the checklist in pairs to check what they have learned. Points which directly address grammar and structures are marked with a G. There is a **Lernzieltest** sheet in the Resource and Assessment File (page 115). Encourage pupils to look back at the chapter and to use the grammar section to revise what they are unclear about.

You can also use the **Lernzieltest** as an end-of-unit plenary.

Wiederholung

This is a revision page to prepare pupils for the **Kontrolle** at the end of the chapter.

Resources
CD 3, track 33

Hör zu. Wo ist das? (1–6) (AT1/3)

Listening. Pupils listen to the recording and, after each question, identify which building/place on the map they are being directed to.

1 – *Guten Tag. Wo ist hier [beep], bitte?*
 – *Also. Gehen Sie geradeaus und nehmen Sie die erste Straße rechts.*
 – *Danke schön.*
 – *Bitte sehr.*
2 – *Hallo. Wo ist [beep], bitte?*
 – *Geh geradeaus und nimm die zweite Straße links.*
 – *Danke.*
 – *Bitte.*
3 – *Entschuldigen Sie, bitte. Wo ist [beep]?*
 – *Gehen Sie geradeaus und nehmen Sie die erste Straße links.*
 – *Danke schön.*
 – *Bitte sehr.*
4 – *Guten Tag. Wo ist [beep], bitte?*
 – *Geh geradeaus und nimm die dritte Straße rechts.*
 – *Danke.*
 – *Bitte.*
5 – *Wo ist [beep], bitte?*
 – *Geh geradeaus und nimm die dritte Straße links.*
 – *Danke.*
 – *Bitte.*
6 – *Guten Tag, wo ist [beep]?*
 – *Gehen Sie geradeaus und nehmen Sie die zweite Straße rechts.*

Answers
1 d – die Post
2 b – das Schwimmbad
3 a – das Verkehrsamt
4 f – der Bahnhof
5 c – der Park
6 e – die Kirche

2 Partnerarbeit. (AT 2/3)
1.4b/Y7

Speaking. Working in pairs, pupils create four dialogues, following the model and illustrations given, between customer and vendor at a snack stand.

3 Wie ist die richtige Reihenfolge? (AT 3/3)
2.1/Y7

Reading. Pupils read the leaflet about Leipzig, and arrange the illustrations in the order that they are mentioned in the text.

Answers
c, g, e, l, k, b, i, d, a, j, h, f

4 Was machst du in den Sommerferien? Schreib acht Sätze. (AT 4/4–5)
2.4b/Y7 2.4b/Y8

Writing. Pupils write a paragraph about their real or imaginary plans for the summer holidays, using the present tense to talk about the future. Most pupils should aim to form compound sentences and include opinions.

SELF-ACCESS READING AND WRITING AT TWO LEVELS

A Reinforcement

1 Wo geht man hin? (AT 3/2 AT4/1)
`2.1/Y7`

Reading. Pupils read the notes giving directions, refer to the map, and copy the correct word from those provided, to show where they are being directed to.

> **Answers**
> 1 das Verkehrsamt
> 2 der Bahnhof
> 3 das Schwimmbad
> 4 das Rathaus
> 5 die Kirche

2 Ordne das Gespräch. (AT 3/3) `2.1/Y7`

Reading. Pupils work out the correct order for the lines of a conversation at a snack bar. They could then write out the conversation.

> **Answers**
> b, e, a, d, f, c

3 Schreib die Tabelle ab und ordne die Wörter der richtigen Kategorie zu. (AT 3/1 AT 4/1)
`4.2/Y7`

Reading/Writing. Pupils make a copy of the grid, and write each item of vocabulary in the correct column.

> **Answers**
>
> | In der Stadt | Transport | Wo? | Essen | Trinken | Land | Großstadt |
> |---|---|---|---|---|---|---|
> | Schwimmbad | Zug | Straße | Wurst | Tee | die Schweiz | Bern |
> | Markt | Auto | links | Senf | Bier | Irland | Berlin |

4 Schreib noch drei Wörter für jede Kategorie. (AT 4/1)
`4.2/Y7`

Writing. Pupils write three more ideas of their own in each column, referring back through the chapter for ideas if necessary.

B Extension

1 Ist das Osnabrück oder Quakenbrück? (AT 3/4)
`2.2a/Y8`

Reading. Pupils scan the texts about two places in North Germany, and decide whether each picture represents what is said about Osnabrück or Quakenbrück. Some pictures apply to both places. They record the answers in a simple grid.

> **Answers**
> Osnabrück: c, d, e, g, i, k
> Quakenbrück: a, b, d, f, g, h, j, k

2 Richtig (R), Falsch (F) oder nicht im Text (N)? (AT 3/5)
`2.2a/Y8`

Reading. Pupils read the texts in greater detail, and decide whether each statement is true, false, or not mentioned. Pupils could re-write the false sentences correctly.

> **Answers**
> 1 falsch (Großstadt)
> 2 richtig
> 3 nicht im Text
> 4 falsch (jeden Freitag)
> 5 richtig
> 6 nicht im Text

3 Schreib Pläne für einen Tag in Quakenbrück. (AT 4/5) `2.4b/Y7 2.4b/Y8`

Writing. Pupils write imaginary plans for a day in Quakenbrück. Remind them that the present tense can be used to talk about the future, and that they should take ideas for activities from the text. Encourage them to use *wir* as well as *ich*. Some pupils may be able to include clock times, and to form compound sentences.

6 Workbooks

Übungsheft A, Seite 52

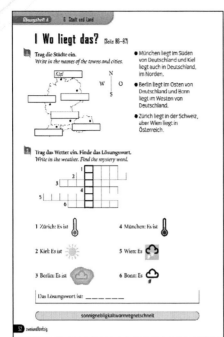

1 (AT3 Level 2)

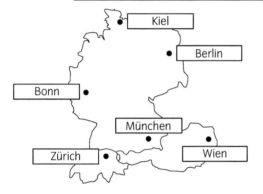

2 (AT4 Level 1) 1 warm 2 sonnig 3 neblig 4 kalt 5 schneit 6 regnet

Das Lösungswort ist wolkig.

Übungsheft A, Seite 53

1a (AT3 Level 3)
Liebe Katrin, in meiner Stadt gibt es einen **Bahnhof** und drei **Supermärkte**. Wir haben auch ein **Schloss** und ein **Rathaus**. Es gibt auch drei **Kirchen** und einen **Markt**. Schreib bald, Mani

1b (AT3 Level 3)
Town hall: 1, Market: 1, Church: 3, Castle: 1, Station: 1, Supermarket: 3

2 (AT4 Level 3) 1 Das Schloss? Man kann mit dem Taxi fahren. 2 Das Schwimmbad? Man kann mit der Straßenbahn fahren. 3 Nach Bonn? Man kann mit dem Flugzeug fliegen. 4 Nach Berlin? Man kann mit dem Zug fahren. 5 Der Markt? Man kann zu Fuß gehen. 6 Die Kirche? Man kann mit dem Bus fahren.

Übungsheft B, Seite 52

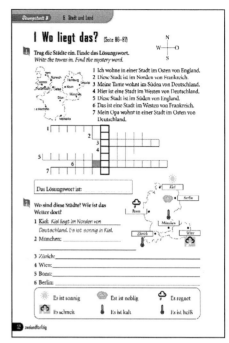

1 (AT3 Level 2) 1 Norwich 2 Calais 3 München 4 Bonn 5 Portsmouth 6 La Rochelle 7 Leipzig

Das Lösungswort ist Hamburg.

2 (AT4 Level 3)
1 Kiel liegt im Norden von Deutschland. Es ist sonnig in Kiel. 2 München liegt im Süden von Deutschland. Es ist kalt in München. 3 Zürich liegt in der Schweiz. Es ist heiß in Zürich. 4 Wien liegt in Österreich. Es schneit in Wien. 5 Bonn liegt im Westen von Deutschland. Es regnet in Bonn. 6 Berlin liegt im Osten von Deutschland. Es ist neblig in Berlin.

Übungsheft B, Seite 53

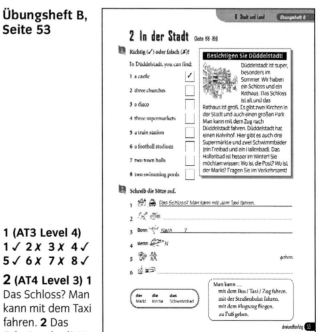

1 (AT3 Level 4)
1 ✓ 2 ✗ 3 ✗ 4 ✓ 5 ✓ 6 ✗ 7 ✗ 8 ✓

2 (AT4 Level 3) 1 Das Schloss? Man kann mit dem Taxi fahren. 2 Das Schwimmbad? Man kann mit der Straßenbahn fahren. 3 Nach Bonn? Man kann mit dem Flugzeug fliegen. 4 Nach Berlin? Man kann mit dem Zug fahren. 5 Der Markt? Man kann zu Fuß gehen. 6 Die Kirche? Man kann mit dem Bus fahren.

**Übungsheft A,
Seite 54**

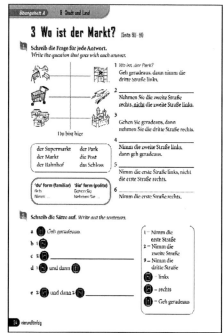

1 (AT3 Level 2, AT4 Level 2) 1 Wo ist der Park? **2** Wo ist der Bahnhof? **3** Wo ist die Post? **4** Wo ist der Supermarkt? **5** Wo ist der Markt? **6** Wo ist das Schloss?

2 (AT4 Level 2–3) 1 Geh geradeaus. **2** Nimm die erste Straße links. **3** Nimm die zweite Straße rechts. **4** Nimm die erste Straße links und dann geh geradeaus. **5** Nimm die zweite Straße rechts und dann die zweite Straße links.

**Übungsheft B,
Seite 54**

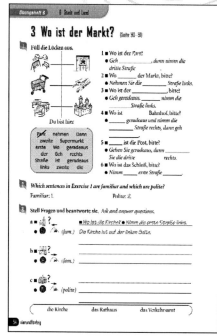

1 (AT3 Level 3, AT4 Level 3) 1 Wo ist der Park? – Geh **geradeaus**, dann nimm die dritte Straße **links**. **2** Wo **ist** der Markt, bitte? – Nehmen Sie die **erste** Straße links. **3** Wo ist der **Supermarkt**, bitte? – Geh geradeaus. **Dann** nimm die **zweite** Straße links. **4** Wo ist **der** Bahnhof, bitte? – **Geh** geradeaus und nimm die **zweite** Straße rechts, dann geh **geradeaus**. **5 Wo** ist die Post, bitte? – Gehen Sie geradeaus, dann **nehmen** Sie die dritte Straße **rechts**. **6** Wo ist das Schloß, bitte? – Nimm **die** erste Straße **rechts**.

2 (AT3 Level 3) *Familiar:* 1, 3, 4, 6; *Polite:* 2, 5

3 (AT4 Level 3)

a ■ Wo ist die Kirche? ● Nimm die erste Straße links. Die Kirche ist auf der linken Seite. **b** ■ Wo ist das Verkehrsamt? ● Nimm die zweite Straße rechts. Das Verkehrsamt ist auf der rechten Seite. **c** ■ Wo ist das Rathaus? ● Nehmen Sie die dritte Straße links. Das Rathaus ist auf der rechten Seite.

**Übungsheft A,
Seite 55**

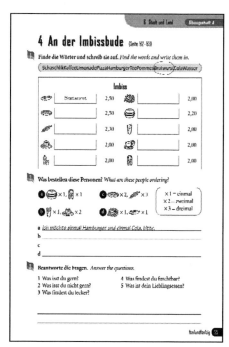

1 (AT3 Level 1, AT4 Level 1) Bratwurst, Pizza, Schaschlik, Kaffee, Wasser, Pommes, Hamburger, Limonade, Tee, Cola

2 (AT4 Level 3) 1 Ich möchte einmal Hamburger und einmal Cola, bitte. **2** Ich möchte einmal Limonade und zweimal Kaffee, bitte. **3** Ich möchte zweimal Pizza und dreimal Schaschlik, bitte. **4** Ich möchte einmal Pommes und einmal Bratwurst, bitte.

3 (AT4 Level 3–4)

**Übungsheft B,
Seite 55**

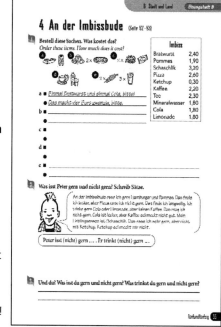

1 (AT4 Level 3) a ■ Einmal Bratwurst und einmal Cola bitte! ● Das macht vier Euro zwanzig, bitte. **b** ■ Einmal Kaffee und zweimal Pizza, bitte! ● Das macht sieben Euro vierzig, bitte. **c** ■ Zweimal Pommes mit Ketchup, bitte! ● Das macht vier Euro vierzig, bitte. **d** ■ Einmal Tee und einmal Mineralwasser, bitte! ● Das macht vier Euro zehn, bitte. **e** ■ Zweimal Schaschlik und dreimal Limonade, bitte! ● Das macht elf Euro achtzig, bitte.

2 (AT3 Level 4, AT4 Level 3) Peter isst gern Hamburger, Pommes und Schaschlik. Er isst nicht gern Pizza und Ketchup. Er trinkt gern Cola und Limonade. Er trinkt nicht gern Kaffee.

3 (AT4 Level 4)

Übungsheft A, Seite 56

Übungsheft B, Seite 56

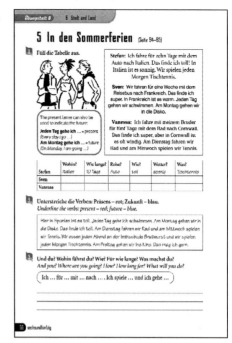

1 (AT3 Level 2) 1 l, e, g **2** b, c, a **3** f, h, d **4** f, c, g

2 (AT4 Level 3) a Ich fliege für zwei Wochen mit dem Flugzeug nach Spanien. In Spanien ist es sonnig. **b** Ich fahre für eine Woche mit dem Bus nach Schottland. In Schottland ist es kalt. **c** Ich fahre für zehn Tage mit dem Zug nach Frankreich. In Frankreich ist es warm.

1 (AT3 Level 4)

	Wohin?	Wie lange?	Reise?	Wie?	Wetter?	Was?
Stefan:	Italien	10 Tage	Auto	toll	sonnig	Tischtennis
Sven:	Frankreich	1 Woche	Reisebus	super	warm	schwimmen / Disko
Vanessa:	Cornwall	5 Tage	Rad	super	windig	Rad / Tennis

2 (AT3 Level 5) *Underlined in red:* ist, gehe, finde, essen, spielen, mag; *Underlined in blue:* gehen, fahren, spielen, gehen

3 (AT4 Level 3–4)

Übungsheft A, Seite 57

Übungsheft B, Seite 57

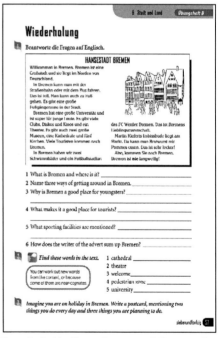

1 (AT3 Level 4) 1 The summer holidays. **2** One week. **3** Northern Portugal. **4** No, with her family. **5** By plane. **6** Go swimming. **7** Go riding. **8** On Wednesday. **9** Go to the cinema. **10** Go to the disco.

2 (AT3 Level 4) Reithalle, Tennisplatz, Lissabon

3 (AT4 Level 3–4)

1 (AT3 Level 4) 1 It's a city in Northern Germany. **2** By tram, by bus, on foot. **3** Big university, lots of clubs, discos, cinemas and a theatre. **4** Two large museums, a cathedral and five churches. **5** Two swimming pools and a football stadium. **6** It's never boring!

2 (AT3 Level 4) 1 Kathedrale **2** Theater **3** Willkommen **4** Fußgängerzone **5** Universität

3 (AT4 Level 4)

**Übungsheft A,
Seite 58**

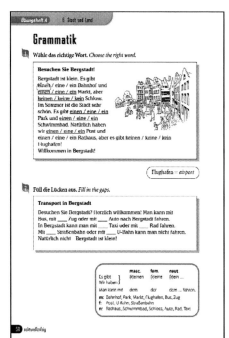

**Übungsheft B,
Seite 58**

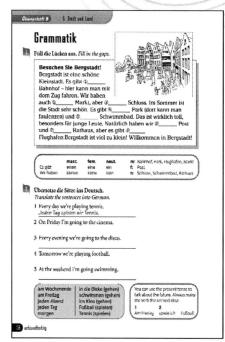

1 (AT3 Level 3) Bergstadt ist klein. Es gibt **einen** Bahnhof und **einen** Markt, aber **kein** Schloss. Im Sommer ist die Stadt sehr schön. Es gibt **einen** Park und **ein** Schwimmbad. Natürlich haben wir **eine** Post und **ein** Rathaus, aber es gibt **keinen** Flughafen! Willkommen in Bergstadt!

2 (AT3 Level 3) Besuchen Sie Bergstadt? Herzlich willkommen! Man kann mit **dem** Bus, mit **dem** Zug oder mit **dem** Auto nach Bergstadt fahren. In Bergstadt kann man mit **dem** Taxi oder mit **dem** Rad fahren. Mit **der** Straßenbahn oder mit **der** U-Bahn kann man nicht fahren. Natürlich nicht – Bergstadt ist klein!

1 (AT4 Level 4) 1 einen Bahnhof **2 einen** Markt **3 kein** Schloss **4 einen** Park **5 ein** Schwimmbad **6 eine** Post **7 ein** Rathaus, **8 keinen** Flughafen.

2 (AT4 Level 4) 1 Jeden Tag spielen wir Tennis. **2** Am Freitag gehe ich ins Kino. **3** Jeden Abend gehen wir in die Disko. **4** Morgen spielen wir Fußball. **5** Am Wochenende gehe ich schwimmen.

6 Resource and assessment file

Arbeitsblatt 6.1

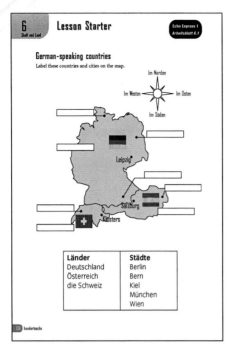

Deutschland – Kiel, Berlin, München; die Schweiz – Bern;
Österreich – Wien

Arbeitsblatt 6.2

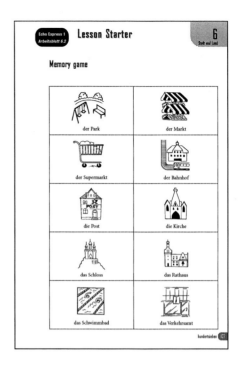

Arbeitsblatt 6.3

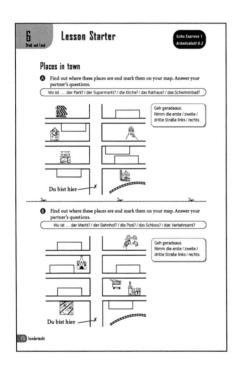

Arbeitsblatt 6.4

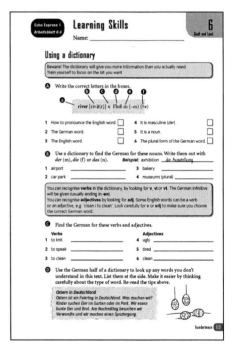

A
1 b 2 d 3 a 4 e 5 c 6 f

B
1 der Flughafen 2 der Parkplatz 3 die Bäckerei 4 die Museen

C
1 stricken 2 sprechen 3 putzen / sauber machen 4 hässlich
5 müde 6 sauber

Arbeitsblatt 6.5

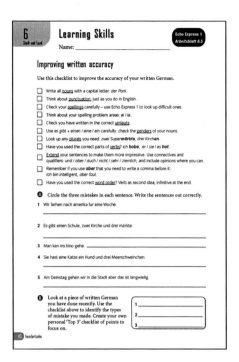

A

1 Wir fa**hr**en nach **A**merika f**ür** eine Woche. **2** Es gibt ein**e** Schule, zwei Kirche**n** und drei **M**ärkte. **3** Man kan**n** ins **K**ino gehe**n**. **4** Sie ha**t** eine Katze, [comma] ein**en** Hund und drei Meerschweinchen. **5** Am D**ie**nstag gehen wir in die Stadt, [comma] aber das ist langw**ei**lig.

Arbeitsblatt 6.7

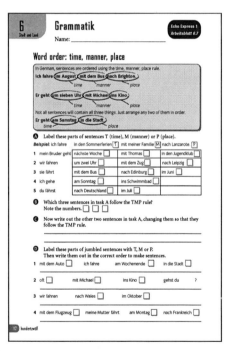

A
1 T M P **2** T M P
3 M P T **4** T P **5** P T

B
1, 2, 4

C
3 Sie fährt im Juni mit dem Bus nach Edinburg.
5 Du fährst im Juli nach Deutschland.

D
1 M T P / Ich fahre am Wochenende mit dem Auto in die Stadt.
2 T M P / Gehst du oft mit Michael ins Kino?
3 P T / Wir fahren im Oktober nach Wales.
4 M T P / Meine Mutter fährt am Montag mit dem Flugzeug nach Frankreich.

Arbeitsblatt 6.6

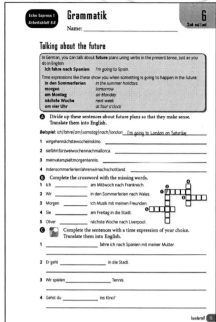

A
1 Wir gehen nächste Woche ins Kino. *We're going to the cinema next week.*
2 Sie fährt für zwei Wochen nach Mallorca. *She's going to Majorca for two weeks.*
3 Mein Vater spielt morgen Tennis. *My father is playing tennis tomorrow.*
4 In den Sommerferien fahren wir nach Schottland. *In the summer holidays we're going to Scotland.*

B
1 fahre **2** fahren **3** höre **4** geht **5** fährt